LEICESTER UNIVERS
AF751282

CZECHOSLOVAK
ACADEMY
OF SCIENCES

# TRENDS OF PRIVATE INTERNATIONAL LAW

SCIENTIFIC EDITORS

Prof. Dr. Štefan Luby
Dr. Otto Kunz

PAVEL KALENSKÝ

# Trends of Private International Law

ACADEMIA
PRAGUE
MARTINUS NIJHOFF
THE HAGUE

PRAGUE 1971

Distribution throughout the world with the exception of socialist countries:

Martinus Nijhoff's Boekhandel en Uitgeversmaatschappij N. V. Lange Voorhout 9-11, The Hague, The Netherlands

© Pavel Kalenský 1971
All rights reserved

No part of this book may be reproduced in any form, by photostat, microfilm, retrieval system, or any other means, without written permission from the publishers

Printed in Czechoslovakia

ISBN 90 247 1221 1

WITHDRAWN FROM
UNIVERSITY OF LEICESTER
LIBRARY

LEICESTER UNIVERSITY LIBRARY

RB m001861

KAL

423 467
11.1.74

# CONTENTS

"La théorie en droit international privé . . . : c'est un combat de nègres, le soir, dans un tunnel."
/M. Gutzwiller, *Rabels Zeitschift,* 1937, p. 326./

". . . Deutsche, Franzosen, Engländer und Amerikaner, stehen sich oft sehr schroff gegenüber. Alle aber vereinigen sich in einem gemeinsamen lebhaften Interesse an den hier einschlagenden Fragen, in dem Bestreben nach Annäherung, Ausgleichung, Verständigung, so wie es sich in keiner anderen Rechtslehre findet."
/Savigny, *System des heutigen Römischen Rechts,* Vol. VIII /1849/, Foreword, p. IV./

# FOREWORD

In the course of the close to twenty years that I have devoted to practical and theoretical work in the field of private international law and the law of international trade, I have been repeatedly and increasingly bothered by the three questions which I am trying to answer in the present study, namely What?, Why? and How?, that is questions concerning the object, reason and method, which are essential in any field of study.

I am fully aware of the fact that it is probably impossible to provide a complete, exhaustive and unequivocal answer to these three questions in the sphere of private international law, and that such an answer should not even be expected in the foreseeable future. I do not say this as an excuse for the shortcomings that undoubtedly exist in my study, but I believe that the considerate and understanding reader will realize the difficulties with which any work concerned with basic, theoretical study of such a complex subject-matter as modern-day private international law must necessarily meet.

Private international law, as a phenomenon of the social superstructure, forms in a way a part of social reality, which calls for a certain juridico-sociological analysis as a starting point. This is contained in the first part of the present study.

Seeking the answer to the three basic questions of contemporary private international law, I also deemed it essential to outline to the reader the historical development of the different concepts of this particular branch of law, for without the knowledge of this history it is impossible to understand the contemporary problems.

The fact that private international law oscillates between public international law and substantive municipal law as it is applied in individual countries creates considerable problems in both theory and practice. I have tried to deal with these problems in the third part of my study, concerning "universalism" and "nationalism" in the doctrine of private international law, as well as in its fourth part, which is devoted to the object and nature of this law and its place in the overall system of law.

The character of private international law, ensuing from the plurality of municipal laws – which also characterize the origin and existence of comparative jurisprudence – inspired me to produce the fifth part of this study, which primarily tries to explain the theoretical problems of comparative jurisprudence but does so – defining its objectives and possibilities – in order to underline at the same time its role in private international law and in the law of international trade.

The sixth and final part of my study is concerned with the substance and nature of application of foreign law, which, in its consequences, represents something of a "culmination" of the conflict rules and which is of utmost importance for the private international law and the general law of every state because the application of a foreign law – even when it is based on a rule of municipal law – disturbs the homogeneity and exclusive character of the municipal law of any country; therefore, I have tried to provide an answer as to the mutual relationship between the municipal law of a state and the applied foreign law.

This structure of my study thus necessitated the consideration of certain problems from different aspects; however, I have done so only to the essential extent called for by the outline of my work.

This book is not an attempt to provide a "legal philosophy" of private international law as a comprehensive system, although I realized that the basic questions I had posed to myself would lead to a study in legal philosophy rather than to a purely juristic treatise; nevertheless, I feel that the reader will understand that this work is concerned with an analysis and explication of the positive rules of private international law only to the extent essential for keeping the scope of the book within reasonable bounds.

My study could not have been produced without the kind and patient understanding and support of all my colleagues and friends from the Institute of Legal Science of the Czechoslovak Academy of Sciences and the Faculty of Law of Charles University, to whom I hereby convey my deepest gratitude.

Prague, October the 9th, 1968.

Pavel Kalenský

# PART ONE

# Private International Law as a Social Phenomenon

## CHAPTER 1

## A General Survey

Private international law (both as a branch of law and as a branch of jurisprudence) occupies in certain aspects a special and unique position among other branches of law and jurisprudence.

On the one hand, stress is being laid on its intricate character given by the complexity and extent of the problems it covers, which range from the sphere of public international law to the sphere of municipal, primarily civil, law; this gives private international law the character of a hybrid and extremely complicated field of law. On the other hand, we must not ignore those authors, who view such an essential part of private international law as the law of conflict of laws "only" as a technical matter which is to provide the judge, in abstract and technical formulas, independent of the existing socio-political and economic conditions, with guidance in settling particular conflicts problems;[1] this, of course, is not to detract from the complexity and subtle nature of these formulas.

However, neither opinion prevents the doctrine of private international law from being characterized – perhaps to an even greater extent than the other fields of jurisprudence – by its speculative nature which frequently leads to abstract and highly

---

[1] See, e.g., the opinion of the outstanding Swiss author M. Gutzwiller, who in his study (remarkable for its actual content) "Le développement historique du droit international privé", *Recueil des Cours,* 1929, Vol. IV, p. 376, writes: "*... le droit international privé est absolument étranger à ces considérations matérielles ... les questions des conflicts des lois civiles renferment un problème juridique, voir technique, abbandonné dans une mesure bien large aux décisions d'un petit comité d'experts.*"

complex theories. This fact, to be true, is not the result of some fancy in nurturing such theories, but reflects the very nature of private international law and ensues from its objects, its scope and the character of the social, objective reality, which private international law governs and from which it proceeds. We should bear in mind from the very beginning that in all its parts, private international law is, in a way, full of contradictions and serious problems, which in their essence ensue from the character of its subject-matter. Most complications probably arise from the fact that private international law involves the legal regulation of social relations which – due to the existence of a foreign or international element contained therein – have a specific international character but in their overwhelming majority are governed by the municipal laws of the individual states, which must give certain, but at the same time very different, regard to the international character of the regulated relationships. This fact – which undoubtedly ensues from the different class and political substance of individual states and their concrete interests -- is the principal source of the disparity between individual municipal rules governing essentially the same or very similar cases or social relations; although the doctrine of private international law must respect this state of affairs, it is typical of it, that it is characterized by certain tendency towards internationality, which is, on the one hand, the heritage of a common legal development (at least a particular one) and, on the other hand, the outcome of the endeavour to obtain a harmonious settlement of the same cases in the greatest possible number of states; this – in our opinion quite natural tendency – is also greatly promoted by the international features whereby public international law influences private international law, as well as by the postulates which ensue at the level of private international law from the calls for the peaceful co-existence of states with different social systems.

Although private international law is at present primarily a part of municipal law, it should not be understood – as a branch of law – as a mere body of rules issued seemingly in an arbitrary manner by each state within the framework of its sovereignty regardless of international links and the conclusions arising from public international law, its principles and rules as regards the definition of the jurisdiction of individual states in treating non-sovereign subjects, irrespective of whether they are their own citizens or aliens. Thus, within these bounds, private international law is considerably influenced by the idea of the international community of states, the principles of general international law, and the assumed reciprocity on the part of other members of the international community, in spite of the fact that this reciprocity does not directly affect the application of foreign law to any particular extent and that its absence does not lead to retortion in the field of the law of conflict of laws.

It may be said that private international law oscillates between the territorial nature of municipal law and the universality of public international law. Although we do not feel that it is possible to prove that private international law is a part of public international law, we cannot ignore the fact that between the two there does exist a relationship of functional connection and interaction, which is quite understandable and warranted by the nature of the social relations governed by private international law.

The private international law of every state – similar as other branches of law – expresses certain class interests and in its substance embodies the will of the ruling class isolated within national boundaries, but at the same time a will which must bear in mind the interests the ruling class within the particular state has with respect to other members of the international community, irrespective of whether states of the same or a different socio-economic character are involved.

For the present, it would probably be wrong and unrealistic to claim that the private international law of every state differs according to whether it governs the relationships of its own subjects to non-sovereign subjects from states of the same socio-economic character or to subject from states whose socio-economic character is different or contradictory. Although certain trends aiming at such a solution cannot be ignored, especially in the sphere of unification or integration of substantive law with a foreign element, which take place primarily in smaller units governed by a uniform economic or political concept, especially one striving at integration, we must, on the other hand, also bear in mind elements of a general character and the ensuing postulates of non-discrimination of states, which is very prominently manifested in private international law, mainly in its classical component part, i.e. the law of conflict of laws.[2]

The element of the class character of law, which is contained in private international law just as it is in other branches of law and which merely acquires a specific expression conditioned by the nature of the social relations governed by private international law, does not erase the "internationality" which is an essential component of private international law and without which this law would lose the *raison d'être* of its existence. Certain features of a general nature typical of private international law, which have been shaped by the postulates of the international community of states, the principles of peaceful

---

[2] We may quote as an example the legal technique used in recent years in the unification proposals of the Hague Conference on Private International Law, which – although rather limited in the participation of member-states and restricted mostly to West European states – frequently instructs the states that have adopted certain conflicts rules to apply such rules towards other states, even those which are not members of the Conference or, although members, have not adopted the respective rule. Thus, e.g., the important Convention on the Law Applicable to International Sale of Goods, dated June the 15th, 1955 *(Convention sur la loi applicable aux ventes à caractère international d'objets mobiliers corporels),* which entered in force for a number of West European states in 1964, provides for the duty of members states to incorporate the substantive provisions of the Convention in their municipal law. A similar system of unification of the substantive rules governing sales contracts was adopted by the so-called Uniform Hague Laws Governing the Conclusion of International Sales Contracts and International Sales Contract, which provide that the rules contained therein should be applicable irrespective of the citizenship of the parties to the contract and of whether the state whose citizen the party is had ratified the respective convention or not; it is, of course, problematic whether these laws have a real chance of becoming at least a particular, unified law of international sales contracts for example in such an economically important area as the European Economic Community.

co-existence and the principles of public international law, have, in the course of historical development, established in the private international law of individual states certain constant rules, basically influenced primarily by the postulates of a rational and just settlement of the most typical cases – especially in the law of conflict of laws – which are sometimes called the principles of private international law. The special importance of these principles is, in addition, spurred by the fact that the private international law of many states is an unwritten law or, at the most, is governed very briefly and vaguely in a few provisions of Civil Codes dating from a period when the intensity of international contacts between the nonsovereign subjects of different states had been insignificant compared with the present state of affairs; this fact, too, spurs the endeavour to generalize the settlement of individual cases of conflict of laws accepted by the courts of different countries and thus to strengthen the trend towards the formulation of certain fundamental rules or principles. Many authors consider as the main such principles of the law of conflict of laws the principle of the free choice of the applicable law by the parties in the sphere of the conflicts law of obligations, or the principle of *locus regit formam actus,* applicable to the formal requisities of legal acts, as well as the principle of *legis rei sitae* applicable to conflicts of law regarding rights *in rem* to immovables and movables. The conclusion made in this connection is formulated primarily by the disciples of the internationalist school and of universalistic tendencies in private international law in the sense that there exist certain general or fundamental principles of private international law which are likened to the importance held in public international law by its general and fundamental principles. In view of the fact that at its present stage of development private international law is primarily of a municipal character, it could, of course, be also deduced that the principles of the law of conflict of laws whose scope and definition are the subject of considerable differences of opinion, are general principles of law, recognized by civilized nations, which constitute, under Article 38 (c) of the Statute of the International Court of Justice, one of the forms of the law to be applied by this court. Although public international law has a very strong impact on private international law, it is, nevertheless, a fact that the sources or forms of private international law, and in particular those of the law of conflict of laws as its substantial part, still have a mostly municipal character; however, this should not lead to the conclusion that there cannot exist any fundamental principles of private international law as a phenomenon existing in all legal systems. Naturally, we do not believe that these principles exist in the form of customary (public) international law as it is used to be the case with the main principles of public international law before the United Nations Charter entered into force; what we have are, in fact, similar principles or rules of the private international law of individual states.

If we consider the function of private international law in contemporary society, we can, most probably, reach the conclusion that the principle of the mandatory co-operation of states in economic, social and cultural matters, as expressed in the United Nations Charter, is also of major importance for the development of private international law. However, a detailed analysis of the fundamental and universal principles of private international law, or of how these principles are formulated in the legislation and judicial decisions of a number of states, would show that their individual appearance in the individual municipal laws is far from identical; we know, for example, of differences existing in the laws of individual states as regards the scope of the choice of the applicable law by the parties in the conflicts law of obligations[3] or as regards the content and limits of any other of the given principles.

It is in private international law, in particular its general part, that we meet – to a much greater extent than in other fields of jurisprudence – with the use of the historical, or at least histo-

---

[3] See the author's book *Obligační statut kupní smlouvy v mezinárodním styku (Conflict of Laws in International Sale).* Nakladatelství Československé akademie věd, Prague, 1960, pp. 70 ff.

rizing, method in the treatment of individual questions; this method of interpretation is customary not only with respect to the development of the doctrine of private international law but also with respect to the study of the treatment of individual questions in substantive law. In our opinion, this method of interpretation has many advantages because it shows private international law as a living and, in its own way, dynamic matter which is constantly developing. Among other things, its advantage also rests in the fact that it makes it possible to point to the social contingency of the legislative treatment of the individual questions and to the dependence of the development of this treatment on changes taking place in the social, primarily economic, conditions.

The birth and growth of private international law in the past are inseparably linked with the development of society under feudalism and capitalism. For the very origin of private international law, as we understand it today, was conditioned by the existence of the city-states of Northern Italy in the 13th to 15th centuries; these city-states gradually suppressed feudal relations of production, then prevailing elsewhere in Europe, in the interest of the emerging bourgeoisie which already then needed free labour. Private international law and its then system — the statutory theory — had reflected from the very beginning the economic life of society at every stage of its development; the fact that in its subsequent development this theory had in many respects acquired retardation tendencies only shows that under the socio-economic conditions which had developed in feudal Europe outside Northern Italy it had often become an instrument used by the ruling feudal class for protecting its interests against the growing power of the emerging bourgeoisie. However, not only the origin but also the subsequent development of the doctrine of the law of conflict of laws clearly indicate how individual ideas and tendencies of this development are conditional upon the socio-economic character of social development.

Thus, for example, Dumoulin, who is a continuator of the postglossators in France, expresses in the sphere of private international law the interest of centralized royal authority and its ally, the emering bourgeoisie in Paris, in eliminating legal particularism in France; the territorial concept of statutes, as understood by d'Argentré, a feudal lord from Brittany, reflects the interests of the feudal aristocracy – mainly in Northern France – fighting against the centralizing trends of the French royal power. The Dutch statutory theory, born after the Peace of Westphalia in 1648, expressed the interests of the Dutch bourgeoisie in the period when it had reached the apex of its economic and political power and when it tried to subject the greatest possible number of legal relations with a foreign element to its own law; the idea of sovereignty, which was being developed in the works of the then Dutch jurists (Grotius in particular), was a reflection of the long struggle of the Dutch Provinces for independence against the feudal Spanish realm. Wächter's and especially Savigny's teachings, which brought to an end the until then prevailing statutory theory in the 19th century, met the interests of the German industrial and commercial bourgeoisie in the period of industrial capitalism. Mancini's national and personalistic theories reflected the struggle of 19th century Italy for unification and for keeping the millions of Italian emigrants tied to their native country. The reception of the Dutch statutory theory by Story in the United States in the early 19th century, which underlined the principle of the territorial validity of laws and international comity as the basis for applying foreign law, became a most useful instrument for American businessmen which had taken over the heritage of the Dutch commercial empire; Story's doctrine subsequently became the basis of the theory of so-called vested rights as the grounds for applying foreign law and as it was formulated by Prof. Beale in the first half of this century.

This necessarily schematic, simplified and incomplete outline of the past development of the law of conflict of laws leads us to the conclusion that it is quite impossible to consider contemporary private international law in isolation and without regard to this development. The question we must ask in this connection could be formulated as follows: "What are the main features of contemporary private international law and what social and economic factors determine and influence these features?" This question must first make us study contemporary private international law as a phenomenon of the social superstructure existing in the legal systems of all states.

Besides what we might call sociological or political aspects, private international law as a whole (and, quite naturally, also the law of conflict of laws as its substantial component part) has, of course, specific problems of its own, which manifest themselves at the legal level and which we might call "legal" problems or – *sit venia verbo* – problems of "legal technique". Naturally, we are fully aware of the fact that the sociological and political premises of private international law very strongly and decisively influence the legal aspects of the given problem. Private international law, as ensues from its specific character and uniqueness even among the other spheres of municipal law on the one hand, and its relationship to public international law on the other hand, also has its specific methodological problems arising from the fact that it is a branch of law, which is based on the plurality of the legal systems of mutually equal sovereign states. The fact that private international law proceeds from the plurality of legal systems results in the situation where, as regards the application of scientific methods of study, the methods of solving concrete cases of conflict of laws, or the prevention of such cases it cannot limit itself only to the methods specific for the other branches of municipal law, or to the methods applied with respect to public international law; best suited to the specific character and, we might say, the very essence of the phenomenon of private international law is the widespread use of the comparative method as well as of the results achieved by comparative jurisprudence, which is essential for contemporary private international law both as regards the solution of concrete cases and the methods of its scientific study.

## CHAPTER 2
## The Legal and Sociological Aspects of Private International Law

### (1) Ontological and Gnoseological Aspects

Private international law as a phenomenon of the social and legal superstructure is marked by specific problems both in its ontological aspect and in its gnoseological aspect. In spite of this fact, however, when studying it, we cannot separate and isolate these two aspects from each other. The general prerequisite of the understanding of private international law from the ontological aspect is its existence as a phenomenon; of course, its knowledge is nothing less and nothing more than the knowledge of people who have acquainted themselves more or less adequately with this phenomenon. It is from this link between the ontological and gnoseological aspects of private international law that we must proceed without, of course, mixing or confusing the two.

From the ontological point of view, private international law, as a social phenomenon, is constantly influenced by a whole conglomerate of conditions – arising, in fact, from the material life of society – and we may say that it can meet its social purpose and function only if this fact (which, of course, is very complex and difficult to understand) is duly respected. However, in contrast to the other branches of municipal law, it is true of private international law – and this fact must be especially stressed in the present period of intensive international contacts – that in the process of its formation it is necessary to take into consideration a much broader scale of social interests and influences, mostly quite complex in their substance and manifestations, than in the case of the other branches of law. The same is true as regards the process of application of private international law which must often place into harmony conflicting laws by specific technical means of its own, such as, e.g., qualification, *renvoi*, public policy, not speaking of the choice of proper points of contact, the application of foreign law, etc.; in the course of this process, the content of a number of concepts and categories of municipal law undergoes certain changes from their normal consideration in municipal civil law, once they come into contact with foreign legal systems.[1]

However, in its ontological aspect, private international law is not only influenced by the material conditions of the life of society, as the matter is sometimes simplified, but it is at the same time a complex cultural phenomenon and a part of the legal culture of society, which is inspired by a number of factors, for example of ethical and philosophical nature, and by their evaluation; it is only thus that we should understand the statement that private international law is "after all" influenced by the material conditions of the life of society at the given stage of its development. In this connection we should point to yet another fact which is of utmost importance for understanding the foundations of private international law. When we speak of the impact of the material conditions of the life of society on the origin and process of application of any branch of municipal law, we usually have in mind only the material conditions of life in the given state, within the national boundaries. The situation is much more complex in the case of private international law. There, society and the material conditions of its life are not restricted to the bounds of a single nation. They are of a much broader scope which involves a wide range of international factors and elements, which constitute the conditions of life of society in the international framework. Under the present conditions of intensive international contacts, every state, when formulating and applying private international law, must pay increased attention to the aforesaid conditions and judge them most objectively. Any arbitrary and subjectively orientated ap-

---

[1] This is the substance of the idea of what is known as the autonomous or comparative qualification of legal institutions, underlined by Rabel and Becket.

proach, influenced by short-range and frequently utilitarian interests, with which we also meet in the sphere of private international law, may, in the end, have quite negative effects.

Since private international law is concerned with the regulation of the legal relationships of non-sovereign subjects – i.e. natural and juristic persons – with a foreign element and under the conditions of the international life of society, it has, also as a phenomenon of the social superstructure, a highly complex character of inter-related and interacting interests of individual states and their concepts of governing the social relations of non-sovereign subjects including a foreign element. If we make a closer study of the relations between the individual and society as it appears in the sphere covered by private international law, we find that the justified interests of individuals are respected in a special manner, specific for private international law, with which we meet, with certain variations and differences, in the legal systems of practically all states. For the conflict-of-laws rules give individuals a broad opportunity to determine themselves, under certain conditions, what law is to govern their legal relations (as a rule those involving contracts). Althougth manifestation of will may, e.g. in the municipal civil law of all states, derogate the optional rules of the law, the very phenomenon of determination of the applicable law by the subject of the respective legal relations is more than a mere transposition of contractual freedom in the civil-law sense; it is a specific phenomenon precisely because it involves the regulation of social relations which are characterized by the fact that they are linked with several (two, at least) state sovereignties and legal systems.

### (2) Private International Law as a Social Phenomenon

The private international law of every state, as well as private international law in the broader sense, as a phenomenon of the social superstructure, must always be studied and viewed also as a phenomenon arising from the given economic and political *milieu*, as a social phenomenon in the true meaning of the term; what is most obvious, are its links with not only the national but also the international life of society, where, precisely at the present time, we can note the growing importance of relations in which the subjects of rights and obligations are nonsovereign subjects, i.e. natural and legal persons. From this aspect, private international law, as a phenomenon existing in the legal systems of all states, has a number of general premises and features.

Although – in contrast to many authors – we do not consider private international law, as a category of law, to be a supranational phenomenon in its existence and theoretical concept, we must not ignore the common or similar features of this phenomenon from the ontological aspect; of course, these features are differently understood, respected and promoted by individual states as legislators both in the formulation of the law and its application, mostly in dependence on the prevailing social and economic conditions.

Thus, if we view private international law from the point of view of its specific features both at the ontological level and as regards the legal "expression" and respect for these premises, we can see that it has indeed much in common in the legal systems of different countries. Nevertheless, we believe that it would not be warranted to go in the juristic view and study of private international law as a whole or of its individual problems (both general and specific) beyond the limits of considering the phenomenon with the help of the comparative method and to resort to a natural-law understanding or interpretation based on the idealistic endeavour to have private international law common to all mankind and substantiated only by postulates of rationality or justice. Similar constructions, or their reflections in the various codifications and unification efforts so often typical of international law, would have hardly any chance of success when confronted with the positive private international law of the individual states, and would be contrary especially to the class nature of every law, including private international law.

Therefore, just as any other branch of law, private international law, too, must respect social reality; in this sense, all that applies to other branches of law as regards their relations with the material conditions of the life of society, applies to private international law as well. Private international law, as any body of law, is an expression of the will of the ruling class; the fact that it expresses the interests of the ruling class (or the interests of the whole people in an advanced socialist society), determined by the material and other conditions of its life, means among other things, that attention must be paid to the necessities arising in this connection from the fact that it governs relationships which are characterized by the existence of a foreign element. The private international law of every state must therefore also respect among other things — although to a different extent and, perhaps, for different reasons — the existence of the international community of states, characterized by the principle of peaceful co-existence of states, as well as the fact that its object is the regulation of the relations between non-sovereign subjects in the international life of society. It is precisely in this respect that private international law differs from other branches of municipal law and is very closely connected with elements of co-existence, which play a substantial role in contemporary public international law. Here also rests the core of the development of private international law we have witnessed in the past decades.

The fact that private international law must respect the conditions arising in international contacts does not mean, of course, that we agree with the assertions that its formation and future development are not to be substantially influenced by the political and economic interests of the individual states which formulate private international law, but by the "supra-class", "all-human" interests of the international community. Although international division of labour and international economic relations are an objective phenomenon and its objectivity is not modified even by the fact that these relations are maintained between states with opposing economic systems, nothing has changed as regards the correctness of Marx's thesis concerning the specific character of international relations as derived, unoriginal relations of production.[2] We must proceed from this initial, characteristic feature of the international economic situation and international relations, if we are to underline the fact that individual states continue to play a major role in the formation of contemporary private international law. In spite of the existing trends towards international division of labour and in spite of the objective character of this division, it remains a fact in the period of the existence of independent and sovereign states, that the primary relations of production are still being shaped within the framework of these individual states and that it is the interests and will of the individual ruling classes in the respective states, which determine to what extent these primary relations of production are to be placed in harmony with the objective need of an international division of labour. The interests of the individual ruling classes also determine the consideration of the position and interests of the ruling classes in other states in promoting the international division of labour and international economic relations. Thus, if conditions are to be created for developing international division of labour, we cannot ignore the manifestation of the will of the ruling classes in the individual states of the international community of states. Naturally, the will of the ruling classes in the individual states, and thus the will of the individual sovereign states, must be also manifested in the sphere of formation and application of private international law, and we may say that conditions for the future development of this law may be created at the present on this basis only.

This situation and the stress laid on the role played by sove-

---

[2] See K. Marx, *A Critique of Political Economy* (Czech edition), Prague, 1953, p. 178; here Marx points to the fact that economic systems proceed from the simple, such as labour, division of labour, etc., to the state, international exchange and a world market. Marx thus distinguishes between the international conditions of production, international division of labour, export and import, and the sum total of the conditions under which bourgeois society exists and functions in the form of a single state.

reign states and their class interests in the field under study does not, however, mean that today, any state can ignore certain given premises and facts in the sphere of private international law. These are, basically, the premises of the existence and origin of private international law, or those derived therefrom, and their proper understanding and utilization continue even today to be a prerequisite for the development of private international law.

### (3) The Prerequisites of the Origin and Existence of Private International Law

It is generally known that most textbooks and systems raise as the conditions of the origin and existence of private international law on the one hand the fact that there exist in the world parallel to each other many sovereign states with different legal systems and, on the other hand, that the citizens of these states, who are non-sovereign subjects – i.e. natural and legal persons – establish contacts and relations of civil law (or family law), labour law or procedural character.[3] Of course, it should be seen that the two aforesaid preconditions are far from being static and that in the past decades they have undergone a very dynamic development.

Contemporary private international law must bear in mind this development but must do so in its own, specific manner. Therein lies, essentially, its contribution to the needs of the contemporary international life of society.

Present-day private international law must proceed from the fact of the parallel existence of a number of sovereign states and their legal systems, without, of course, ignoring the fact that these states form an international community of states, which is governed by the rules and principles of public international law,

---

[3] See R. Bystrický, *Základy mezinárodního práva soukromého, (Principles of Private International Law)*, Prague 1958, pp. 11 ff.

both customary and embodied in treaties; naturally, this raises some consequences for the states in the sphere of formation and application of private international law, which could not have been felt at the time when private international law was only emerging and which were far from as intensive as they are today even before the Second World War, when the private international law of most capitalist states had only acquired the main features of its contemporary shape.

The obvious dependence of private international law on the economic and political conditions prevailing in every state and on the international life of society has made even Western authors increasingly depart from the position held, for example still in the 1920's, by Gutzwiller,[4] according to which private international law, as a technical aid essential for the judge, was quite independent of the material conditions of the life of society.

However, in order for private international law to attain its present importance both for individual states and for international co-operation and relations between non-sovereign subjects, the two basic conditions of its origin and development had to undergo certain progress. This progress had its beginning in the existence of a number of city-states, especially in Northern Italy of the 12th and 13th centuries, which only very slowly rid themselves of their character of originally closed units, mostly in connection with the emergence of the urban bourgeoisie and commerce which was then beginning to grow and erode the isolation of the individual entities. But in order for private international law to progress further, it was necessary for the initial, sporadic contacts between non-sovereign subjects subordinated to the laws of different states and juridically exceeding the boundaries of a single jurisdiction to grow to a certain level both quantitatively and as regards the general and essential character of such contacts for the life of society. This development continued parallel with the transformation of closed state entities (originally urban or feudal) into entities

[4] See *Recueil des Cours,* 1929, Vol. IV, p. 376.

which could not consider contacts between the natural and legal persons from different states and subjected to different laws as an exception from normal legal practice, but viewed them as a normal necessity which was warranted in modern times by the internationalization of production and commercial exchange and by the need of such internationalization for the vital interests of every state as well as for the unity of mankind. Of course, in the present period we must proceed from the fact that in the historical and sociological view of the past development, the synthesis between the plurality of states and the unity of mankind must be understood so, that the unity of mankind are at present realized precisely through the plurality of the existing states; this opinion seems to us to act also as the driving force behind the endeavour to promote and develop the legal regulation of the social relations between non-sovereign subjects, which transcend the boundaries of a single state and wich are governed by private international law.

Although the heart of private international law are relations between non-sovereign subjects (natural or legal persons), we must keep in mind that the settlement or regulation of these relations, which in their sum total are becoming – precisely in view of the internationalization of production and commercial exchange, and of the whole life of society in general – one of the major component parts of international relations, must not be based only on the utilization of the legal institutions inherent to the individual legal systems for the purpose of regulating the relations arising between individuals within the framework established by the sovereignty of individual states; it is precisely the character of the contacts and relations governed by private international law in the broader sense, which requires that, given the observance of respect for the sovereignty of individual states, solutions should be sought in international regulation of problems of substantive law and conflicts of law, whose essential co-ordination and harmony can be ensured only by a consensus of the will of sovereign states. In this respect, the legal community of modern-day sovereign states – even though the class character of these states may differ and they may belong to different socio-economic systems – can do much for the full development and progress of the human society within the international scope. The international legal community of states may in this connection provide for an effective legal regulation of the relations arising between non-sovereign subjects and thereby contribute to the practical realization of the demands ensuing from the peaceful co-existence of states and their duty to co-operate with each other.

### (4) Private International Law and the Plurality and Co-Existence of States

There is a close relationship between private international law as a phenomenon in the sphere of the legal superstructure, which is common to the legal systems of all states, and the international legal community of states which are the agents of its progress. On the one hand, this relationship involves the fact that the harmony of rules governing conflict of laws in the individual legal systems, for which private international law has been striving in the past decades both in the field of the selective function of the law of conflict of laws and as regards the endeavour to prevent conflicts between attempts to unify the substantive law governing relations with a foreign element, can help evoke among the non-sovereign subjects of the relationships governed by private international law a consciousness of a legal relation, which is the antithesis of xenophobia. Naturally, private international law is not to be used to spur any tendencies which might try to ignore or negate the fact that under the present situation it is necessary to proceed even in the endeavour to promote the progress of private international law from the plurality of sovereign states and their differing legal systems. The primary role of private international law as a phenomenon common to the legal systems of all states is to introduce into the relationships of non-sovereign subjects, which are its object, a certain order which, while respecting the basic political and legal premises of contemporary society, would strive for the attainment of such solutions to problems of conflict-of-laws rules and substantive law, that would promote co-operation among states and their peaceful co-existence. Although the private international law of every state – as any body of law – expresses the interests of the ruling classes in the respective states, which are inseparably linked with its existence, the postulates arising from the co-existence of states and from their duty to co-operate, as envisaged in particular by the United Nations Charter, are common to all states at the legal (although not political) level.[5]

The demands ensuing from the co-existence of states with different politico-economic systems and from the obligation of states to co-operate with each other act, in the period when there exist next to each other states with a different class character and substance, as a real force affecting the development of contemporary private international law both within the sphere of municipal law and in international efforts and proposals aiming at the unification of private international law. These demands can overcome the political and social elements obstructing the progressive development of private international law, be it the xenophobia arising in a number of states from excessive nationalism, or idealistic tendencies which ignore the fact that the international community of states consists of sovereign states with a different class substance. In reality, the often proclaimed, alleged progressivity of the supranational tendencies must prove itself as a useless instrument in promoting the progress of private international law precisely because it ignores the basic premises of contemporary international politics. The fact that at the present there exist within states with different socio-economic system and in different geographical regions strong integration

---

[5] See, in particular, Article 1, No. 3, of the Charter: "The purposes of the United Nations are ... to achieve international cooperation in solving international problems of an economic, social, cultural or humanitarian character, and in promoting and encouraging respect for human rights and for fundamental freedoms for all without distinction as to race, sex, language, or religion."

tendencies in an often highly developed form,[6] which, as a rule, have also, quite naturally, brought about a development of private international law within the given group of states, in no way affects the extreme importance of overall and truly universal relations among all states, irrespective of their politico-economic systems and groupings to which they at present belong for the progress of private international law. The needs of economic integration in entities, which are usually limited in a certain manner may require the attainment, within their framework, of such a degree of legal regulation, which by far exceeds the bounds of regulations which are not conditioned by such a high degree of integration; this applies both to the various rules adopted within the framework of the European Economic Community and, for example, to the level of unification of the rules governing international sales contracts within the framework of the General Conditions of Delivery of the Council of Mutual Economic Assistance. However, these particular regulations and their indisputable importance for the relationship arising within the individual integration groupings may at the same time serve as a means essential for the general progress of private international law; this progress and its final success undoubtedly depend on the need of world-wide economic contacts, which is of an objective character.

Private international law has therefore necessarily become a certain legal expression of international co-operation of primarily economic character and dependent on its intensity, which, however, as a phenomenon of the social superstructure, has its own, specific legal problems, characteristic of its existence, but which are quite often being presented as allegedly legal problems only. However, the influence of the character of the intensity of international co-operation on the individual legal or "only legal" problems of private international law is, in fact,

---

[6] What we have in mind are the European communities (i.e. the European Economic Community, Euratom and the Coal and Steel Union), the European Free Trade Association, the Council of Mutual Economic Assistance, the integration trends in Africa and Latin America, etc.

quite easy to determine. We might quote many examples to demonstrate this fact; but let us mention, by way of illustration, only the changes in North American judgments on the extraterritorial effects of Soviet nationalization decrees following the *de iure* recognition of the Soviet Union by the United States in the 1930's, or the development of the rules governing international sales contracts after the Second World War, which, besides expressing the conditions arising from international trade within the framework of the individual integration groupings, also underlines the elements of universal international commerce.

On the one hand, the relations between private international law and international co-operation is of such a nature, that private international law, as a phenomenon of the social superstructure, is conditional in its existence and development upon international co-operation and its intensity. On the other hand, of course, there could be no successful international co-operation and, in particular, contacts between non-sovereign subjects subordinated to the laws of different sovereign states, if the legal expression of international co-operation, which private international law undoubtedly is, were not objectively summed up in the form of a system of legal rules. While, therefore, private international law is the outcome of certain prerequisites of a sociological character, its continued existence is essential for the growth of relationships and contacts between non-sovereign subjects subordinated to different legal systems and living in different states. We could, in this respect, compare private international law and its importance to the importance of motor oil for the proper functioning of a combustion engine; if the engine lacks oil or if the lubrication system fails, the engine cannot operate.

While with respect to legal relationships between natural and legal persons under municipal law within the sovereign territory of a single state, not affecting the law of another state, international co-operation is a factor which does not directly influence these relationships and, at the most, touches on them only indirectly, it is essential for legal relationships involving the laws of several states, which are governed by private international law. The growing intensity of international co-operation is accompanied by a gradual differentiation between purely municipal relations, not containing any foreign element, which are governed by the respective branches of municipal law, which do not envisage the existence of a foreign element in the relationships they govern, and relations with a foreign element, which are governed by private international law, either by conflict-of-laws rules, procedural rules, so-called direct municipal-law rules or internationally unified rules; thus, the rules of private international law include all rules which envisage the existence of a foreign element in the social relations governed by them. It is thereby that the rules of private international law in their present form and at the present stage of development differ – according to almost unanimous opinion – from the rules of other branches of law, governing private-law relationships of a purely municipal nature.[7]

## (5) The Problem of Foreign Element in Legal Relations

As may be seen, a major role is being played in the definition of social relationships governed by private international law, as well as in the differentiation between these relationships and relations governed by "purely municipal" branches of law, by the existence of an international or foreign element involved in the former. The international or foreign element contained in the social relations governed by law may be defined quite factually, such as, for example, the location of a thing abroad; however, besides this possibility of defining the foreign

---

[7] See, e.g., the opinion of the French theoretician, H. Battifol: "L'objet général du droit international privé ... est l'ensemble des règles applicables aux seules personnes privées dans les relations de la société internationale." (*Traité élémentaire de droit international privé,* Paris, 1955, p. 3.)

element, there is also the possibility of using for its definition criteria of a personal nature, such as foreign citizenship or domicil of a subject of the respective relation. In our opinion, it would be proper, in defining the foreign element, to proceed both from criteria of territorial location and from criteria of a personal nature, the essential factor for its existence in the given relation being the fact that some of its elements affect the sovereignty and laws of more than a single state. The existence of a foreign element in legally governed social relations may take various forms and configurations which it is difficult (and, for our purposes, quite superfluous) to specify precisely because of their great variety. It is, however, certain that the relation between the facts of a case and more than a single state sovereignty (and more than a single body of law) creates the basis for the international character of such a relation. Thus, for example, the subjection of a person subjected to the law of a certain state on the basis of personal criteria (citizenship, domicil) to the territorial sovereignty of another state, where such a person finds itself, is one of the most frequent causes of the international character of the relations established either by the activity of such a person as a subject of the legal relations or through legal events concerning that person; the same is true of the location of things or rights in other countries. There is one thing, which is typical of the existence of a foreign element in all possible configurations that may occur; the existence of a foreign element in a given relation requires a certain human activity or a legal event involving a human agent. We may therefore sum up this problem by saying that the existence of a foreign element in a legal relation is the result of human activity (in the broadest sense) and that it is inseparably linked with man and his activities; this link between the foreign or international element and human activity is naturally manifested especially in cases where the foreign element does not directly ensue from certain characteristics of man, who, as a rule, acts as the object of a legal relation (e.g. as an alien in another state), but also in cases where the foreign element exists in the legal relationship e.g. on the basis of the location of a thing or a right abroad, which could have only taken place on the basis of human activity.

We may say in general, that the rather common assertions that a prerequisite of private international law is, on the one hand, the existence of several equal states and their laws, and, on the other hand, contacts between individual non-sovereign subjects belonging to these entities (i.e. natural and legal persons), describe the substance of the origin and existence of private international law as a phenomenon of the social superstructure only in a most general sense.

This summary opinion is augmented in the modern understanding of this question by additional aspects, especially sociologically-political aspects. What we have primarily in mind in this respect are the facts arising from the current situation, where the unity of the human community (not in the abstract sense) is being realized through the plurality of states of a different class character, which are under the obligation to co-operate with each other. If we study more deeply the manifestations of the human activity, which is typical of the mutual contacts between non-sovereign subjects subordinated to different states and their laws, and which constitutes the substance of the relationships governed by private international law, we find that the existence of a greater number of state entities as a politico-sociological phenomenon, and the fact that the social relation governed by the law is linked with these entities, forces the individual to act in these relations in a manner which differs in its specific way from behaviour in relations arising within the individual state entities without a foreign or international element; the manner of this behaviour is directly influenced by the legal expression of the policy pursued by the individual state entities and is different, for example, in cases of their mutual mistrust or relative isolation and cases of their co-operation.

These then are the prerequisites on which rests the very existence of private international law as a phenomenon of the social superstructure; it is these prerequisites, which make all the states of the international community respect this fact in one way or another. The universal, superstructural phenomenon of private international law is therefore being realized in the specific approach used by different states to the solution of the same, or at least similar, social situations, which is characteristic of their legal systems and becomes their part.

## (6) Prospects of Development

Without being able to rely in this connection on the results of an empirical, sociological research, we may underline – on the basis of the above theoretical and sociological considerations – certain aspects which may help throw some light on the prospects of the future development of private international law.

We may generally sum up that in the study of the social contingency of private international law, we meet under the present conditions of the international life of society with a broader scale of interests and influences which are characteristic of contemporary private international law and which we do not encounter when studying the social contingency of the other branches of municipal law.

What we have primarily in mind is the growing volume of contacts between non-sovereign subjects of different states which cross the frontiers of the individual state entities. This fact calls for a new view of the life of the individual subjects under the conditions of the advancing internationalization of production and exchange of goods, and, together with the objective phenomena of international political life, such as the emergence of new states and the creation of larger entities, usually on the basis of economic integration, forces the existing private international law to adjust itself constantly to the needs of the international life of society.

Thus, the private international law of every state is determined in its individual manifestations, as well as in the extent to which it stresses the selective function of the law of conflict of laws or the regulation by substantive law of relations with a foreign element, both economically and socio-politically. Both these forms of contingency of private international law are, naturally, interlinked; in view of the general nature of this link we do not find it necessary for the purposes of the present study to discuss these questions in detail.

In the development of private international law we may trace periods with the prevailing trend towards stressing the principle of territoriality and, as a consequence, towards a relative limitation of the applicability of foreign law; this is done by subordinating all persons and all things located on the territory of the state, whose court is to decide the given case, through various means of legal technique and methods common to private international law, to the law of that state. In other periods and under different conditions we can see, on the other hand, that the accent laid on the teritorial principle (which undoubtedly is to some extent warranted and proper) has been replaced by concepts which, as a rule, have been based on elements of a personal character and have made the application of foreign law easier. The contemporary private international laws of individual states mostly contains the features of their initial concepts; on the one hand, we could point to the territorial concepts of Anglo-American law, proceeding from the heritage of territoriality in the theories of the 17th century Dutch authors, or, on the other hand, to the personal criteria of French or Italian laws.

In this connection we must ask whether the past concepts of private international law, which originated in Europe and the United States, can meet the social needs of present-day world and the international life of its society, characterized by revolutionary changes in the political, economic and social spheres after the Second World War. These include primarily the internationalization of production and exchange of goods as well as of the whole life of society to an extent which only recently would have seemed unbelievable; to this we must add the formation of new states whose number has more than doubled compared with the number of sovereign states in existence before the Second World War. The founding of a new state has thus far almost always led to the creation of a new legal system and thus also of a new private international law in accordance with the well known fact that there are as many private international laws in the world as there are sovereign states. This, of course, is a trend which seems to be contrary to the theoretical efforts manifested most intensively in the doctrine of private international law – even though with different motives and in different modalities – which we might generally describe as an endeavour to obtain a universal validity of individual, theoretically warranted solutions and therefore as an endeavour to bring gradually closer together the private international laws of the different coutries. These efforts are also promoted by the economic integration taking place in a number of mostly geographically formed groupings of states in different parts of the world. This economic integration is undoubtedly an objective phenomenon and is a necessary consequence of the internationalization of production and exchange of goods, which also has an objective character. This fact does not mean, of course, that the economic substance and the methods of operation of the individual integration groupings can be placed on an identical level; these groupings considerably differ, as in the case of the integration of the West European capitalist states within the European Economic Community on the one hand, and the socialist integration realized within the framework of the Council of Mutual Economic Assistance, on the other hand. This fact also produces major differences in the field of the legal regulation of these integration processes, which must be borne in mind as an objective phenomenon.

It seems therefore, that the current period in the development of private international law may be characterized as a period of confrontation between the standard heritage of the past, which is manifested in the plurality of the individual private international laws, and the endeavour to adopt a broader, unifying concept of individual rules, which would lead to a closer identity of the municipal laws in the given sphere. In this connection we should therefore expect a gradual formation of private international laws within certain groupings of states, mostly dependent on progressing economic integration; this applies primarily to those sectors, which are in their substance important for the purposes of integration (while other sectors will probably be ignored).

Bearing in mind the probability of a development determined by the call for peaceful co-existence of states and the obligation of all states to co-operate with each other, we believe that, on the one hand, we must not overlook the class substance of individual states and their groupings, which always manifests itself in the legal sphere, but, on the other hand, we must not obstruct in the field of private international law the adoption of solutions which are acceptable on the broadest possible basis. The relatively high degree of efforts to formulate a common private international law in the West European integration groupings, the socialist integration in the member countries of the Council of Mutual Economic Assistance, the Anglo-American concepts, and the differences between these phenomena indicate a tendency towards the formation of the aforesaid entities in the sphere of private international law as well. On the other hand, of course, the rapid pace of the process of formation of new states in the past years, connected with growing economic co-operation and international division of labour, provide the conditions for the inclusion in the private international laws of individual states and their groupings of basic solutions which would make possible their broadest possible acceptance. Although it would be wrong and illusory to try to force through at the supranational level the adoption of universalistic trends at the present period, when the unity of mankind is being realized through the plurality of states with a different class substance, we should not ignore the fact that it is precisely demands raised for co-operation and co-existence between these states, which act as elements promoting the rapprochement of the individual concepts of private international law.

The progress of private international law therefore directly depends on the forms of the international organization of the human society and, we may say, on the initial concepts of this organization. These questions are mostly left aside as superfluous in the study of private international law at universities and in its general, common presentation. But in its historical survey we must pay attention to the differences arising from these initial concepts.

Thus, the concept of the absolutely perfect system of Roman law[8] brought into being in the period of Rome's increased contacts with the neighbouring tribes and nations the *ius gentium* as a universally applicable law. The fall of the Roman Empire and the resulting disintegration of the organization of the society of those days led to the assertion of personal "tribal laws" which had to be ascertained in each individual case; their plurality was such that it made Agobardus, the Bishop of Lyon, comment in his letter to king Louis the Devout that it often occurred that five men sitting together at a table were each under a different law.[9] As, subsequently, the Christian community of European feudal states of the early Middle Ages began gradually to form, based in its legal superstructure on the reception of Justinian's codification, the post-glossators began to form the concept of the statutory theory which also contained (thanks to the Roman heritage) strong elements of Christian universalism. After the changes through which the Italian, French and Dutch statutory concepts had passed — influenced in their whole by the individual stages of development of the feudal and eventually bourgeois society — emergence of bourgeois states in the modern sense, as well as the concept of sovereignty of these states, led in the 19th century to the plurality of individual private international laws, relatively independent of each other; because of the then prevailing international situation, this state of affairs could not change even after the founding of the Soviet Union. Only the present state of plurality of states with different class substance on the one hand, and the high degree of political and economic organization of these states on the other hand, dictated by the demands of co-existence, co-operation and internationalization

---

[8] Comp. Cicero's statement (*De oratore*, Lib. I, cap.. 44, § 197): "*Incredibile est quam sit omne ius civile praeter hoc nostrum incinditum ac poene ridiculum.*"

[9] See Brunner, *Deutsche Rechtsgeschichte*, 1st ed., Leipzig, 1887, Vol. I, p. 259.

of the whole life of society, seems to indicate that we have reached the threshold of a new concept, which must also deeply affect the development of private international law.

We can demonstrate already on the development of private international law in the capitalist period the changes that had occurred, as a result of the transformation of the industrial capitalism of the first half of the 19th century into the advanced capitalism and imperialism of the late 19th and early 20th centuries, not only in some of the initial concepts of private international law but also in individual conflict-of-laws rules,[10] where the direct influence of the economic transformations is easily traceable. In the present period, when there exist in the world several socio-economic formations and systems of ownership, a number of additional changes will take place in connection with international economic co-operation between the states belonging to these systems and their groupings; the future of these changes is only beginning to take shape.

Other factors, which also affect the development of private international law and its changes, are the existing political and ideological conditions; their influence on private international law must not be underestimated especially as regards its initial concepts and their formation. Precisely under the impact of these political conditions, private international law has become, in a way, a political matter. Changes taking place in such political categories as, for instance, state sovereignty, the idea of international communities, the relation between the individual and the state (his own or a foreign one), or the concepts of universally recognized human rights, quite naturally leave an indelible imprint on private international law, just as changes of an economic character. This influence is reflected not only in the formation of the initial concepts but also in a number of rules of seemingly "technical" character only; these factors play a direct, major role in the shaping of the opinion on what is to be understood under "public policy", what is the ideological expla-

---

[10] For a description of these changes see Part Two of the present work.

nation for the application of a foreign law by the domestic court, how theory is to explain the law of conflict of laws, the solution of the question whether a concrete case involves a violation of public policy, etc.

Thus, contemporary private international law, viewed as a phenomenon of the social superstructure, is characterized by highly diversified elements typical of the current stage of its development. On the one hand, it includes elements which in their present shape represent a culmination of the centuries-old tradition of this whole sphere of law which has become an integral part of the legal culture of the whole human society. This heritage of the past, mostly formed under different socio-economic conditions than those prevailing today, is, on the other hand, the subject of a dynamic development influenced by the transformation of the whole international life of society, from which private international law ensues and whose important aspects it governs. One of the features of this transformation is the gradual differentiation of social relations containing a foreign element from relationships of a "purely municipal" nature, which leads in its consequences to the situation where private international law has ceased to be only a law of conflict of laws and is also gradually becoming a substantive private international law. The current stage of development of private international law, influenced by the changes taking place in the international life of the human society, will undoubtedly require the expenditure of great effort in its scientific study and in municipal and international legislative activity; the fundamental problem of this activity will be the determination of the extent to which the established scientific and methodological approach to the solution of individual questions – often characteristic of the individual, initial concepts of private international law, formed in the past – can satisfy the urgent social need and demands which the highly advanced internationalization of the life of our society places on the private international law of our days.

•

As we have already mentioned, the problems of contemporary private international law are deeply influenced by the historical development and transformation through which private international law has passed in the course of the seven or eight centuries of its existence. Therefore, before we discuss the problems of the concept of contemporary private international law, we shall try to outline their historical development at least in a brief survey.

PART TWO

# Historical Development of the Concepts of Private International Law

## CHAPTER 1

## The Situation Prior to the Emergence of the Statutory Theory of Private International Law

### (1) The Law of the Slave State and Conflicts of Law

The earliest origin of the law of conflict of laws, which today forms the core of private international law, can be traced to the emergence of tribal laws in Italy in the period following the disintegration of the Roman Empire.[1]

It is only then that we can note the appearance of problems which didn't occur at the time of the united Roman Empire and the validity of Roman law (irrespective of whether this law was the *ius civile* or the *ius gentium,* which was specifically designed for legal relationships involving non-Roman elements). This original situation did not change even after the proclamation of the edict issued in 212 A. D. by Emperor Caracalla, who granted all freemen in the Roman Empire fully-fledged Roman citizenship; this edict was, of course, issued at a time when the old *ius civile* had already merged to quite an extent with the more modern *ius gentium* which was created for the needs of commercial contacts.

During the existence of the Roman Empire and in the period of the slave system in general, the conditions for the formation of a law governing conflict of laws were missing; the closed character and sanctity of the individual legal systems, ensuing from the original identity between law and religion, were typical

---

[1] Some authors, such as Lewald, *Conflicts des lois dans le monde grec et romain,* Athens, 1946, point, however, to the existence of questions of conflict of laws in ancient Greece, Rome and elsewhere (e.g. ancient Egypt).

of that period and resulted in the exclusion of foreigners and relationships with a foreign element from the domestic rule of law. Although in the Roman Empire there existed many relations with a foreign, or rather non-Roman, element (at least in the period preceding Caracalla's edict), there did not exist – at least according to the Romans – several laws of states which respect each other, which, together with the existence of civil-law relations with a foreign element, are the prerequisites of the formation of private international law.[2] Roman law was considered to be the most perfect of all, as claimed by Cicero, who, when comparing Roman law with the laws of Lycurgos, Dracon and Solon, came to the conclusion that, "*incredibile est quam sit omne ius civile praeter hoc nostrum inconditum ac paene ridiculum*".[3] Even after Caracalla had issued his edict in 212 A. D., when only barbarians were considered to be *peregrini*, rules governing conflict of laws were not included in Roman law.[4]

In Roman law we thus meet with the tendency to impose this

---

[2] See, e.g., Lunts, *Mezinárodní právo soukromé (Private International Law)*, Czech translation from the Russian, Prague, 1952, p. 45, Krčmář, *Úvod do mezinárodního práva soukromého (Introduction to Private International Law)*, Prague, 1906, p. 37 and *Základy Bartolovy a Baldovy teorie mezinárodního práva soukromého (The Bases of Bartolus' and Baldus' Doctrine of Private International Law)*, Prague, 1910, p. 12, 3rd ed., M. Wolff, *Das internationale Privatrecht Deutschlands*, Berlin–Göttingen–Heidelberg, 1965, pp. 2 and 3.

[3] Cicero, *De oratore I*, 44, 197. Quoted from M. Wolff, *Private International Law*, 2nd ed., Oxford, 1950, p. 20; also see Lunts, *Mezinárodní právo soukromé (Private International Law)*, p. 47.

[4] Although some passages in the Digest point to the necessity of deciding certain matters on the basis of local customs *(mos, consuetudo loci,* or *provinciae)*, such as in, Dig. 33.1.21, 26.7.7.10, 17.1.10.3; however, M. Wolff, *Private International Law*, p. 20, believes that this simply means that gaps in treaties and testaments should be filled in this manner. For opinion on conflicts in the laws of Antiquity see Mitteis, *Reichsrecht und Volksrecht in den östlichen Provinzen des römischen Kaiserreichs*, 1891, pp. 120, 161; Lewald, *Conflicts* (he points to the appearance of the idea of autonomy even in ancient Egypt); J. Beyssac, *Les conflicts des lois à Rome*, Bordeaux, 1888; Cybichowski, *Das antike Völkerrecht*, Breslau, 1907.

law on all legal relations settled by Roman lawyers; when we bear in mind the endeavour of the Roman Empire towards world domination, we should not be surprised that this endeavour is parallelled by the expansionist character of Roman law in the sphere of civil-law relations.

## (2) The Emergence of Tribal Laws and the Personal Principle

The Germanic invasion of Italy in the 5th century destroyed the unity of the Roman Empire and also resulted in the temporary extinction of the universal, territorial validity of Roman law. Instead of a single, vast empire, there appeared (although not always in a legally defined form) a number of smaller territorial, relatively isolated, entities which began to be governed by their own laws. The peoples who invaded Italy from the north and established their rule on the conquered territories brought with them their own laws which were, of course, inferior to the highly detailed Roman law.

At the time when Lombard rule came to an end in Italy at the end of the 8th century and was replaced by the rule of Frankish kings, regulations began to be issued, which were binding on a territorial basis. Besides these regulations, the rule was observed — as a custom as well as on the basis of formally issued decrees — that unless a generally binding regulation was in force, a man should live in accordance with his tribal law.[5] However, after the fall of the Frankish realm and before the founding of the Holy Roman Empire, the growing complexity of the situation and life forced out Lombard law in favour of Roman law which could better serve the needs of the then society than the former. This trend was spurred by the belief in the universal validity of Roman law, which was also promoted by the opinion, strongly asserted only since the 11th century,

---

[5] See Krčmář, ***Základy, (Bases)***, p. 19; also the sources and bibliography listed there in footnotes Nos. 7 and 8.

that the Holy Roman Empire founded by Charlemagne was a direct continuation and heir of the ancient Roman Empire.[6] At the same time, however, the tribal laws continued to remain in force. This gradually gave rise to the problem, initiated by the multiplicity of the tribal laws, which law should govern legal relationships containing a foreign element. This problem was settled on the basis of the personal principle according to the tribal laws of the parties.

Initially, every ethnic group was bound by its own tribal law which governed the legal relationships of all its members. The means of ascertaining the tribal law was the *professio iuris,* that is the answer to the question *qua lege visis?*, raised during judicial proceedings; the answer may have been, for example: "*Ego ex gente Romanorum, professus sum ex lege Romanorum vivere*". However, the *professio iuris* also appears outside judicial proceedings, especially in written documents. The multiplicity of the tribal laws was such, that it was criticized by Bishop Agobardus in the already quoted statement, in which he said that often five men might walk or sit together, every one of them under a different law.

### (3) Feudalism and the Territorial Principle

The subsequent formation of feudal entities on the territory of the Roman Empire brought to an end the personal principle; the feudal lord exercised, as a rule, authority over all persons found on the territory he ruled. The law of the given territory therefore applied to all individuals on that territory, irrespective

---

[6] This process is described in detail by Neumeyer, *Die gemeinrechtliche Entwicklung des internationalen Privat- und Strafrechts bis Bartolus,* Vol. I, Munich, 1901, pp. 59 ff. See also the views put forward by Koschaker, *Europa und das römische Recht,* 2nd ed., Munich, 1953, p. 17 (as regards the relationship between Charlemange's empire and the Imperium Romanum) and p. 38 (as regards the subsequent view that the German emperors were the successors of the Roman emperors).

of their tribal origin. The legal status of the inhabitants depended on their ties with the territory. The personal principle was replaced by the territorial principle, which was directly conditional upon the emergence of the feudal system. The territorial principle was then also applied to the question of conflicts of laws. However, the minute possibility of the occurrence of such questions was due to the economic isolation of the individual feudal entities and to the fact that contacts between the population of these entities were almost non-existent.

Nevertheless, the application of the territorial principle did not completely erase the difference between the local population and aliens, or between old and new members of the feudal entity, as indicated, for example, by the institution of the mediaeval feudal law known as *ius albinagii (droit d'aubaine),* under which the ruler confiscated the estate of a deceased alien. However, according to unanimous opinion, a lack of sources from this period prevents us from learning whether under such a situation the alien law may not have been taken into consideration at least to a limited extent.

As the territorial principle grew in its application, the knowledge of the old tribal laws gradually disappeared. Personal law, expressed by the law of a person's tribal origin, was replaced in the law of conflict of laws by a new criterion, proceeding from the link between the individual and his country, the criterion of his domicil, which eventually prevailed.

Parallel with this process, however, respect continued to grow towards Roman law as a universal source of law; its knowledge was being restored on the basis of manuscripts then discovered. Roman law became the subject of intensive study especially at Italian universities, primarily in Bologna, and the trend towards recognizing it as a universally valid body of law continuously grew.

## CHAPTER 2
# The Emergence and Initial Progress of the Statutory Theory

## (4) The Economic and Political Prerequisites

As early as from the Roman period, the fertile Lombard Plain and the cities of Northern Italy – Pisa, Milan, Bologna, Venice, Genoa, Florence, Parma, Padua, Modena, Ferrara, Siena and others – ranked among the richest commercial centres trading with areas north of the Alps and with overseas lands. The wealth of these urban centres, originally incorporated in feudal systems, encouraged the emerging bourgeoisie to supplement its growing economic power with a special political status, free of the feudal fetters, in order to obtain cheap labour from the adjacent rural areas. The beginning of the 11th century saw the beginning of the process of liberation of these cities from their feudal episcopal or secular overlords; after administrative and judicial authority had been transferred to the city administrations, this process culminated in the Peace Treaty of Constance in 1183, concluded between the union of Lombard cities and Emperor Frederic I, Barbarossa. This peace meant for the Italian cities their *de facto* separation from the central authority of the Holy Roman Empire which maintained only formal sovereignty over them. The rights granted to these cities under the Peace of Constance included the right of their own legislative competence.[1] Most of the cities of Northern Italy became independent city-

---

[1] See Krčmář, *Základy (Bases)*, pp. 34 ff., with the express quotation of the wording of the Peace Treaty of Constance: "*Nos imperator Fridericus et filius noster Henricus Romanorum rex concedimus vobis civitatibus locis et personis societatis regalia et consuetudines vostras tam i civitate quam extra civitatem ... etc.*" On p. 39 Krčmář points, however, to the continuing autority of imperial legislative power, which also included the authority to abolish and amend the city statutes.

states which issued their own laws *(statuta)* necessitated by their rapidly growing commercial contacts; this, in turn, resulted in a steadily increasing number of legal relations containing a foreign element. The equal position of the individual urban entities and the diversity of their laws gave rise to problems which today are included in private international law. The universal law observed by the North Italian cities continued to be Roman law, but the *statuta* issued by the individual cities could derogate Roman law under the principle *lex posterior derogat legi priori.* And between the city statutes and the Roman law there still existed municipal consuetudinary law which included both Roman and Germanic elements.[2]

(5) The Glossators

In the period when the school of the glossators – the true restorers of Roman law – had flourished most, the problem of application of the laws of the individual city-states to relationships containing a foreign element was at first settled in favour of the validity of the law of the court making the decision *(lex fori).*[3]

Only later (in about 1200), the opinion was put forward, that in the case of a conflict between the laws of the individual cities, the judge should apply the law he found better.[4]

---

[2] *Ibid.*, pp. 53 and 54.

[3] See Gutzwiller, *Recueil des Cours,* 1929, Vol. IV, p. 299; also Meijers, "L'historie des principes fondamentaux du droit international privé à partir du Moyen-Age", *Recueil des Cours,* 1934, Vol. 49, p. 593.

[4] Gutzwiller, *Recueil des Cours,* 1929, vol. IV, p. 301, quotes Magister Aldric as the author of this opinion and as the actual founder of the doctrine of private international law: "*... quaeritur si homines diversarum provinciarum, quae diversas habent consuetudines, sub uno eodemque iudice litigant, utrum earum iudex qui iudicandum suscepit sequi debeat? Respondeo eam quae potior et utilior videtur, debet enim iudicare secundum quod melius ei visum fuerit*". Also see Krčmář, *Zá-*

The basic text which served as the basis for the promotion of the views raised by the glossators and post-glossators on private international law was the law *Cunctos populos* from the book *De summa Trinitate* of Justinian's Code (C. J. 1,1,1), which begins with the following words: "*Cunctos populos quos clementiae nostrae regit imperium in tali volumus religione versari, quam divum Petrum apostolum tradisse Romanis religio* ...". This text was used to deduce scholastically that the legislator intended to make his rules binding only upon his subjects. The *glossae* commenting this text (in particular the famous gloss of Accursius from the early 13th century) brought to an end the initial validity of the *lex fori*. Accursius comments as follows: "*argumentum: quod si bononiensis conveniatur Mutinae, non debet iudicari secundum statuta Mutinae quibus non subest, cum dicat 'quos nostrae clementiae'.*"[5] This example shows how scholastically the first principles of the statutory theory of private international law had been deduced, in particular the principle that the territorial validity of the *lex fori* applied only to citizens and not aliens. Roughly at the same time, when Accursius wrote his gloss, Carolus de Tocco formulated quite unequivocally their rule "*statuta non ligant nisi subditos*".[6]

## (6) The Post-Glossators

The origins of the actual statutory theory of private international law were inseparably linked with the activities of the post-glossators and were marked by their casuistic and scho-

---

*klady (Bases)*, p. 117. The same author, however, names in his "Beiträge zur Geschichte des internationalen Privatrechts," *Zeitschrift zur Jahrhundertfeier des österreichischen ABGB*, 1911, Vol. 2, p. 141, Jacobus Balduini as the founder of the science of private international law.

[5] See Neumayer, *Entwicklung*, Vol. II pp. 76 and 63; Gutzwiller, *Recueil des Cours*, 1929, vol. 19, p. 303.

[6] Schnitzer, *Handuch des internationalen Privatrechts*, Basel, 1957, Vol. I, p. 7.

lastic methods of interpretation;[7] on the other hand, they deserve credit for having largely borne in mind – in contrast to the glossators – also the needs of legal practice, created by the growing commercial contacts.

Typical of the theory and methods of the post-glossators in the sphere of private international law was their effort to find solutions for conflicts of laws according to the content of the legal relationships involved. Therein lay the beginning of the actual statutory theory of private international law, characterized by a differentiation of the conflicts criteria according to whether the case involved a conflict between personal, real or, subsequently, also mixed statutes.

It is remarkable, and it also points to the economic necessity which gave rise to individual conflicts solutions, that the effort to formulate conflicts criteria applicable to all types of the given relationships did not manifest itself until the sphere of the law of obligations had gained some prominence.[8] Thus, economic necessity brought into being the conflicts principle which provided that contracts were to be governed by the law of the place where they had been concluded, irrespective of the persons which were the contracting parties.

After a thorough study of old manuscripts, Neumeyer came to the conclusion that the credit for the formulation of this principle did not belong to the legists but to authors on canon law, without, however, excluding the possibility that the principle had been taken over from an older civil-law specialist.[9] Thus Johannes Faventinus, a canonist, asserted as early as at the end of the 12th century that contracts should be governed by the law of the place of their conclusion. The same opinion was held

---

[7] The casuistic method of the post-glossators and their typically scholastic arguments later met with a strong oposition especially among the humanists. See Sommer, *Prameny sokromého práva římského (Sources of Roman Private Law)*, 2nd ed., pp. 758–159.

[8] Gutzwiller, *Recueil des Cours*, 1929, Vol. IV, p. 304; Neumeyer, *Entwicklung*, Vol. II, p. 83.

[9] Neumeyer, *Entwicklung*, Vol. II, pp. 84, 135 ff. Also see Gutzwiller, *Recueil des Cours*, 1929, Vol. IV, p. 305.

by another authority on canon law, Bernardus Papiensis.[10] There is no need to discuss here the question which so greatly intrigued Neumayer, namely whether the credit for developing the principle of application of the *lex loci conclusionis* should go to the canonists or legists. It is a fact, however, that this principle was fully elaborated and developed by the post-glossators.

The texts on which the post-glossators based their arguments regarding the law of obligations were two fragments from the Digest. One was the law *Si fundus* (Dig. 21, 2, 6): "*Si fundus venierit, ex consuetudine eius regionis in qua negotium gestum est pro evictione caveri oportet.*" This involved the principle applicable to guaranty for eviction in sales of immovables. The other was the law *Contraxisse* (Dig. 44, 7,21): "*Contraxisse unusquisque in eo loco intelligetur in quo ut solveret se obligavit.*" We shall demonstrate further below how the post-glossators made use of texts on Roman law for deducing principles which the original authors undoubtedly never had in mind, and how in this manner they formed for practical purposes the foundations of a completely new doctrine.

Once the principle of applicability of the law of the place of the contract, irrespective of the personal statute of the contracting parties, had been adopted, practical needs brought forth a new principle, arising from the necessity of subjecting also aliens to the procedural law of the adjudicating court in contrast to the possible application of a foreign substantive law. This drew a clear dividing line in international legal contracts between the substance and the form of proceedings, and created the categories of substantive law, determined *ad litem decidendam*, and procedural law *ad litis ordinationem*, which was always to be applied to the consideration of procedural questions.[11] At the

---

[10] Neumeyer, *Entwicklung*, Vol. II, pp. 136 ff.

[11] Jacobus Balduini is universally recognized as the author of this distinction. See Neumeyer, *Entwicklung*, Vol. II, pp. 85 ff.; Krčmář, *Beiträge*, p. 41, and *Základy (Bases)*, pp. 112 ff., where he describes Jacobus Balduini as the father of private international law. – The text quoted by Neumeyer reads as follows: "*aut consuetudo est ad litis ordinationem aut ad litem decidendam introducta si ad litis ordi-*

end of the 13th century, the application of the *lex fori* to questions regarding procedure was generally accepted throughout Italy.[12]

However, we may describe as the period of a true flourishment of the theory of private international law only a somewhat later period, when the doctrine of the school of the post-glossators had developed in its full scope; this school is characterized by the names of Dinus, Jacobus de Arena, Oldradus (who was the teacher of the famous Bartolus), Jacobus Buttrigarius, Jacobus de Ravanis (de Révigny), Petrus de Bellapertica (de Belleperche), Cinus, Guilielmus Durantis, Albericus de Rosate, Joannes Faber, and, finally, Bartolus de Sassoferrato, Baldus de Ubaldis, and others.[13] This school was marked by the already noted trend towards an exploitation of the authority of Roman law – scholastically interpreted – for obtaining practical solutions.

The fact that in further discussion we shall primarily concentrate on the development of and changes in the concepts of private international law with regard to the law of obligations is due to the fact that it is in this field, marked by the closest ties with the reality of international economic relations, that the changes in the individual concepts are most noticeable; on the other hand, in the sphere of private and family laws, where religious and national traditions often play a decisive role, as well as in the sphere of rights *in rem*, marked by the prevalence of the principle of *lex rei sitae*, this development and its impact are not as prominent.

---

*nationem, puta ut libellus detur ... qualiter procedatur in causa et tunc spectatur consuetudo quae est in foro iudicio, aut est introducta ad litem decidendam, puta an venditor teneatur ad duplam et tunc inspicitur consuetudo loci ubi contractum est.*"

[12] Meijers, *Recueil des Cours,* 1934, Vol. 49, p. 596.

[13] An analysis of the doctrine of these and other authors can be found primarily in Lainé, *Introduction au droit international privé contenant une étude historique et critique de la théorie des statuts et des rapports de cette théorie avec le Code civil,* Paris, Vol. 1 (1886), Vol. 2 (1892), and the two listed works of Krčmář.

## (7) Bartolus and Baldus

We should first take note of the opinions of the famous Bartolus de Sassoferrato (1313—1357) who is universally recognized as the father of the statutory theory and as the man who first made the distinction between personal and real statutes. It was he, who logically supplemented and systematically completed the views of his predecessors and produced his own, albeit incomprehensive, theory of private international law.[14]

Bartolus considered a case where an action for failure to perform a contract made by a foreigner in Perugia was entertained in the place of the foreigner's origin. Under his interpretation of *Si fundus,* Bartolus reached the conclusion that the form of the contract *(solemnitas contractus)* had to be governed by the law of the place where the contract was made. Questions of procedural law *(litis ordinatio)* were to be considered according to the law of the forum. However, where the substance of the case *(ipsius litis decisio)* was to be decided upon, Bartolus underlined the necessity of further distinction.

The natural consequences of the contract, which could have been envisaged under the contract at the time of its conclusion, were to be governed by the law of the place of the contract. Here, too, Bartolus applied the law *Si fundus.* Under the law of the place of the contract he understood the law of the place where the contract had been made rather than the law of the place where it was to be performed *(locus contractus est in loco ubi celebratus contractus non in loco in quem est collata solutio* — an argument based on the law *Contraxisse).* However, as regards consequences arising after the conclusion of the contract

---

[14] See Lainé, *Introduction,* Vol. I, pp. 133 ff. and Krčmář, *Základy (Bases).* — The work of Bartolus is discussed in monograph form by C. M. S. Woolf, *Bartolo de Sassoferrato,* Urbino, 1935. Passages from Bartolus' commentary on the Codex, which contain the essence of his statutory doctrine, were published by Meili, "Die theoretischen Abhandlungen des Bartolus und Baldus über das internationale Privatrecht und Strafrecht", *Zeitschrift für internationales Privat- und Strafrecht begr. von Böhm,* Vol. 4, 1894, pp. 260 ff., 340 ff., 446 ff.

from negligence or delays, these were to be governed by the law of the place where the contract was to be performed or, where this was not specified, by the law of the forum.[15]

These opinions of Bartolus indicate the clear distinction he made between the form of the contract and the solemnities concerning the conclusion of the contract; he also distinguished between substantive and formal laws and between application of the law of the place of the contract and the law of the place of its performance, depending on whether normal or irregular consequences of the contract were involved.[16]

Bartolus was also of the opinion that prescription was to be governed by the law of the place of performance of the contract and annulation by the law of the making of the contract in cases where the abolishment ensued from the contract proper.[17]

In another place Bartolus also considered questions concerning capacity to acquire rights or to perform legal acts. He reached the conclusion that as regards the latter, the statute of the city was binding upon its citizens no matter where they may have found themselves. As for the former, the local statute was applicable only on the territory of the respective place.

Bartolus devoted special attention to the extraterritorial effect of legal prohibitions outside the scope of criminal law; he made a distinction between prohibitions to perform certain acts violating a specific form (e.g. prohibitions to make testaments or to perform certain negotiations in a different form than in the presence of two witnesses), which, in his opinion had only territorial effect, prohibitions under substantive rules or made in view of the nature of the case (e.g. the prohibition imposed on a co-owner to sell his share without the consent of the other co-

---

[15] Lainé, *Introduction,* Vol. I, p. 136.

[16] This distinction made first by Bartolus serves to this day as the basis for the distinction made by contemporary French authors between *effets* and *suites* as the consequences of a contract, and between the application of different laws depending on what consequences are involved in the given case. See Batiffol, *Les Conflicts de lois en matière de Contrats,* Paris, 1938, p. 70.

[17] See Lainé, *Introduction,* Vol. I, p. 136.

owner), which had extraterritorial effect, and finally, a third type of prohibitions relating to the character of the respective person; in these cases, however, where a *prohibitio favorabilis* was to protect a particular person (e.g. a person below a certain age could not make a testament), the prohibition had extraterritorial effect irrespective of where the person found itself; on the other hand, where the prohibition was a *prohibitio odiosa,* it had only territorial effect (e.g. a prohibition denying daughters the right to inherit).[18]

Baldus de Ubaldis (1327–1400), who was a disciple of Bartolus, eleborated in particular on Bartolus' arguments regarding capacity to acquire rights and perform legal acts. [19] He also clearly defined the law which was to govern questions of capacity. It was not the *lex originis* but the *lex domicilii;* this may be explained by the fact that domicile was a much more practical criterion for determining capacity under conditions of highly developed trade than the *lex originis;* an additional factor was the formal subjection of the North Italian cities to the Holy Roman Empire in spite of their *de facto* independence.

## (8) Bartholomeus de Saliceto, Paulus de Castro, Rochus Curtius

The most prominent among the followers of Bartolus and Baldus, who had made their own contribution to the development of the conflict rules governing primarily the law of obligations, was Bartholomeus de Saliceto (†1412); following the example set by his teachers, he arrived in his commentary on the law

---

[18] Gutzwiller, *Recueil des Cours,* 1929, Vol. IV, p. 310. A detailed analysis and criticism of these views of Bartolus are offered by Lainé, *Introduction,* Vol. I, p. 146.

[19] On Baldus see Lainé, *Introduction,* Vol. I, pp. 166 ff., and Krčmář, *Základy (Bases);* Baldus' writings on statutory theory are quoted by Meili, *Zeitschrift für internationales Privat- und Strafrecht,* Vol. 4 (1894), pp. 454 ff.; Baldus and his work are also the topic of *L'opera di Baldo,* published by the University of Perugia in 1901.

*Cunctos populos* at the conclusion that questions arising from contracts should be considered according to the law of the place where the respective contract had been made.[20]

However, Saliceto also concerned himself with the question of whether the law of the place where the contract was made should also be applied in cases where the contract was to be performed in a different place; this was a disputed problem based on interpretations of the law *Contraxisse*, which permitted the application of the law of the place of performance.[21] Saliceto, just like Bartolus, advocated the place of the making as the decisive criterion, but added the observation (used to this day by advocates of the *lex loci conclusionis*) that it would be unjustly hard towards the parties to the contract, to apply to their contract a law whose rules had probably been unknown to them. He also shared the opinion of his teacher Bartolus, expressed in the distinction the latter had made between regular consequences of a contract (which were to be governed by the law of the place of the making) and irregular consequences (which were to be governed by the law of the place of performance, if it had been specified, or, if not, by the *lex fori*).

Paulus de Castro (†1441) who was a disciple of Baldus, used as an argument for the validity of the *lex locis conclusionis* a parallel between the birth of a man and a contract,[22] asserting that contracts, just as individuals, should be subjected to the law of their origin, i.e. the law of the place where the contract was made *(quia talis contractus dicitur ibi nasci ubi paciscitur, et, sicut persona ratione originis ligatur a statutis loci originis, ita et actus).*

Rochus Curtius (†1495), who was but an epigon of his more famous predecessors and the last of the Italian post-glossa-

---

[20] Lainé, *Introduction,* Vol. I, pp. 178 ff.; Batiffol, *Contrats,* p. 21.

[21] The sentence *"Contraxisse unusquisque in eo loco intelligetur in quo ut solveret se obligavit"* lends itself to a dual interpretation: one favouring the place of the making of the contract, the other the place of its performance.

[22] Lainé, *Introduction,* Vol. I, pp. 188 ff.

tors, put forward the idea that the *lex loci conclusionis* should be the basic principle governing conflict problems of the law of obligations because the parties had tacitly chosen the law of the place of performance as the applicable law.

Naturally, Curtius was not asserting the principle of a free choice of the applicable law by the parties, as it might seem at first look; for all the Italian post-glossators proceeded from the principle of the *lex loci conclusionis,* and Curtius merely provided a supporting argument to explain this fundamental principle.[23] The question of choice of the applicable law by the parties, which could supersede the law that would be otherwise applicable under the usual criteria, did not appear in its crystallized form until the 16th century, when it was raised by the French lawyer Charles Dumoulin.

## (9) Conclusions

A comparison made between the doctrine of the glossators, who laid the foundations of private international law, and the conclusions reached by the post-glossators shows that the latter had actually developed a wholly new doctrine which is generally described in the history of private international law as the statutory theory. This theory subsequently also became a method of private international law, which was further developed by French and Dutch jurists and had not been abandoned until the 19th century.

Although the post-glossators had used typically scholastic and casuistic methods and elaborated on cases mechanically taken over by later authors from earlier authors, expanding them into extensive distinctions and subdistinctions, there is no doubt that

---

[23] Batiffol, *Contrats,* p. 22; Caleb, *Essai sur le principe de l'autonomie de la volonté en droit international privé,* Paris, 1927, p. 133; Niboyet, *"La Théorie de l'autonomie de la Volonté", Recueil des Cours,* 1927, Vol. I, p. 8.

in their period their work meant progress. They used the authority enjoyed by Roman law to help break down the barriers of enclosed feudal units, hampering legal contacts, in the interests of the emerging bourgeoisie under new political and economic conditions. In place of the rigid principle of territoriality, inherent to feudal economy, they freed the way to the application of the principle of personality, which was in keeping with the growing occurrence of cases containing a foreign element.

The progressive character of the doctrine developed by the post-glossators is perhaps best reflected in the solution of conflict problems in the sphere of the law of obligations. Nothing could suit better the needs of growing commercial contacts than the applicability of the personality principle to cases involving the capacity of the contracting parties; the same was true of the validity of the law of the place of the making of the contract, in most cases involving obligations. The same law was also applied to questions of the form of contracts (which were then mostly made between persons present), which pomoted the feeling of assurance that the commercial transaction was concluded in good and proper form and that its validity could not be contested for lack of form.

Thus the work of the post-glossators was in keeping with the characterization voiced by Friedrich Engels in his treatise on the disintegration of feudalism and the growth of the bourgeoisie: "The re-discovery of Roman law brought about a division of labour between the priests, who had served as legal advisors in the feudal period, and jurists who were not ecclesiastics. These new jurists essentially represented the burghers; thus the law they studied, lectured on and practiced was in substance of anti-feudal character and, in a certain sense, was of a bourgeois nature. Roman law is a classical legal expression of the life and conflicts of society governed by purely private ownership to the extent where no subsequent legislation could improve on it in any substantial way. However, in the Middle Ages, bourgeois ownership was still strongly affected by feudal restrictions and, for example, was mostly based on privileges; in this respect, Roman law was still far above the then prevailing bourgeois situation. The future historical development of bourgeois ownership could only follow the trend – as it did – towards purely private ownership. However, this development had to find a powerful driving force in Roman law which already contained all that the bourgeoisie of the later Middle Ages strove for, then still unwittingly."[24]

---

[24] Engels, *O rozkladu feudalismu a rozvoji buržoasie (The Disintegration of Feudalism and the Development of Bourgeoisie*, Prague, 1951, p. 14.

# CHAPTER 3
# French and Dutch Statutory Theory

## (10) Charles Dumoulin – the French Successor of Bartolus

Many post-glossators and successors of Bartolus were of French origin or were active on the territory of present-day Southern France. However, the economic and political situation in Northern Italy and France differed. In contrast to the city-states of Northern Italy, where feudalism had been liquidated for all practical purposes, the economic situation in France was dominated by the continued existence of feudal relations which were relatively stronger in the north of the country than in the south. The period of the activity of the followers of the post-glossators in France was at the same time the period when the individual French provinces, ruled by feudal lords, were being integrated into a politically united state, the subsequent absolute monarchy. The urban commercial elements, concentrated primarily in Paris, were interested both in the creation of a single, national market and in the unification of the country.[1] The emerging and growing bourgeoisie thus became the natural ally of royal authority in the latter's struggle for the subjection of the powerful feudal magnates and the curtailment of their privileges. As for French law, Roman law – in contrast to Northern Italy – did not enjoy the authority of the law in force and at the most merely influenced the creation of the consuetudinary law (called *coutumes*) existing in the southern provinces of France.

The most prominent of the successors of the post-glossators in France was Carolus Molinaeus (Charles Dumoulin – 1500–1566) who also made the greatest contribution to the development of the theory of settling conflict of laws in the sphere of the law of

---

[1] Lunts, *Mezinárodní právo soukromé (Private International Law)*, p. 52.

contracts.[2] His work is interesting primarily because it raises, for the first time, the question of choice of the applicable law by the parties to the contract; this question was no longer understood as a subsidiary and auxiliary explanation of the validity of the *lex loci contractus celebrati* (which already appeared in the works of Rochus Curtius) but as a separate conflict criterion.[3]

Dumoulin used the method developed by the post-glossators (especially in his comments on Justinian's Code which had been published at the time of his stay in Tübingen where, as a Huguenot, he had fled to escape religious persecution); he distinguished between statutes according to whether they governed the form of legal acts or whether they concerned a different, substantive law. When discussing the substance of contracts, Dumoulin developed his theory of autonomy of will. In his opinion, the supreme law in the sphere, of the law of contracts was the will of the parties; if such will was not expressed, it had to be sought in the circumstances under which the parties were making their contract; the place where the contract was made was only one but not the only such circumstance; the others included the domicile of the parties and similar facts.[4] In arguing in favour of this conclusion, Dumoulin referred to a case where the owner of real property located in Germany sold the property on his journey in Italy. And in his legal argumentation he made use of the well-known law *Si fundus;* at the same time, however, he pointed to the fact that the place of the making of the contract .was often a chance one, especially in cases where the

---

[2] For Dumoulin's personality and his work in general see Lainé, *Introduction,* Vol. I, pp. 223 ff., F. Meili, "Argentraeus und Molinaeus und ihre Bedeutung im internationalen Privat- und Strafrecht", *Zeitschrift für internationales Recht,* V, 1895, pp. 363, 371, 452, 554 and a reprint of the works of Dumoulin and d'Argentré.

[3] Caleb, *Essai,* pp. 132 ff., Niboyet, *Recueil de Cours,* 1927, Vol. 1, p. 9; Lunts, *Mezinárodní právo soukromé (Private International Law),* p. 52; Bagge, "Les conflict de lois en matière de contrat de vente de biens meubles corporels", *Recueil des Cours,* 1928, Vol. V, pp. 134, and 135, Meijers, *Recueil des Cours,* 1934, Vol. 49, pp. 637 ff.

[4] Lainé, *Introduction,* Vol. I, pp. 229 and 230.

parties did not make the contract in the place of their common domicil.[5]

In his *Consilium LIII* (which he wrote before his commentary), Dumoulin also discussed the will of the parties not expressly made.[6] Here he assigned to an assumed (tacitly made) marriage contract the same importance as if the contract had been made expressly; in doing so, he referred to argumentation based on sound reason.[7]

Dumoulin also made an important distinction between a contract of sale as conceived from the viewpoint of the law of obligations and its effects under substantive law; he reached the conclusion that the sphere of the choice of law should differ according to whether the former or the latter case were involved.[8]

Dumoulin's teachings, which proceeded from the idea that in the sphere of the law of obligations the will of the parties was the law, at the same time promoted yet another principle, so frequently abused today in the search for the hypothetical will of the parties in most legal systems, namely that the will of the parties – unless expressly made – should be sought according

[5] *Iste est proprius casus et verus intellectus D. 1. 6. de evictionibus D. 21. 2., in qua dicitur venditorem teneri cavere secundum consuetudinem loci contractus, quod est intelligendum non de loco contractus fortuiti, sed domicilii, prout crebrius usuvenit immobilia non vendi peregre, sed in loco domicilii, lex autem debet adaptari ad casus vel hypotheses quae solent frequenter accidere, nec extendi ad casus raro accidentes.* – See the reprint in Meili, "Argantraeus und Molinaeus und ihre Bedeutung im internationalen Privat- und Strafrecht", *Zeitschrift für internationales Recht* (Böhms Ztschr.), 1895, Vol. V, p. 556.

[6] The case involved the problem whether community of property existing under the Paris custom between spouses who had not made a marriage contract, also applied to property located within the sphere of a law governing matrimonial property relations in a different manner.

[7] *"Primum in sano intellectum nullum habet dubium quin societas semel contracta complectatur bona ubicumque sita sine nulla differencia territoriali quemadmodum quilibet Contractus sive tacitus sive expressus ligat personam et res disponentes ubiques."* This *Consilium* subsequently became the topic of a lively discussion in the French and Dutch literature on private international law; it was critized primarily by d'Argentré.

[8] See Bagge, *Recueil des Cours*, 1928, Vol. V, p. 135.

to the circumstances of the case, and that the law deduced from this will should also govern the questions which in the opinion of Bartolus should be governed by the law of the place of performance.

In Dumoulin's doctrine the principle of the validity of the *lex loci conclusionis* therefore lost its imperative character; Dumoulin thus became the first jurist to oppose the rigidity of *a priori* given points of contact in the sphere of the law of obligations and to advocate the principle of a certain flexibility in considering problems of conflict of laws, which was broadly applied in legal practice especially in later years because it met the needs of growing international trade.

It should be noted that some authors often fail to grasp the significance of Dumoulin's teachings and try to lessen his importance even as the originator of the principle of autonomy of will; in doing so, they refer to the fact that Dumoulin himself views choice of law as an *a posteriori explanation* of a practically useful solution rather than as a separate conflict criterion meeting the requirements of logic and justice,[9] or simply stress that Dumoulin's contribution rests in the fact that he had taken the step which neither Salicetus nor Curtius had dared to make, when he admitted that the assumption of the validity of the *lex loci conclusionis* could be reversed by the circumstances of the respective case;[10] on the other hand, L. A. Lunts quite properly notes that "Dumoulin's teachings reflected the interests of the merchants since they enabled their representatives to overcome legal particularism by private agreement; thus the customs observed in Paris as a centre of commerce could be applied in Brittany, Normandy and other provinces which lagged behind in their economic and legal development."[11]

---

[9] See, e.g., Lainé, *Introduction*, Vol. I, pp. 232 ff.

[10] See Batiffol, *Contrats*, p. 23. On the other hand, Dumoulin's importance is correctly assessed e.g. by Martin Wolff, *Das internationale Privatrecht Deutschlands*, p. 15.

[11] See Lunts, *Mezinárodní právo soukromé (Private International Law)*, p. 53. The author points out that Dumoulin's doctrine had been quite advanced for its period.

## (11) Reaction to Dumoulin's Doctrine — D'Argentré

Although Dumoulin's argumentation reflects certain respect for the territorial character of the consuetudinary law of the individual French provinces even as regards consideration of questions of capacity,[12] the strictly territorial character of the *coutumes* upheld by the feudal lords of the outlying provinces immediately evoked a reaction to Dumoulin's doctrine.

The chief representative of this reaction in the doctrine of private international law was d'Argentré (1519—1590), a nobleman and jurist of Brittany, who tried to uphold in full the privileges of the feudal barons against central royal authority which was supported by the growing Paris bourgeoisie. In his opinion, all consuetudinary law was "real" *(les coutumes sont réelles),* which meant that in the sphere of the law of conflicts of law it had an almost absolute territorial character and validity.[13]

In his Commentary on Article 218 of the Collection of Legal Customs of Brittany d'Argentré opposed all trends (both of the Italian post-glossators and Dumoulin) which recommended a broader application of the personal principle to the detriment of the territorial nature of local legal customs and which supported the idea of a uniform, generally valid body of law.[14]

D'Argentré fully abandoned the determination of the applicable law according to the specifications of the Italian school of which he spoke with contempt. He himself settled problems of conflict of laws differently according to whether the conflict affected real statutes, personal statutes or mixed statutes. Real statutes concerned real property in all legal relations, no

---

[12] For detail see Meijers, *Recueil des Cours,* 1934, Vol. 49, *L'historie des principes fondamentaux,* pp. 651 ff.; Meijers studies the effects of territoriality on personal statutes to which most post-glossators attached extraterritorial effects.

[13] For detail see Lainé, *Introduction,* Vol. I, p. 291.

[14] Article 218 of the *coutumes* of Brittany dealt with the right of the testator to bequeath (donate) one third of his estate to other persons than his heirs. D'Argentré considered primarily the problem whether this right also applied to property located outside the territorial scope of the respective *coutumes.* See Lainé, *Introduction,* Vol. I, pp. 311 ff.

matter whether they involved rights *in rem,* obligations or succession; conflict problems were to be settled uniformly by the simple application of the law of the place where the respective thing was located. The personal statutes were of an exclusive nature and according to d'Argentré's doctrine could apply to persons only and not to persons in connection with things (e.g. to questions of majority, etc.); they could be granted extraterritorial character and be applied to individuals finding themselves outside their home territory. The mixed statutes were concerned to some extent with both persons and things; the relationship to persons was of a subsidiary nature and the relationship to things gave these special statutes a territorial character, which, in turn, resulted in the application of the local law.[15] In d'Argentré's opinion, nothing in the sphere of legal relationships to real property could be governed by the private will of the parties, nor could such relationships be governed by other law than that of the place where respective property was located *(lex rei sitae).* This very division of the statutes and the setting of rigid conflict criteria, primarily of the *lex rei sitae,* indicate the intensity with which d'Argentré opposed the penetration of elements of a foreign law into the local *coutumes.* In the sphere of relations involving the law of obligations d'Argentré recognized only expressly stated will and did not operate with the concept of an assumed (or tacitly expressed) will of the parties.

The teachings of d'Argentré and his numerous followers demonstrate how it was still possible at the time when feudalism was losing its firm hold to act in the sphere of the legal superstructure against progressive tendencies which were in keeping with the economic interests of the growing bourgeoisie. But the success of these reactionary endeavours was more than doubtful even in France herself; Dumoulin's doctrine clearly prevailed especially in judicial decisions.[16]

---

[15] See Lainé, *Introduction,* Vol. I, pp. 316 ff.; Gutzwiller, *Recueil des Cours,* 1929, Vol. IV, pp. 323 ff.; Meijers, *Recueil des Cours,* 1934, Vol. 49, p. 648.

[16] This was admitted even by such an admirer of d'Argentré's theory as Lainé, *Introduction,* Vol. I, p. 340.

## (12) French Authors of the 18th Century

The teachings of the French authors living in the 18th century, such as, in particular, Boullenois or Bouhier, also reflect a clear tendency to develop further the heritage of the Italian post-glossators and of Dumoulin in the sphere of considerations concerning the conflict rules relating to the law of obligations. Thus Boullenois subjected the conditions of the validity of the contract to the law of the place of its making, while the effects of the contract were to be governed primarily by the law of the place of performance.[17] Boullenois was also fully aware of the chance that often affected the choice of the place of the making of the contract, referred directly to Dumoulin's arguments on this point, and recognized Dumoulin's idea of the choice of the applicable law by the parties, which he considered as the most suitable for practical needs. Bouhier, another 18th century French jurist, referred to Dumoulin when he recommended the idea of the choice of the applicable law by the parties, which was to be considered in the first place when solving problems of conflict of laws.[18] Similarly abandoned was the once subjection of the mixed statutes to the territorial law; in contrast, Bouhier deduced that the personal element was to be given priority in these cases.[19]

The teachings of these authors reflected already in full the interests of the bourgeoisie on the eve of the French Revolution.

## (13) The Statutory Theory in the Netherlands

The long struggle of the Dutch provinces and Flanders for liberation from the feudal domination of the Spanish monarchy and the Dukes of Burgundy, inspired by ideas of independence and

---

[17] Batiffol, *Contrats,* p. 24; Lainé, *Introduction,* Vol. II, p. 13.

[18] Lainé, *Introduction,* Vol. II, p. 66.

[19] *Ibid,* p. 72.

state sovereignty, could not but find a reflection also in the theory of private international law developed by what is known as the Dutch statutory school. The teachings of the French advocate of the territorial character of most statutes, Bertrand d'Argentré, had found already earlier quite a number of followers among Dutch jurists.[20] But it was not until the final confirmation of Dutch independence, that is after the Peace of Westphalia in 1648, that the theories of Paul Voet (1619–1677), Ulric Huber (1636–1694) and Johann Voet (1647–1714), the son of Paul Voet, began to develop; these are today universally defined as Dutch statutory theory.[21]

All these authors, who expressed quite different views in rather protracted discussions on what was actually the content of real, personal and mixed statutes, proceeded from a uniform proclamation of the territorial principle as the main criterion for solving conflicts of laws.

It is truly remarkable how the territorial principle, which in d'Argentré's concept had been used to defend the privileges of the feudal *coutumes* of the French provinces against the growing power of the Paris bourgeoisie, was a century later applied by jurists representing the highly developed Dutch bourgeoisie, standing at the peak of its naval and commercial power, to governing the extensive international commercial and financial contacts, concentrated in the cities and ports of the Netherlands, as much as possible by the domestic law. The bourgeoisie, which in the period of its growth in Northern France and Italy had made use of all possibilities for undermining the validity of the territorial principle in order to facilitate its commercial penetration of other countries, could a few centuries later use its eco-

---

[20] This was true especially of Burgundus, Rodemburgh and Stockmans, whose work is discussed in detail by Lainé, *Introduction,* Vol. I, pp. 395 ff.

[21] For a general characterization of the Dutch school see Lunts, *Mezinárodní právo soukromé (Private International Law),* pp. 54 ff.; Gutzwiller, *Recueil des Cours,* 1929, Vol. IV, p. 325; Lainé, *Introduction,* Vol. II, pp. 95, 96; M. Wolff, *Private International Law,* Oxford, 1950, 2nd ed., pp. 22 ff.; Schnitzer, *Handbuch,* pp. 11 ff.

nomic power in the Netherlands for re-asserting the territorial principle for the purpose of justifying and enforcing the application of its own law in its dealings with foreign commercial partners.

The Dutch authors were helped in this endeavour by a masterful exploitation of the idea of sovereignty, developed in the work of Grotius. The idea of sovereignty of states and their laws was used by the Dutch jurists in the sphere of private international law for destroying the universal character of the statutory theory. They set aside the previous opinion that, proceeding from the general validity of conflict rules, the state was obliged to apply in some cases foreign law, to which also corresponded its right to claim that in similar cases adjudicated abroad its own law be applied. On the other hand, the Dutch jurists asserted that the application of foreign law was not a legal obligation but that it was the prerogative of every state to choose whether it would apply the foreign law or not. If it chose to apply it, it did so only on the basis of mere international comity *(comitas gentium)*.

Johannes Voet did, however, admit that an absolute application of the territorial principle would have the effect that under this principles one state would abolish acts of other states and vice versa, which would result in mutual detriment caused to subjects of the states concerned.[22] Only this concern for the interests of its own subjects, the Dutch authors claimed, was the actual reason why the state granted some extraterritorial effect to foreign law on the basis of international comity. When stating the grounds for international comity, Huber also outlined the fundamental idea of the theory of vested rights,[23] under which extraterritorial recognition should also be granted to rights acquired under a specific law. In the course of time this theory also became established in English and especially American law where it was promoted by Joseph Story. The economic reasons underlying the acceptance of the idea of international comity as

---

[22] Lainé, *Introduction,* Vol. II, p. 103.

[23] Bagge, *Recueil des Cours,* 1928, Vol. V, p. 138.

the ground for the application of foreign law are more than obviously reflected in the works of English and American authors.

However, in the sphere of the law of obligations, the Dutch theory — in spite of its insistence on the territorial principle — represented certain progress compared with the views held by d'Argentré. The first step in this direction was taken by Paul Voet when he included among the mixed statutes rules governing the form of legal actions,[24] which, in fact, provided the opportunity for taking into account also the personal principle. Paul's son Johannes concerned himself in his commentary on the *Pandecta* especially with the effects of the autonomy of will of the parties in choosing the applicable law.[25] However, he excepted from the free choice of the contracting parties statutes concerned with general benefit and *bons mœurs* which could not be derogated by the will of the parties; thereby he also laid the basis of the subsequently so disputable concept of public policy. On the other hand he admitted that the parties could preclude by express or tacit agreement the effect of statutes, provided that the provisions of the statutes served purely private interests and did not contain any prohibition.[26] Thus, the Dutch statutory theory began to make a distinction between optional rules, mandatory rules, and rules constituting the highly disputable category of public policy.

The Dutch statutory doctrine represented the beginning of the end of the idea of a uniform, universally binding private international law, as developed by the post-glossators.[27] The ideas of state sovereignty and international comity, which had

---

[24] Lainé, *Introduction,* Vol. II, p. 99.

[25] Gutzwiller, *Recueil des Cours,* 1929, Vol. IV, p. 327, especially footnote No. 1, on the same page.

[26] Lainé, *Introduction,* Vol. II, p. 106.

[27] Nevertheless, remnants of these views of the post-glossators survived for quite some time yet in the works of German authors writing on private international law; these authors were influenced by the general validity of Roman law in the form of the *usus modernus pandectarum.* This concept survived in Germany essentially until the 19th century when it was abandoned by Wächter and Savigny.

struck deep roots in the Dutch statutory doctrine, brought into being as many private international laws as there are legal systems in the world. Conflicts of laws began to be understood as international rather than inter-regional conflicts. The nationalistic isolationism, of which the Dutch statutists are sometimes being accused, was reduced in the sphere of the law of obligations to the minimum by the promotion of the free choice of the applicable law by the contracting parties; there is no doubt, of course, that the economic preponderance of the Dutch necessarily resulted in the choice of Dutch law in commercial contracts. The growth of international trade literally forced the Dutch authors not to obstruct the trend towards extension of the "free" choice of the applicable law by the contracting parties.

## (14) Echoes of the Statutory Theory in Germany

Germany, which more than any other country was divided into a large number of small territorial units, naturally offered fertile soil for the solution of many problems of private international and especially inter-regional law. However, the German authors, who may all be described as followers of first the post-glossators and later the Dutch doctrine, and of whom note should be taken of Joachym Mynsinger, Andreas Gaill, David Mevius and Samuel Stryck (who followed the post-glossators' doctrine), Henric de Coceji and Hofacker (who advocated the Dutch doctrine), had little of the originality and inventiveness typical of the post-glossators, Dumoulin, d'Argentré, or the Dutch statutists.[28]

Outstanding among the authors who concerned themselves with conflicts in the sphere of the law of obligations was Nico-

[28] These German authors are discussed in particular by F. Meili, *Geschichte und System des internationalen Privatrechts im Grundriss*, Leipzig, 1892, pp. 35 ff.; Wächter, "Über die Collision der Privatrechtsgesenze verschiedener Staaten", *Archiv für die civilistische Praxis*, 1841, pp. 230 ff., and Gutzwiller, *Recueil des Cours*, 1929, Vol. IV, pp. 392 ff.

laus Hert (Hertius). He advocated in this sphere a broad application of the *lex loci conclusionis,* but, in his opinion, this law could not be applied if it ran counter to the public law of the state of the forum, or if the foreign contracting party did not know the laws of the place where the contract was made.[29]

The German statutory doctrine was included in its essence in Bavaria's Maxmillian Code of 1756 and in the Prussian *Landrecht* of 1794.[30] But except for the proclaimed principle of *locus regit formam actus,* relating to form, the aforesaid codes of law did not settle the question which substantive law should be applied in cases of conflict in the sphere of the law of obligations.

## (15) Final Conclusions Regarding the Statutory Theory

In spite of the economic and political transformations which had taken place in Europe from the early 14th century to the end of the 18th century – the period generally designated in the history of private international law as the period of the domination of the statutory doctrine – all the authors of those days had in common the method of dividing statutes into categories of real, personal and mixed statutes (although their criteria for this categorization differed and sometimes were diametrally opposed) and of searching for a uniform conflict principle for each category of statutes.

As regards the quest for a uniform conflict criterion to govern relationships under the law of obligations, the statutory theory laid the basis for the growth of ideas which are still being developed or advocated in different forms and under different influences. As for the consideration of the form of contracts, there

---

[29] Gutzwiller, *Recueil des Cours,* 1929, Vol. IV, p. 331, and Wächter, *Archiv,* pp. 281 ff.

[30] See M. Wolff, *Das internationale Privatrecht Deutschlands,* pp. 18 and 19.

was an almost unanimous acceptance of the principle *locus regit formam actus*, although the authors did not concern themselves very much with the problem whether this principle should be applied in its obligatory or optional sense. On the other hand, the distinction made by Bartolus between regular effects of contracts (i.e. those, which may be envisaged already at the time the contract is made) and irregular effects (i.e. those, whose basis is laid only after the making of the contract) did not assert itself as a steady and firm criterion. Nevertheless, the deductions made by the different authors of the statutory school of thought resulted in the *a priori* acceptance of Bartolus' principle of applicability of the law of the place of the making of the contract as the basic criterion for settling conflicts in the sphere of the law of obligations; this principle has survived until today especially in legal systems dominated by Roman law.

The problems arising from the lack of uniformity in dividing individual statutes and from the weakness of the *a priori* understood principle of applicability of the law of the place of the making of the contract were in most cases solved with the help of Dumoulin's formulation of the possibility of a free choice of the applicable law by the contracting parties not only on the basis of an express stipulation but also by tacit or even hypothetical agreement between the parties, as it was accepted and promoted by the Dutch authors. Questions of capacity were governed by the personal statute of the contracting party, determined by his domicil.[31]

Although the Dutch jurists, as the first to do so, began to view conflict of laws as being primarily of an international character, and by their concept of international comity as a ground for the possible application of foreign law paved the way for the subsequently universal acceptance of the principle of "municipal" laws of conflict of laws, private international law

---

31 Domicil was replaced by citizenship only in the *Code civil* of 1804 and in the Austrian General Civil Code of 1811; this development undoubtedly better met the needs of the emerging unitarian bourgeois states and was also influenced by 18th century ideas of natural law.

still did not lose in that period its universal character, deduced from the universal authority of Roman law and, subsequently, also from the principles of natural law. Only the 19th century, which was the century of bourgeois codifications of civil law, brought this concept to its end.

The deductions brought forth by the statutory doctrine, which were in keeping with the objectives of the emerging bourgeoisie in the period preceding the growth of industrial capitalism, were in some instances included in the few provisions of the 19th century codifications, concerned with the law of conflict of laws. Under the influence of Joseph Story, the Dutch statutory doctrine eventually provided the basis for the American and English understanding of private international law.[32] The statutory doctrine thus became, for all practical purposes, the basis of all the other development trends of private international law.

---

[32] See sub-chapter 23 of the present study and Lunts, *Mezinárodní právo soukromé (Private International Law)*, pp. 56 ff., which offers an excellent outline of the development of the Anglo-American concept of private international law.

## CHAPTER 4
# Development in the Period of Capitalism

### (16) General Comments

In the period of capitalism, when the bourgeoisie had already seized power, we can trace the endeavour of the new ruling class to regulate by legislation civil-law relations; thus, the 19th century is being properly called the century of bourgeois codifications of civil law in most European and many non-European (especially Latin American) states. These major legislative tasks, which expressed a synthesis of the economic and political power of the bourgeoisie, were doubtlessly initiated by changes in ownership relations, by the fact that the feudal form of ownership had changed into capitalist ownership.[1]

The list of these civil codes would be long, beginning with the Prussian *Allgemeines Landrecht* of 1794 (which also codified other fields of law) or the French *Code civil* of 1804, and ending with the German Civil Code of 1896 or the Swiss Civil Code of 1907.[2] The enactment of these codes ended the era of the domination of Roman law as a universally valid and applicable law. However, in the sphere of private international law, the first

---

[1] Knapp, *Vlastnictví v lidové demokracii (Ownership in the People's Democracy)*, Prague, 1952, pp. 70 ff.

[2] The French *Code civil* was introduced in Belgium in 1807. Then followed the Austrian Civil Code in 1811, and the Dutch Civil Code of 1838; the Civil Code of Haiti, enacted in 1825, was almost literally patterned after the French model, just as the Civil Code of Peru of 1852, the Greek Civil Code of 1856 (no longer in force today), the Italian one of 1865 (also no longer valid), and the Rumanian Civil Code adopted in the same year. Then followed Portugal (1867), Uruguay (1868), Argentina (1869), Colombia (1873), Costa Rica (1887), Spain (1888), Germany (1896), Japan (1898), Nicaragua (1903), Honduras (1905), Switzerland (1907), and many other states.

codifications of civil law did not proceed beyond the enactment of some of the principles previously arrived at by the statutory doctrine on the basis of the already described method.

## (17) The French and Austrian Civil Codes

An expression of what had been beyond any doubt typical for the statutory doctrine – but with the conflict criterion of domicil being replaced by the criterion of citizenship – is the still valid Article 3 of the French *Code civil.*[3] The French *Code civil* ignores, however, completely the question which law is to govern relations under the law of contracts, nor does it even formulate the universally recognized principle *locus regit formam actus,* which, although included in the original proposal, was eventually left out of the final draft; the whole sphere of law of conflict of laws was thereby left to be regulated by the courts which turned it into a veritable jungle.

Although the Austrian Civil Code is relatively more specific than the *Code civil* as regards provisions governing conflict of laws and contains a number of rules of private international law (Sections 4, 33 to 37, 400), here, too, it was extremely difficult to find a conflicts criterion applying to matters involving the law of obligations because of the vagueness and contradictions of the provisions of Sections 33 to 37, as well as because of the lack of uniformity in judicial decision.[4] A novel rule, enacted for the first time, was the precedence given to the law which is more favourable as regards the validity of the contract (Section 35 of the Austrian Civil Code).

---

[3] *Les lois de police et de sûreté obligent tous ceux qui habitent le territoire. – Les immeubles même ceux possédés par les étrangers, sont régis par la loi française. Les lois concernant l'état et la capacité des personnes régissent les Français, même résidant en pays étranger.*

[4] See also Walker, *Internationales Privatrecht,* Vienna, 1926, pp. 361 ff.; P. Steinlechner, "Zur Würdigung der Bestimmungen des österreichischen ABGB über die örtliche Geltung der Gesetze", *Festschrift zur Jahrhundertfeier des ABGB,* 1911, Vol. II, pp. 60, 83 ff.

Thus, viewed from the aspect of the development of private international law in general and the solution of conflicts in the sphere of the law of obligations in particular, the enactment of the French *Code civil* and the Austrian Civil Code did not mean, in substance, more than just the fact that the basic conclusions arrived at by the statutory doctrine were – and that only partially – embodied in national rules governing conflict of laws.

## (18) Wächter

Wächter, whose ideas were of major importance in the general theory of private international law because he put to a definite end the statutory doctrine and proclaimed the existence of municipal laws governing conflict of laws, did not make a special contribution either to the method of solving concrete conflicts of laws in the sphere of the law of obligations.[5]

## (19) Savigny's Theory

A major turn in the doctrine of private international law was brought about by the theory developed by the German authority on Roman law, Friedrich Carl von Savigny, in the eighth volume of his work on the systems of contemporary Roman law.[6]

---

[5] In his articles "Über Collision der Privatrechtsgesetze verschiedener Staaten", published in the *Archiv für civilistische Praxis* in 1841 and 1842, Wächter did set forth a method for solving conflicts of laws on the basis of municipal conflict rules, in the spirit of municipal laws or the law of the forum, but contributed very little to the positive solution of such conflicts. See also Gutzwiller, *Recueil des Cours,* 1929, Vol. IV, p. 352, and Lunts, *Mezinárodní právo soukromé (Private International Law),* pp. 60 ff.

[6] F. C. von Savigny, *System des heutigen Römischen Rechts,* Vol. VIII, Berlin, 1849.

Under the influence of German idealistic philosophy (mainly Leibniz and Kant), the already seventy-year old Savigny formulated in his work for the first time a uniform, basic criterion for solving all problems of conflict of laws, a principle which was universally valid and on the basis of which it would be possible to settle any question involving a conflict of laws. The principle was the localization of legal relations in space.

Although Savigny proceeded from the idea of the universal validity of Roman law *(usus modernus pandectarum)*, in contrast to the authors advocating the statutory theory, he did not seek the justification for the application of foreign law in Roman law, nor did he try to seek criteria for such application in the classification of legal rules on the basis of their object into categories of real, personal and mixed statutes.

Savigny proceeded from concrete legal relations and from the *a priori* accepted fact that every law, every legal relation is localized in space; he called this localization the seat of the legal relationship *(Sitz)*.[7] He considered it therefore natural and practical that conflicts of laws of independent states should be settled by the application of the law of that territorial unit, to which the respective legal relation is closest by its localization. This was Savigny's universal solution; its purpose was to obtain in the solution of conflicts of laws the same result in all states and under all laws.[8]

In Savigny's opinion, the existence of private international law and the fact that all states apply in some cases foreign law were basically due to the existence of the international community of nations which were in mutual contact.[9] Savigny thus appeared as a founder of the supranational theory of private

---

[7] See Savigny, *System*, pp. 14 ff., in particular, p. 108; also see Lunts, *Mezinárodní právo soukromé (Private International Law)*, p. 61; M. Wolff, *Das Internationale Privatrecht Deutschlands*, p. 21, and Gutzwiller, *Der Einfluss Savignys auf die Entwicklung des Internationalprivatrechts*, Freiburg, 1923, p. 12.

[8] Savigny, *System*, p. 27.

[9] *Ibid*, p. 27.

international law[10] and at the same time as a firm opponent of the Dutch statutory doctrine which sought the justification for the existence of private international law only in international comity.

Savigny's justification for the application of foreign law, as well as its general formula, were in keeping with the endeavours of the bourgeoisie which was then proclaiming the principles of "free capitalism". His efforts to obtain a uniform solution under all systems of law through the localization of the respective legal relation expressed the interests of the then bourgeoisie in promoting international trade.

Of major importance was especially Savigny's theory concerning the solution of conflicts in the sphere of the law of obligations, which became the basis for teachings developed by other authors. Savigny underlined the difficulty of answering the question where an obligation was actually localized,[11] as well as the problem of specifying what was actually the object of an obligation, the difficulties arising from the fact that an obligation involved a relationship between several subjects, and, finally, the problem of determining the applicable law as regards the mutual obligations of the contracting parties.[12]

Savigny viewed as the substance of an obligation the activity of the debtor aimed at performance, while the co-operation of the creditor was for him only a subsidiary matter.[13] A characteristic feature of an obligation was the typical link between the local law and the place of the forum which, in turn, was again sought and determined according to the person of the debtor. Savigny thus combined the determination of the applicable law and the place of the forum, and deduced that from the establishment of the obligation, the attention of the parties concentrated on its performance and on the place of such performance,

---

[10] Nussbaum, *Grundzüge des internationalen Privatrechts,* Munich and Berlin, 1952, p. 20.

[11] *Ibid.,* p. 201.

[12] Savigny, *System,* p. 201; Gutzwiller, *Einfluss Savignys,* p. 23.

[13] Savigny, *System,* p. 202.

where the place of the forum was also to be sought, if necessary, on the basis of a voluntary submission of the parties.[14]

In the actual analysis of what was to be understood under the term place of performance, he stressed the will of the parties, either expressly stated or ensuing from the circumstances of the case, as the main factor in determining the place of performance.[15] In this analysis he first proceeded from cases where the place of performance had been determined by expressly stated will, and then he sought the place of performance in cases where it had not been specified in the obligation, constantly being guided by the mutual link between the places of performance and the court or rather their identity;[16] he finally reached the conclusion that the law of such a place was also the law that should be applied in solving problems of conflict of laws.[17]

As regards the determination of the applicable law in cases involving the law of obligations, Savigny set forth detailed rules.[18] The broad application of the autonomy of will of the

---

[14] Savigny, *System*, p. 208: "*...und es liegt daher im Wesen der Obligation, dass der Ort der Erfüllung als Sitz der Obligation gedacht, dass an diesen Ort der besondere Gerichtsstand der Obligation durch freie Unterwerfung verlegt wurde.*"

[15] *Ibid.*, p. 211.

[16] The link between the place of the forum and the place of performance in Savigny's arguments is conditional upon the validity of Roman law in Germany *(usus modernus pandectarum)*.

[17] Savigny, *System*, p. 246.

[18] *Ibid.*, p. 247.

(a) In cases where the place of performance was determined by the will of the parties, the law of that place was to be applied according to Savigny;

(b) if the obligation arose from normal commercial transactions carried out by the debtor, the law to be applied was to be the law of the place where such transactions were being made;

(c) if the obligation ensued from a single act of the debtor in the place of his domicil, the applicable law was the law of this place, irrespective of any subsequent change of domicil by the debtor;

(d) if the obligation arose from a single act of the debtor outside the place of his domicil but under circumstances indicating that performance

parties, advocated by Savigny, indicated that his doctrine expressed the interests of industrial, "free" capitalism.

Savigny recommended that questions of capacity to legal acts be governed by the law of the place of domicil.[19] He also concerned himself with the question whether the interpretation of contracts should not possibly be governed by a special local law (i.e. a law different from the law of the place of performance), but reached the conclusion that this did not involve the question of application of the local law, but a question of interpretation aiming primarily at the ascertainment of the true intent of the contracting parties. The local law (i.e. primarily the law of the place of performance) was to be applied, in his opinion, to questions of limitation of action; at the same time, Savigny rejected the opinion of older authors (especially Huber) that prescription was a matter of procedural law, which should always be governed by the law of the forum.[20]

Savigny accepted basically only two exceptions from the application of the *lex fori solutionis,* which should have been also applied to the question of validity of an obligation. The first exception, in favour of consideration of validity according to the *lex fori,* seemed to him warranted under the condition that the validity of the obligation would be hampered by a strictly positive, mandatory rule (such as prohibition of usury or enforcement of debts from games).[21] The other exception involved cases where the parties had chosen a different law than that of the place of performance.

Savigny devoted special attention to the form of legal acts and to an analysis of the principle *locus regit actum.*[22] He con-

---

could be expected to be made in that very same place, the applicable law was the law of that place;

(e) if none of the aforesaid conditions existed, the applicable law was the law of the debtor's place of domicil.

[19] *Ibid.,* pp. 134 ff.; as regards obligations in particular, see pp. 263 ff.

[20] *Ibid.,* p. 273. Huber's concept is accepted to this day by English and American courts.

[21] *Ibid.,* p. 275.

[22] *Ibid.,* pp. 348 ff.

sidered this principle to be a part of the universally valid consuetudinary law; in his opinion, the importance of this principle lay in the fact that it was sufficient for the form to be in keeping with the law of the place of the making of the contract, even if a different form was prescribed in the place where the act was localized; at the same time he favoured an optional application of this principle and its application even in cases where the observance of a foreign form would mean acting *in fraudem legis,* i.e. escaping the law otherwise governing the form of action.[23]

## (20) The Influence and Importance of Savigny

As the founder of the historical school of law and opponent of natural law, Savigny greatly influenced through his works the whole future development of the doctrine of private international law, and many of his theories and ideas were incorporated in conflict rules or judicial decisions.

The law of the place of performance, which in Savigny's opinion was to govern relations under the law of obligations, became the decisive law under the decisions of German courts and, as regards the effect of contracts (not as regards their making and validity) also under Swiss judicial decisions, unless, of course, the parties had expressly or tacitly agreed on the application of a different law. However, the rigid application of the law of the place of performance primarily by the German courts caused the statute of mutual obligations – and thus especially contracts of sale – to split according to whether in a specific case a party was to be viewed as the debtor or creditor, which meant that in most cases the obligations of the creditors and debtors were governed by different laws.

Savigny's theories have been criticized to this day. An obvious weakness of his doctrine is his thesis on the application of the

---

[23] *Ibid.*, pp. 350, 358.

law of the place of performance; its untenability was demonstrated precisely in the highly developed practice of international trade when conflicts of laws regarding synallagmatic obligations had to be solved.[24]

Among the French authors, Savigny's basic concept was criticized very sharply by Niboyet.[25] Savigny's initial idea of the international community and the private international law ensuing therefrom could not, naturally, prevail in the struggle between individual capitalist states. But even those parts of Savigny's doctrine, which were acceptable to the legislators and courts of industrial capitalism as regards practical solutions of conflicts of laws, underwent considerable changes in the era of financial capitalism.

Savigny's doctrine influenced primarily the Civil Code of Saxony, adopted in 1863, which was the first body af law to accept the applicability of the law the place of performance to the solution of conflicts in the sphere of the law of obligations.[26] Savigny's views also served as the basis for the civil codes of some of the Swiss cantons.[27] But Savigny's opinion, which wanted to provide the same protection to bourgeois interests in all countries in the era of free capitalism, failed to prevail in the introductory law to the German Civil Code of 1896, which contains the rules of German private international law.[28] For these rules do not even contain any mention of solution of conflict of laws

---

[24] Brinz, the German authority on Roman law, spoke contemptuously of the "seat" of obligations and aptly noted with respect to Savigny's doctrine of obligations: *"Entweder sie sitzen überhaupt nicht, oder sie sitzen auf zwei Stühlen."* (Brinz, *Lehrbuch der Pandekten,* Vol. I, 1873, p. 102, quoted from Gutzwiller, *Einfluss Savignys,* p. 359.

[25] Niboyet, *Cours de droit international privé français,* Paris, 1949, pp. 392 ff.

[26] Section 11 of the Civil Code of Saxony read as follows: *"Forderungen werden nach den Gesetzen des Ortes beurteilt, an welchem sie zu erfüllen sind."* See Gutzwiller, *Einfluss Savinys,* p. 107.

[27] *Ibid.,* p. 108. The cantons were those of Zürich, Schaffhausen and Zug.

[28] See Sections 7 to 31 of the introductory law to the German Civil Code.

in the sphere of the law of obligations, although the original draft of these rules (known as the Gebhard proposals) contained a clear reference to the law of the place of performance quite in keeping with Savigny's doctrine. These proposals so displeased Bismarck that he even banned their publication. The rules concerned with the law of obligations were omitted from the subsequent draft when it was discussed in the German Federal Council, apparently because Savigny's idea of a harmonious solution of conflict problems in all states and in the international community was no longer in keeping with the interests of German monopoly capital which was striving for world domination.[29]

Savigny's influence was not manifested only in German law, or in Swiss legislation, but his doctrine also became a major factor influencing the Anglo-American,[30] French and Italian laws of conflict of laws.[31]

---

[29] See Lunts, *Mezinárodní právo soukromé (Private International Law)*, p. 61. Similarly, the system of one-sided conflict rules in the introductory law to the German Civil Code chose as the basic criterion citizenship rather than domicil, which was recommended by Savigny. For details see, in particular, Walker, *Internationales Privatrecht*, 4th ed., Wien, 1926, pp. 58 ff., and Nussbaum, *Deutsches internationales Privatrecht*, Tübingen, 1932, pp. 27 and 28. The interest of German big business in suppressing the originally progressive rules proposed in the initial draft had to be admitted even by this German author. It is remarkable that while the German Federal Council adopted the provisions of the substantive law without any changes, the rules governing conflict of laws had to be thoroughly re-written without any explanation. Nussbaum feels that the reason for this move was the "cosmopolitan" character of the original proposals which were fully based on Savigny's doctrine.

[30] Gutzwiller, *Einfluss Savignys*, pp. 109–131, and M. Wolff, *Private International Law*, p. 37, who points especially to the fact that Savigny recommended domicil as the decisive conflict criterion, whereby he came close to the opinion of English and American authors and jurists.

[31] Gutzwiller, *Einfluss Savignys*, pp. 132–149, lists among the authors influenced by Savigny's doctrine Asser, Rolin, Despagnet, Audiner, Bartin, and others.

## (21) Mancini and His "National" School

The doctrine developed by the Italian jurist and politician Pasquale Mancini (1817–1888) directly reflects the influence of the economic and political situation of Italy of those days with her division into a number of small territorial units. Mancini's doctrine expresses the idea of the national and political unification of Italy which had tried for years to free herself of the fetters of political atomization and impotence.

In his famous Turin lecture on nationality as the foundation of international law,[32] Mancini asserted as a fundamental thesis, that nationality rather than the state constituted the foundation of international law. Public and private international laws appeared to Mancini as branches of some broader international laws which he understood as being a part of a universal law of mankind. In private international law, the personal element, expressed by nationality as understood by Mancini, constituted the guiding principle; its purpose – in Italy's situation – was to preserve the legal link between the millions of Italian emigrants and their native country.

In private international law, Mancini divided the rules of private law into two categories. The first category was made up of "essential private law" *(il diritto privato necessario)*, where nationality was the decisive conflict criterion; this category of rules governed all matters which somehow affected the personal status of the individual, i.e. primarily relations under personal, family and inheritance laws. This category of legal rules

---

[32] The text of the lecture, entitled *"Della nazionalità come fondamento del diritto delle genti"*, was published in Mancini, *Diritto internazionale,* Prelezioni, Naples, 1873, pp. 5 ff. It should be noted, however, that in Romanesque languages nationality and citizenship are usually expressed by the same term (*nazionalità, nationalité*, etc.). It is therefore necessary to determine in a specific case according to context, what the author has actually in mind. While Mancini proceeded from nationality, this "nationality" undoubtedly overlapped with the concept of citizenship. This is how we should understand the term "nationality" as it is used in the works of Romanesque authors.

was influenced and, one might say, directly dictated by national tradition, and the individual's will could change nothing in it. The second category of rules was made up of "voluntary private law" *(il diritto privato voluntario),* which included primarily the rules of the law of obligations; in this category of rules, the contracting parties could fully assert their freedom of will, which was manifested not only in the sphere of optional rules of substantive law, but also in the sphere of the law of conflict of laws, where the parties could subject their relations to any foreign law, provided that this was not contrary to the territorial public order. It is only natural that in this sphere of "voluntary private law", Mancini did not consider as decisive only expressly stated will but also manifestations of will that could be deduced from the circumstances of each specific case.

Although both Mancini and Savigny advocated the concept of a supranational, universal private international law, Mancini was quite critical towards Savigny's doctrine.[33] One major point on which the two authors disagreed was precisely the concept of localizing obligations in the seat of the debtor, which had been promoted by Savigny and which Mancini had unfavourably analyzed in his opinion calling for the conclusion of an international agreement which would govern international law of obligations and demonstrating on examples the instability of the localization advocated by Savigny.[34]

Mancini's doctrine had many supporters especially in Italy and France, and provided the theoretical background for the Italian codification of private international law, contained in the introductory provisions of the Italian Civil Code of 1865. In the sphere of conflicts relating to the law of obligations, this influence was manifested in the provisions of Article 9 of the intro-

---

[33] Gutzwiller, *Einfluss Savignys,* pp. 152 ff.

[34] Mancini, "De l'utilité de rendre obligatoires pour tous les Etats sous la forme d'un ou de plusieurs traités internationaux, un certain nombre de règles générales de droit international privé pour assurer la décision uniforme des conflits entre les différentes législations civiles et criminelles", *Clunet,* 1874, p. 287; see also Gutzwiller, *Einfluss Savignys,* p. 153.

ductory part of the Civil Code of 1865, Article 58 of the Italian Commercial Code of 1882, as well as Article 25 of the introductory part of the now valid Italian Civil Code; all these provisions refer to the common citizenship of the contracting parties, unless the parties expressed a different will.[35] In general, the importance of Mancini's doctrine was manifested mainly in the fact that it represented – at least on the European Continent – the final prevalence of citizenship as a conflict criterion in place of domicil which had been previously applied and also recommended by Savigny.

The most outstanding among Mancini's non-Italian disciples[36] was the French author André Weiss, whose theory is the most systematic and consistent. Weiss proceeded from the assumption that a rule concerned with "private" interests always aimed at the benefit of individuals; the second premise from which he proceeded was the thesis that only the activity of those persons

---

[35] Article 9, par. 2, of the introduction to the Italian Civil Code of 1865 provided as follows: "The substance and effects of obligations shall be governed by the law of the place where they had been concluded and, in the event that the foreign contracting parties have the same nationality, they shall be governed by their municipal law. In all cases where it would appear that the parties had expressed a different will, such will shall be respected."

Article 58 of the Italian Commercial Code of 1882 did not mention the will of the parties at all and subjected commercial obligations to the law of the place of their conclussion or to the common citizenship of the parties.

Article 25, par. 1 – *Disposizioni sull'applicazione delle leggi in generale* – of the Italian Civil Code of 1942 (its conflict rules had been in force already since 1939) provides as follows: "Contractual obligations shall be governed by the municipal law of the contracting parties, if such law is common to them; if not, they shall be governed by the law of the place where the contract was made. However, in all cases the differing will of the parties shall be respected." *("Le obbligazioni che nascono da contratto sono regolate dalla legge nazionale dei contraenti, se è comune; altrimenti da quella del luogo nel quale il contratto è stato conchiuso. E'salva in ogni caso la diversa volontà delle parti.")*

[36] Of the Italian followers of Mancini note should be taken of Espersone, Catellani and Fiore. In France there were Audinet and André Weiss, and in Belgium Laurent.

for whom the law had been enacted could be governed by such law (i.e. citizens of the respective state). However, according to his doctrine, it is also obvious that the law must regulate this activity of the aforesaid persons everywhere and in all legal relations; exceptions and modifications of these principles were dictated by the demands of international public order, by the generally valid rule of *locus regit actum*, and by autonomy of will.[37]

Weiss's doctrine also supplied the basic idea to the subsequent advocates of the primary validity of the law of citizenship, especially Zitelmann and Frankenstein.

The importance of the national school of law for the law of obligations and, in particular, for the problem of defining the scope within which the contracting parties have the possibility of freely choosing the applicable law, lay in the distinction it made between "necessary" and "voluntary" private law, the distinction between optional and mandatory rules, which, according to Mancini's disciples, could not be eliminated by a mere manifestation of will of the parties. This distinction gave later rise to the well-known dispute between the advocates of a "limited" and "unlimited" choice of the law to be applied to relations under the law of obligations, which marked the whole future development of the question of choice of law and which is still alive.

## (22) Joseph Story and His Doctrine

The American judge Joseph Story (1779–1845), the author of the Commentaries on the Conflict of Laws, became the founder of doctrine typical first of the North American and subsequently also English understanding of private international law.

In contrast to the speculative method used by authors on the

---

[37] See André Weiss, *Traité théoretique et pratique de droit international privé,* Paris, 1912, Vol. III, p. 68. For a characterization of his doctrine also see Blagojević, *Medjunarodno privatno pravo,* Beograd, 1950, p. 84.

European Continent, which was undoubtedly a heritage of the statutory school, Story built his conclusions on an analysis of judicial decisions settling conflicts between the laws of the individual States of the Union.[38] Since the English Common Law did not provide the answer to problems arising from conflict of laws,[39] Story had to proceed from concrete North American materials, but he also relied on a thorough knowledge of such older authors as, in particular, Huber, Voet, Rodenburgh, Boullenois, or Bouhier. In spite of his positivistic analysis of judicial decisions, which Story primarily studied, he also stressed the need of formulating fundamental principles which would facilitate co-operation between individual states in the field of international legal contacts. For Story these fundamental principles were the axioms of the Dutch statutory school;[40] it was primarily the principle of the territorial validity of laws, which best suited American and English commercial interests, which had taken

---

[38] It is in the law of the North American states that we meet for the first time in the Anglo-American sphere of law with the necessity of settling problems of conflict of laws; this fact was due to the partial differences existing between the laws of the individual States of the Union, although they were essentially all the Common Law of England with only some exceptions.

[39] For the reasons why England had no rules governing conflict of laws until the 19th century see Lunts, *Mezinárodní právo soukromé (Private International Law)*, pp. 56 ff., and Gutzwiller, *Recueil des Cours*, 1929, Vol. IV, p. 340. (Thus, for example, the oldest English decision in the sphere of conflict of laws, *Robinson v. Bland*, dates from as late as 1760.)

[40] See Story, *Commentaries on the Conflict of Laws*, 8th ed., Boston, 1883, p. 8: "It is plain that the laws of one country can have no intrinsic force, *proprio vigore*, except within the territorial limits and jurisdiction of that country. They can bind only its own subjects, and others, who are within its jurisdictional limits, and the latter only, while they remain therein. No other nation, or its subjects, are bound to yield the slightest obedience to those laws. Whatever extra-territorial force they are to have, is the result not of any original power to extend them abroad, but of that respect, which from motives of public policy, other nations are disposed to yield to them, giving them effect, as the phrase is, *sub mutuae vicissitudinis obtentu*, with a wise and liberal regard to common convenience and mutual benefits and necessities."

over the heritage of the Dutch commercial empire, and the ensuing doctrine of international commity.[41] Story's teachings served as the basis for the later doctrine of Prof. Beale, which is prevailing in the United States today and which is based on the theory of protection of what is called vested rights.[42]

The practicism and pragmatism of Story and his disciples (including, in particular, Prof. Beale), did not produce a specific theory for solving conflicts of laws in relations arising under the law of obligations; instead these authors left the field wide open to the courts and their general trend to extend the application of the domestic law to foreign parties. As regards the consideration of questions of capacity to legal acts, the territorial concept of Joseph Story resulted in the situation where questions of capacity were judged, as a rule, according to the law of domicil rather than the law of citizenship; this tied the masses of North American immigrants to North American law.

English and American judicial decisions concerned with the law of conflict of laws proceeded from as early as 1760 (the decision of Lord Mansfield in *Robinson v. Bland*) from the presumption that in making their contract, the parties intended to subject the contract to a particular law. This decision also provided the starting point for Story who, however, used the presumptive will of the parties only as an argument for explaining *ex post* why this or that particular law had been applied.[43] Story advocated the consideration of questions regarding the validity of a contract according to the law of the place where the contract was made,[44]

---

[41] For the basic features of the Anglo-American doctrine see Lunts, *Mezinárodní právo soukromé (Private International Law)*, pp. 56 ff.

[42] See Lunts, *Mezinárodní právo soukromé (Private International Law)*, p. 58, and Nussbaum, *Grundzüge*, pp. 24 ff. Protection of acquired rights constitutes the main theoretical idea of Beale's system (Beale, *A Treatise on the Conflict of Laws*, New York, 1935) and of the American Restatement of the Law of Conflict of Laws, for which Prof. Beale was the rapporteur.

[43] See Batiffol, *Contrats*, p. 32.

[44] Story, *Commentaries*, § 242 (p. 325): "Generally speaking, the validity of a contract is to be decided by the law of the place where it is made."

and supported this argument by the presumption that every person making a contract in a particular place had submitted to the law of such a place and tacitly agreed that the same law would also be applicable to the contract.[45]

The same methods is, in fact, also used by American courts to explain the fact that they based their decision on the case under consideration e.g. on the law of the place of performance.

The territorial principle and thus also the basic application of the domestic law, the consideration of questions of capacity and personal status according to the law of domicil, and the absence of uniformity of the rules governing relationships under the law of obligations, which characterize the Anglo-American concept of private international law, provide a fitting instrument to these economically strong states to extend their application of law onto their foreign, mostly economically weaker commercial partners.[46]

•

This historical survey of the older doctrine of private international law (a survey necessarily incomplete, the author must admit) points to certain solutions typical of its contemporary problems. The common, legal heritage of the statutory theory first saw the division of private international law into positivistic and nationalist concepts, typical of the development of this law in the nineteenth and the first half of the twentieth centuries. However, these trends could not erase the features which

---

[45] *Ibid.*, § 261 (p. 348): "The ground of this doctrine, as commonly stated, is that every person, contracting in a place, is understood to submit himself to the law of the place and silently to assent to its action upon his contract... It would be more correct to say that the law of the place of the contract acts upon it independently of any volition of the parties."

[46] See Lunts, *Mezinárodní právo soukromé (Private International Law)*, pp. 59 ff.

are characteristic of the private international law of all states and which provide a link for all the municipal laws governing conflict of laws.

The subsequent development of the doctrine of private international law has been deeply marked until this day by the latent conflict between "universalism" and "nationalism". For this reason, we shall concern ourselves in the following parts of this study with this fundamental problem of the contemporary development of private international law, which is sometimes described as a "crisis" of private international law, and shall try to point to a possible solution of this problem.

# PART THREE

# "Universalism" and "Nationalism" in the Modern Doctrine of Private International Law Especially in Non-Socialist States

## CHAPTER 1
## Introduction

### (1) General Survey

The hybrid nature of private international law as a social phenomenon oscillating between the polarity of universality influenced on the one hand by general international law and, on the other hand, by the municipal character of the applied substantive law almost precludes the possibility of placing the basic trends of the contemporary doctrine under a single common denominator which could result in a unanimously accepted synthesis. Nevertheless, this state of affairs does not mean that an attempt should not be made to determine the basic, characteristic features of the individual doctrines and trends, and thus to specify the characteristic differences between them. Although many of the proclaimed doctrines and trends are clearly of a speculative nature, it would be an illusion not to see how this speculative nature – which is so typical in many respects of private international law – is influenced by historical, political, economic and, last but not least, by legal factors. For this reason we shall try to make a survey of the contemporary doctrines of private international law, which – in view of the background from which the individual doctrines proceed – would divide them into certain groups and trends in accordance with their basic orientation; in doing so, we shall leave aside differences which we do not consider essential in this connection, but which certainly exist within the individual groups and which may sometimes be of considerable importance as regards the solution of specific problems.

As we shall see further, these are primarily differences which have arisen relatively lately in the bourgeois doctrine of public and private international law, where we have witnessed the well known conflicts between the monistic and the dualistic theories and their individual shades. In socialist theory the problem of the conflict between nationalism and universalism has not gained such prominence, undoubtedly due to the fact that the basic theoretical and philosophical view proceeds from other positions than those held by contemporary doctrine in the capitalist states. Nevertheless – as we shall further explain[1] – especially Soviet doctrine has seen a dispute between the advocates of the opinion that private international law is in its substance a part of international law in general, and their opponents who conclude that it forms an integral part of the municipal law of every state. However, since socialist doctrine unequivocally rejects the view on the supranational character of international law (no matter how motivated), the Soviet discussion was held in a different spirit than the dispute which is the topic of this part of the present work.

Without trying to anticipate in this place the conclusions of this analysis, we believe that all trends – of which many have currently lost their originally clear-cut character – are typified, especially in recent years, by the effort to achieve a "rapprochement" of differing views, in particular of those, which are important for practical application in the sphere of private international law; this, of course, cannot hide the differences existing between the original, theoretical positions. The original irreconcilability of the individual concepts has recently been replaced in the whole sphere of private international law by practical realism which is generally viewed as an effective instrument for settling individual, practical questions, which could not be otherwise settled on a possibly general basis, should starting theoretical positions be rigidly adhered to. This state of affairs does not, of course, mean that this realistic effort to achieve progress in solving concrete problems should be interpreted as a victory for pragmatism, or eclecticism, as a trend in legal phi-

---

[1] See Part Four, Chapter 3, sub-chapter 3 of the present work.

losophy, which is being promoted or which has even prevailed in contemporary private international law.

Realism in private international law may be generally characterized as opposition against *a priori* and dogmatic concepts, be it the *a priori* dogmas of the statutory theory and deductions of concrete conclusions made from these dogmas, or the *a priori* dogma of the territorial nature of all law, on which Beale had built his system of American private international law, a system which has been fought by American legal doctrine and practice with greater or lesser intensity since the 1930's. This realism proceeds mainly from the analysis of individual factual and legal configurations, which seeks a just and acceptable solution; this analysis is undoubtedly based on the rational approach which was pomoted in the private international law of the last century by Savigny. If realism is to be effective, it must respect the given situation which leads to the rejection of all apriority; no other procedure is possible in a sphere where it is necessary to proceed simultaneously from the territorial validity of the municipal law, the political interests of individual states which have created it, and from the positive nature of the sources of the law, and at the same time to try and find a solution or solutions, which would harmoniously govern factual configurations occurring in the international life of individuals and society as a whole. Besides opposing *a priori* dogmas, such realism must also combat the formally positivistic subjection of relations governed by private international law exclusively to categories of municipal civil or private law, irrespective of the postulates that ensue from the existence of an international element in these relations, which turns them into a separate and specific category. Similarly, note must also be taken of the trends in judicature and of individual decisions; it should, however, be remembered that a just decision is hampered as much by slavish casuistry as it is by *a priori* solutions voluntaristically projected into individual, concrete situations. Realism is naturally determined by the current historical situation and is fully aware of it.

The realistic approach to the problems of private international law may at the same time be considered as a certain effort to solve the antinomy between conceptual jurisprudence and interest jurisprudence in the given sphere. At the same time, realism tries to attain an adequate degree of positiveness of private international law or, rather, its objectivity in the system of positive conflict rules (and possibly also substantive or procedural rules). The realistic approach to the solution of concrete problems as well as of the basic questions of private international law as a whole, must in the end result lead to the question of the very function of private international law in the life of human society in its international aspects, as well as regards the non-sovereign subjects of the relations governed by private international law. If the internationalist school views private international law as a subdivision of public international law, which settles conflicts between individual sovereignties (frequently in an *a priori* manner), the realistic approach represents an effort to define the scope wherein the individual states, as sovereigns, can act as regards the relations – with a foreign element – between physical and legal persons who are their subjects. This effort is concretely manifested as the effort to formulate generally accepted and universally valid conflict rules, and to achieve widespread unification of substantive law. It is obvious that this effort does not merely aim at a formulation of abstract postulates, but at a very concrete and important activity precisely in view of the fact that it reflects that aspect of co-existence between states belonging to the international community which directly affects individuals who are the subjects of different state sovereignties.

### (2) Basic Historico-Sociological View

This realistic view of the questions of contemporary private international law must naturally be in keeping with a realistic assessment of the basic concepts accepted thus far, which proceed from certain socio-political conditions that have evolved in the course of development of the human society. As already noted, contemporary private international law is the product of a number of development stages. This does not, of course, apply to the past centuries only, but also to what we might call the "modern history" or an analysis of contemporary doctrinal tendencies or concepts — the subject of this chapter. We shall consider as "contemporary doctrinal trends of private international law" those doctrines, which have been propagated since the end of the First World War. This period does not, of course, represent a single unit from the historico-sociological aspect, which fact therefore calls for its periodization. We feel that for the purpose of the following analysis and the understanding of the different doctrines, it is appropriate to divide the era since the end of the First World War into the periods 1918—1932, 1933—1939, 1939 to 1953, and 1953 until the present. This division is not haphazard, for we believe that the aforesaid periods have certain characteristic features which will help us better understand and evaluate the doctrinal trends emerging in those years.

The very first glance at the above periodization makes rather obvious the histor.-sociol. background of the individual doctrines.

Thus, the first period (1918—1932) covers the years of the postwar, well-developed internationality with its prevailing idealistic and universalistic tendencies, which were based on the presumed strength of the system established by the League of Nations; the only element "disturbing" the unity of this idealistic prospect was the existence of the first socialistic state in the world and the existence of new ownership relations towards the means of production. These factors could not be ignored but at the same time no "satisfactory" compromise could be made with them within the framework of the idealistic universalism. Consequently, they had to be fought in the field of private international law by promoting one's own law to the detriment of the foreign law with the help of frequently very subtle methods and technical means. This period, too, was characterized by a great upsurge in the activity of governmental and non-governmental institutions concerned with private international law, such as the Hague Conference on Private International Law, the International Law Association, the Institute of International Law, the Rome Institute for Unification of Private Law, etc.

On the other hand, the period 1933—1939 with the advent of

fascism and the resulting interational political situation brought to an end the postwar peace system and was characterized by a retreat from the idealistic, universalist tendencies. Instead, stress was laid on individual manifestations of etatism. This process was paralleled by a restriction of the universalistically oriented work of the aforementioned international institutions and eventually its complete stagnation. This period was also marked by great preponderance of etatistic doctrines of private international law (in contrast to doctrines tending towards internationalism and universality).

The third period (1939–1953) is the period of the Second World War and the elimination of its consequences. It is only natural that this period was characterized by a still greater tendency to stress etatistic features in private international law, although we should not overlook the fact that in the shadow of this tendency there was a renaissance of universalist trends, especially under the impact of the hope spurred by the aims and the work of the United Nations Organization. At the same time there were some manifestations of a supranational character, which appeared especially in some theories. Of course, in the Cold War period these tendencies could not be realized, so that the etatist trends as a whole continued to prevail.

The period which began with the year 1953 is a period in which international economic integration began to grow — first on a regional basis — and began to influence seriously the practical and theoretical development of private international law. This development has progressed thus far most in the West European economic communities, where there has been a substantial harmonization and unification of those branches of municipal law, which are of primary importance for the status of non-sovereign subjects in these particular units. Although economic integration has not progressed in other parts of the world and among the states of the socialist system as far as in the states belonging to the three West European communities, it is obvious that international economic integration has become in recent years an objectively valid economic trend which is making headway everywhere, even though with different intensity and in different forms. This process cannot but influence private international law to an extent which will necessarily affect all its future development. Economic integration cannot be realized either in capitalist or in socialist states without an essential coordination of private international law and public international law, which are the primary instruments for realizing the integration by means and methods which they alone dispose of. The rapprochement of legal systems and possibly their unification in the individual regions (just as their harmonization) are unthinkable without an extensive utilization of comparative jurisprudence, which has become a characteristic feature of contemporary private international law.

In the recent period we have also noted some essentially new features in legislative activity regarding private international law as well, both in the sphere of legislation materializing in the form of municipal legal regulations and in the international sphere. While in the 19th century and the beginning of the 20th century, the process of making private international law positive frequently involved the destruction of individual concepts and disturbing their former unity, the past decades have seen even in municipal legislation very prominent tendencies towards the rapprochement of the individual systems both as regards the solution of concrete problems and the overall approach to the problem as a whole.[2] This strengthens the international character

---

[2] Thus, for example, such highly important parts of Czechoslovak private international law, as the whole set of conflict rules regarding the law of obligations, are marked by the endeavor to achieve such a rapprochement by realizing in essence the proposals agreed on in the respective field by the Hague Conference on Private International Law; the same holds true of other spheres, such as the provisions governing international commercial arbitration, provisions governing international civil procedure, etc. For comments on identical features appearing in the new Polish private international law see, for example, Kalenský–Steiner, "K novému polskému mezinárodnímu právu soukromému a procesnímu ("On the New Polish Private International Law of Civil Procedure"), *Časopis pro mezinárodní právo (Czechoslovak Journal of International Law)*, No. 2/1966, pp. 121–137.

of private international law. This is parallelled by a considerable internationalization of the doctrine and an international debate on its individual basic problems, such as the application of foreign law, qualification, *renvoi,* etc. Other attempts to solve the problems on an international basis are made in the sphere of what is konwn as the law of international trade, to which the author has pointed on more than one occasion.

At the same time we can see a considerable intensification of the activities of international governmental and non-governmental organizations concerned with private international law, or completely new institutions are being established, whose existence seemed to be a Utopia only a few years ago, such as the United Nations Commission for International Trade Law (UNCITRAL), which has a vast field of activity; a new role which is currently of great importance for the development of private international law is also played by the international organizations established by states for purposes of economic integration, whose work is expanding in breadth and depth alike.[3]

The current period might therefore be called a period of development of private international law, which necessarily overcomes its classical concept of primarily a conflicts of law, while promoting the process of substantiation in which an increasingly greater scope of social relations containing a foreign element is becoming the object of special rules differing from rules of a

---

[3] See, for example, the author's studies "K základním právním problémům Evropského hospodářského společenství" ("Basic Legal Problems of the European Economic Community"), *Studie z mezinárodního práva, (Studies in International Law),* Vol. 9 (1964); "Rada vzájemné hospodářské pomoci ve světle mezinárodního práva" ("The Council of Mutual Economic Assistance in the Light of International Law"), *Rozpravy ČSAV (Transactions of the ČSAV),* 1962; *Právní otázky řízení zahraničního obchodu členských států RVHP, (Legal Aspects of the Management of Foreign Trade Between the Member States of the Council of Mutual Economic Assistance),* Prague, 1966, p. 175; "Ke koncepci právní úpravy zbožních vztahů mezi podniky pro zahraniční obchod členských států RVHP" ("The Concept of the Legal Regulation of Commodity Relations Between Foreign Trade Enterprises of the Member States of the Council of M.E.A."), *Studie z mezinárodního práva (Studies in International Law),* Vol. 11 (1966), pp. 103–135.

municipal character, which do not have a foreign element. The objective of this tendency is to prevent the occurrence of conflicts of law primarily with the help of internationally unified, substantive, "direct" rules, but also through the rapprochement and harmonization of individual municipal rules. Currently, we should not, of course, cherish any illusions that we can attain the ideal state where a thus created private international law could be in effect as something of a new *ius gentium;* therefore, the law of conflicts of law will continue to preserve its importance as an essential part of private international law.

Under the current situation, the doctrines of private international law are also influenced by the assessment of the role played by this law in the international life of society and of its social function which rests not only in the fact that private international law serves individual states as one of the legal instruments of their international policy, but also in the fact that it creates the conditions for everyday peaceful relations between non-sovereign subjects from different states, which represent a very substantial part of the international life of society, a part that helps promote friendly relations among states. Special aspects arise in this connection as regards the role played by private international law in the peaceful co-existence of states with different socio-economic systems. In the interest of peaceful co-existence of these states, we must most critically appraise all that hampers such co-existence, particularly in the field of recognizing the legal effects of the existence of the socialist economic system and socialist ownership relations, which are manifested also in the capitalist states.

If we make a closer analysis of the individual doctrines and trends that have come to the fore since the end of the First World War, we may characterize them as a constant tug-of-war between internationalist and universalist trends on the one side, and trends which put greater stress on the municipal nature of the individual private international laws on the other side. In this contest both these main tendencies have prevailed at one time or another – in a quite obvious dependence on the international situation – without, however, either of them succeeding to suppress the other one completely. While various trends that may be termed "nationalistic" and which proceed from the municipal character of the individual systems of private international law promote theories guided by the specific features of the individual systems of law and by the specific links existing between every private international law and the legal system of the respective state, the internationalist trends put greater stress on the connections with public international law, being mostly guided also by supranational concepts. Naturally, there exists a number of doctrinal shades between the two major groups. A separate, autonomous tendency is the "third", "autonomist" or "comparative" school of private international law.

The above division of the individual doctrines is, of course, very general, as the analysis of the individual doctrinal trends will show us. In this analysis we shall concentrate on

(1) the universalist trends,
(2) the "nationalist" trends, and
(3) the so-called "third" or "autonomist" school of private international law.

# CHAPTER 2
# The Main Views of the Doctrine of Public International Law on Private International Law

## (3) Basic Division

While in the field of public international law the opinion has prevailed at least recently, which may be called universalist, private international law is dominated – with a few exceptions regarding the theoretical approach to its subject matter – by a rather opposite opinion.

If we are to consider internationalist trends in the theory of private international law, we must first discuss some concepts of public international law, which may serve as a basis for an explanation of the concepts of private international law. Many of these doctrines oppose the separation of public international law and private international law, which they consider to be an *a priori* one, and, on the contrary, advocate a unity of the two laws, mostly arguing that private international law forms a "subdivision" of public international law.

One of the arguments put forward in support of this theory is that in the whole sphere of international law it is not possible to divide the law into public and private, as it is otherwise common in the sphere of municipal law. Another fact that is being asserted is that most municipal laws, too, do not clearly specify whether private international law belongs into the sphere of private or public law. Thus, for example, the advocates of this theory argue that French private international law includes under the definition of its object also such categories of public law as citizenship *(nationalité)* and the legal status of aliens *(condition des étrangers)*.

In West European literature on private international law we frequently meet with the assertion that private international law is a part of international law in the broader sense, which is divided into public and private law, and that this so defined sphere of law must be separated from the sphere of municipal, public and private law.[1] This serves as a basis for the claim that the "internationality" of private international law requires that it be viewed as a part of public law.[2]

From the viewpoint of the proper doctrine of private international law, this opinion is, of course, a rather secondary one and many leading authorities are opposed to it. These authorities, whose opinion we shall discuss further in this study, demonstrate that private international law is private law which is merely a continuation of municipal private law.[3] Although this dispute concerning the position of private international law among different branches of law is seemingly of an academic nature only, it is a dispute which is most important for theoretical elucidation of the problem and for the future development of private international law, because it provides the basis for clarifying the main internationalist and universalist positions on the one hand, and the trends called "nationalist", "etatistic" or "particularistic" on the other hand, which concentrate primarily on the *sedes materiae* as regards the definition of the relationship between private international law and public international law.

From the viewpoint of the doctrine of public international law, we can see – as far as the definition of its relationship to private

---

[1] This proceeds from older French legal opinion. See, for example, Foelix—Demangèst, *Traité du droit international privé, ou du conflit des lois de différentes nations en matière de droit privé*, 4th ed., Paris, 1866.

[2] See André Weiss, "Existe-t-il un droit international privé?", *Mémoires de l'Académie de droit comparé*, Vol. I, pp. 177 ff.

[3] See, for example, the opinion of Raape, *Internationales Privatrecht*, Berlin–Frankfurt, 1950, p. 3; Melchior, *Die Grundlagen des deutschen internationalen Privatrechts*, Berlin–Leipzig, 1932, pp. 50 ff.; Nussbaum, *Deutsches internationales Privatrecht*, pp. 14 ff.; Schnitzer, *Handbuch*, Vol. I, p. 22; Arminjon, *Précis de droit international privé*, 3rd ed., Paris, 1956, p. 11; Wolff, *Das internationale Privatrecht Deutschlands*, p. 4; Maury, "Règles générales des conflicts de lois", *Recueil des Cours*, 1936, Vol. 57, pp. 329 ff.

international law is concerned – a very colorful picture lacking uniformity. The internationalists differ in their opinion primarily on how far they adhere to the dualistic or monistic concept, in particular as regards the definition of the relationship between international and municipal laws. Quite naturally, a question which also remains disputable in this connection, is the question whether private international law should be considered a part of international law or of municipal law, or even of both these laws.

Most authors adhering to the concept of the dualistic school[4] hold that the rules of private international law belong to municipal law and that in view of the independence of both international and municipal laws, these rules are irrelevant for public international law.[5] The dualistic concept does not, however, deal with a situation which would arise, if the rules of private international law could be considered a part of both international and municipal laws in a case where the rules of the two laws were contradictory.

The monistic school of public international law, as it is generally known, is basically divided between opinion stressing the primacy of municipal law and opinion underlining the primacy of international law.

Advocates of the monistic trends stressing the primacy of municipal over international law also place beyond any doubt the appurtenance of private international law to municipal law; however, what this theory has failed to clarify is the question

---

[4] E.g. Triepel, *Völkerrecht und Landesrecht,* Leipzig, 1899; "Les rapports entre le droit interne et le droit international", *Recueil des Cours,* 1923, No. 1, pp. 77 ff.; Anzilotti, "Il diritto internazionale nei quadri interni", *Corso di diritto internazionale,* Vol. 1, 1912; Strupp, *Theorie und Praxis des Völkerrechts,* Berlin, 1925, etc.; the opinion of these authors is discussed in Hobza, *Úvod do mezinárodního práva mírového (Introduction to the International Law of Peace),* 1933, Part I, 1933, Prague, pp. 33 ff., and Outrata, *Mezinárodní právo veřejné (International Public Law),* Prague, 1960, pp. 38 ff.

[5] E.g. Triepel, *Völkerrecht und Landesrecht,* p. 274 says: "die Hauptmasse des internationalen Privatrechts ist völkerrechtlich gleichgültig".

whether in the relationship between private international law and public international law the rules of private international law have preference over those of public international law. Although the author has failed to find an express answer to this question, it seems logical that the answer should be in the affirmative.

The situation is different as regards those monistic theories, which accentuate the primacy of public international law. These theories, which prevailed in the doctrine of public international law especially in the period following the Second World War,[6] usually subject the rules of private international law to the rules of the supranational public international law. These views are held, of course, not only by authorities on public international law; there are also authorities on private international law, who assert that the whole body of private international law is but a part of public international law.[7]

Nevertheless, monistic literature is far from unequivocal in this respect. While most authors stress the subjection of private international law to public international law, such an important representative of monistic theory, as Georges Scelle, holds the opposite view, asserting that "it is the legal relationships between individuals, which form the true substance of the international community, and public international law (or the law in effect between governments) has as the substance of its existence merely the task of facilitating relationships between individuals. Public international law serves private international law".[8]

---

[6] Their supportes include many leading authorities, such as Scelle, Duguit, Krabbe, Guggenheim, Verdross, Kelsen, Kunz, Jessup, and others.

[7] See, e.g. Lerebours–Pigeonnière, *Précis de droit international privé,* 5th ed., Paris, 1948, pp. 17 and 57.

[8] G. Scelle, *Manuel élémentaire du droit international public,* 3rd ed., Paris, 1948, p. 19.

### (4) The Concept of Subjection of Private International Law to Public International Law

Most internationalist theories which subordinate municipal private international law to public international law proceed from a certain common basis which links them to a considerable extent and which shapes them into a body of opinion that can be raised to counter the views advocating the independence of private international law or understanding it as a part of municipal private law.

This basis is the existence of the international community of states which is made up of individual states but which is at the same time hierarchically superior to them and within which the rights and obligations of states between each other as well as towards the community are governed by the rules of public international law. The inclusion of states in this international community is viewed as essential and as a thing arising from the very character of the state. The obligation of states towards the international legal community and its other members may be defined as a body of rights and obligations which the state, as a subject of public international law undertakes and whose violation constitutes an unauthorized act or delict for which the state must bear the appropriate burden of responsibility.[9]

From this basic opinion held by the advocates of internationalist theories we may deduce their overall view of private international law. Its dependence on public international law is for them quite obvious and leads them to the conclusion that "private international law is only a sub-division of (public) international law".[10] The dependence of private international law on

---

[9] For the individual theories of public international law, which cannot be analysed here, see Outrata, *Mezinárodní právo veřejné (International Public Law)*, pp. 38 ff.

[10] For these views see also the other parts of the present study as well as the author's study, *"K předmětu a povaze mezinárodního práva soukromého a k otázce jeho místa v systému práva"* ("The Object and Nature of Private International Law and Its Place in the System of Law), *Časopis pro mezinárodní právo (Czechoslovak Journal of International Law)*, 1960, No. 2, pp. 81 ff.

public international law is deduced from the original thesis that the membership of states in the superior international community and the resulting mutual obligations of states also include the obligation of states to apply in certain situations under mutual consent the rules of their municipal laws. A denial of a thus construed obligation of states would also constitute a breach of their obligation to recognize other members of the international legal community and their respective laws, which would be contrary to the fundamental premise of the aforesaid construction. Arguments of a sociological character are used to demonstrate that situations that arise from the mutual, international relations of non-sovereign subjects belonging under different jurisdictions can be settled only by the above method.

These fundamental premises, which are considered to be of an *a priori* character, are used as a basis for deducing other, derived, premises that primarily concern the character of conflict rules. According to the authors of this school, these rules form a part of international law, since they are a part of the law which defines the mutual rights and obligations of states as members of the international legal community, including their claim to have their own substantive law applied before foreign courts and the corresponding obligation to apply foreign law before their own courts. This argument is basically not altered even by the fact that conflict rules are defined in the sources of municipal law; proponents of the internationalist school do not, as a rule, find it difficult to overcome this question, as all their effort is usually directed at proving the existence of customary, treaty and such other conflict rules, which might be considered to be universal legal principles. This standpoint is in most cases promoted by the monistic views held by the majority of these authors. Their postulates may be summed up in general as a call for setling cases with a foreign element on the basis of the above premises in a uniform manner by the courts of one state and throught the uniform application of the same law.

The idealistic and *a priori* speculation which led to the formulation of the (schematic) premises of this school of thought is concluded by the argument that international law (public and, in its own way, also private) is competent to define the conflicts arising between the sovereign authority of individual states. Questions of the character of the sources of private international law, the problem of determining whether public international law does in fact contain customary conflict rules or whether there do exist conflict rules which may be assumed to have the character of universally recognized legal principles, not speaking of the difference between the subjects of the relationships governed by public international law and those governed by private international law, all these are considered by the proponents of this school a set of subsidiary questions which are either ignored in their scheme or are being circumvented by various constructions.

### (5) The Endeavour to Overcome the Extreme Position of Monistic Universalism

The realistic proponents of the internationalist trends are trying to overcome in several ways the problems quite obviously ensuing from the thus defined premises and assumptions, which can hardly stand up under the critical analysis of the proponents of theories that make a distinction between private international law and public international law as two separate spheres. The main trend here is the doctrine which asserts that private international law constitutes one of the external functions of the state.

This doctrinal trend basically recognizes the role played by individual states in governing by their substantive law the relations between non-sovereign subjects, characterized by the presence of a foreign element, and even admits – in contrast to the proponents of the integral internationalist trends – that this role of the individual states is of a primary nature. Its advocates point out that even in the regulation of international relations – both those falling under public international law and those governed by private international law – the state represents the organizational and institutional form which guarantees the maximum effect of the regulation and is, at the same time, irreplaceable by any other legal machinery.

The state as a power, social and legal organization cannot remain inactive in the sphere of international relations where its activity has a creative character. Obviously, these views no longer claim that states are determined by the *a priori* existence of conflict rules of international law, which define conflicts of their sovereign authority, but fully recognize the role played by individual states in creating the political and legal premises of international relations. This role includes among other things, the issuance of conflict rules of municipal law, defining the jurisdiction of the courts with respect to other states, and other matters falling within the scope of private international law; also recognized is the primary competence of municipal courts in applying the rules of private international law. In view of the very small number of conflict rules of customary international law and the vagueness still prevailing as regards their precise formulation and interpretation, especially in comparison with the large number and exact formulation of municipal conflict rules, this state of affairs simply had to be recognized. However, if the correctness of the internationalist doctrine was to be deduced from it, some legal construction had to be devised for this purpose.

The first of the posibilities that offered themselves in this respect was the assertion that the international character of private international law did not ensue from the nature of the formal sources of law or from the character of the authority that made it obligatory, but from its content and function. We must ask, of course, whether this construction is satisfactory to the extent that it can dispel the aforesaid doubts. It cannot, in particular, explain the role played by individual states and their respective laws or courts in formulating and applying private international law, which are factors that – according to other authors – deprive it of the international character. This, however, is countered by the objection – not unsubstantiated in the author's opinion – that through its activity in the sphere of private international law every state fulfills its international role or function, and that when it does so, it is because international law orders it to do it. This assertion is supported by the argument that this sphere of activity of the state is one of primary international relevance.

But the core of the problem does not rest in this international relevance of the activity of the state in the sphere of private international law either. Neither the advocates of the municipal character of private international law, nor the proponents of the internationalist trends claim the opposite. The question is basically one of whether in its activity in the sphere of private international law, the state is bound by certain interests or rules of public international law, which determine this activity either in the direction of the delegation theory, which claims that the jurisdictions of individual states in the sphere of private international law is transferred to the state, or in the direction of the theory of so-called functional duplication, as promoted by Kopelmanas and Wiebringhaus.[11] We shall discuss both these theories in more detail below.

## (6) The Delegation Theory

The delegation theory is based on the idea that the state which is active in the sphere of private international law can do so only because the jurisdiction, which otherwise appertains to the international legal community, has been transferred or delegated to it.[12] This delegation takes place only as a result of the

---

[11] L. Kopelmanas, *La théorie du dédoublement fonctionnel et son utilisation pour la solution des problème des conflicts des lois, Hommage Georges Scelle,* Vol. II, Paris, 1950, pp. 743 ff.; H. Wiebringhaus, *Das Gesetz der funktionellen Verdoppelung* (Beitrag zu einer universalistischen Theorie des International-privat- und Völkerrechts), Saarbrücken, 1955, p. 157.

[12] This is obviously also the opinion held by Guggenheim, *Lehrbuch des Völkerrechts,* 1948, Vol. I, p. 32, who, of course, overlooks the

current situation – which is pretended to be of a transitional character – which due to the provisional non-existence of an international and supranational legislator requires that certain tasks (including those in the sphere of private international law) should be performed by individual states. This situation is an essential but merely provisional phenomenon.

The delegation theory – obviously being also influenced by the dualistic trends – proceeds from the existence of two types of conflict rules. The first group – one that is lower on the scale of hierarchic values – includes conflict rules which are applied by the municipal judge when settling individual cases, i.e. conflict rules which are a part of every municipal law. However, under this theory, the situation is different where international law is created by the state on the basis of jurisdiction delegated to the state. There the state must proceed from conflict rules of a higher level, which, under this theory, allegedly exist beside the conflict rules of municipal law and which define the jurisdiction of the states in conflicts between individual state sovereignties.

The delegation theory therefore basically recognizes the jurisdiction of states and individual state organs in formulating and applying the rules of private international law, but at the same time requires that states should proceed in the formulation of private international law so that the rules should be uniform to the extent that under the private international law of all states only one law should always be applicable to every factual configuration. This very strict concept of the delegation theory must, of course, lose in confrontation with the everyday reality of private international law. That is why certain modifications have been made, clearly influenced by a realistic approach to the problems involved. The modified and moderate form of the delegation theory favors a maximum coordination of the individual, national systems of private international law, at the same

---

fact that the delegation can take place only, if an existing, superior body can delegate its powers to lower bodies that are subordinated to it. Guggenheim changed his opinion, see *Traité de public,* Vol. 1, Geneva, 1953, p. 25.

time advocating maximum cooperation warranted by the international character of the problems to be settled.

Nevertheless, the delegation theory in either form is unable to overcome its basic deficiency, namely the non-existence of a superior, supranational body which could transfer its jurisdiction to subordinate bodies.

### (7) An Assessment of the Monistic and Dualistic Concepts of Private International Law

This brief survey of the opinion held by different representatives of the doctrine of private international law shows that this doctrine is trying to solve the main question with which it is concerned, namely the relationship between public and private international law, primarily in its basic connecting factors; it especially endeavours to determine whether private international law is in fact international law or not.

The opinion held by that part of the internationalist doctrine, which favours the conclusion that private international law is a part of municipal law – in spite of the fact that they are solving questions of factual configurations which are characterized by the existence of a foreign or international element – is based either on the monistic concept laying stress on the municipal law, or on Triepel's dualistic concept; at the same time, of course, the individual authors hold many different shades of the same, basic opinion. The main shortcoming of all these views is the facts that they do not solve the actual problems of private international law and that they all concentrate on conclusions concerning the nature of this law, ensuing from the solution of the relationships between municipal law and international law. Nevertheless – as we shall see further – these are views which quite substantially also determine the basic position of the doctrine of private international law (in contrast to the doctrine of public international law), which, with a few exceptions, does not concern itself with defining the relationship between the two laws, but still proceeds in most instances from the idea that there are as many private international laws in the world, as there are states; the fact that the existence of an international element is considered characteristic of the relations governed by private international law, does not lead most authors to the conclusion that private international law is international law.

The dualistic theory of international law meets with objections that by separating the two spheres of law (i.e. international and municipal law) it does not arrive at the construction of a universally valid law, whereby it disturbs the belief that every law is universal and uniform. The fact that international law and municipal law can exist independently of each other and beside each other makes it possible for rules of municipal law to be contrary to the rules of international law. Objections are also raised against the construction of sources of law, of which some originate from the concurrent will of states and others from the conviction of the municipal legislator, as most authors advocating the dualistic theory hold; what is missing in this theory (mainly acording to the opinion of the advocates of monistic views), is primarily the necessary uniformity, which is essential for the existence of law as a system. This theory is also considered as ineffective as regards the settlement of conflicts between municipal law and international law. The opponents of the dualistic theory try to show that it is impossible and unimaginable to separate international and municipal laws.

According to the critics of the dualistic school, this applies not only to the sphere of municipal and international laws, but even more so as regards the separation of private international law from public international law, which is the logical consequence of the fact that the dualistic trends include private international law in the sphere of municipal law. As we have already shown, interaction between private and public international law is quite essential.

Many of the critical objections raised against the views held by the dualistic school of public international law, which we have just mentioned, may be applied *mutatis mutandis* to the monistic theory favouring the primacy of municipal law. Proponents of monistic trends giving primacy to international law object primarily to the fact that by including private international law in municipal law, the former school achieves a seeming independence of private international law from public international law, which is contrary to reality, as well as the superiority of private international law over public international law. Stressing the role played by states in the creation of international law could, in the view of the opponents of the primacy of municipal law, result in a situation where every state, completely disregarding the interests of other states, could negate within the scope of its jurisdiction, any rule of international law, which would turn the whole sphere of international law into utter chaos. Basically, this school corresponds to the views of the extreme proponents of the particularistic and etatistic theories of private international law, who assert – mostly under the influence of extreme nationalism – that in the sphere of private international law individual states may proceed in a basically arbitrary manner.

We have already mentioned the views of those monists, who favour the primacy of international law and therefore as a rule subordinate private international law to public international law of a universal and supranational character. Very valid objections can be raised against this theory, too. The most serious of these objections rests in the contradiction between this construction and the current situation where individual states play a major role in creating the valid international law in keeping with the principles of state sovereignty. Another objection again aims at stressing the role played by individual states in the formulation and application of private international law. All these objections have led to the effort to overcome the conclusions reached by the proponents of the monistic trends stressing the primacy of international law.[13] We might mention on the sideline that the subordination of private international law to public international law, as proposed in these concepts, creates a situation where the subjects of relations governed by private

---

[13] See above under sub-chapter (5).

international law (i. e. individual physical and legal persons) become subjects in the sphere of public international law, which runs counter to the overwhelming majority of the doctrine of international law, which thus far has denied that an individual could become a subject of public international law, reserving this position to states as the original subjects of public international law and permitting it with respect to some international organizations as derived subjects.

The farthest point in the endeavour to overcome the deficiencies of the monistic school stressing the primacy of international law has thus far been reached by the theory of functional duplication, which is based on the teachings of Georges Scelle, one of the foremost proponents of universalistic tendencies in the interwar period.[14] In the sense of his universalistic concept, private international law must be considered a part of international law, just as the same logically ensues from the theory promoted by other proponents of monistic trends which stress the primacy of international law, we have already mentioned; however, in contrast to most of these authors, Scelle asserted that public international law served private international law.

In the sense of his universalist theory in the sphere of international law, Scelle also considers the relationship between international law and municipal law, subordinating the latter hierarchically to the former. However, at the same time he also proceeds from the fact — corresponding to the existing state of development of international law — that in view of the absence of corresponding international or rather supranational legal institutions, the state must quite frequently perform through its agencies functions that would otherwise appertain to such institutions. The agencies of the state then have jurisdiction of both municipal and international character, depending on whether they are engaged in activities in the municipal or international spheres. This results in what is called functional duplication

---

[14] See, in particular, G. Scelle, *Précis de droit des gens, Principes et systématique,* Vols. I and II, Paris, 1932 and 1934, and his *Manuel élémentaire.*

whenever the agency of a state must be active (quite naturally within the framework of the aforesaid hierarchical subordination of municipal law to international law) in a field where in view of the existing, imperfect state of development of international law an international or rather supranational institution (which, of course, does not exist) should take action. In this respect, therefore, Scelle goes farther than most other authors promoting the universalism of international law in all its forms and with different philosophical motivation.

This interpretation of the construction of functional duplication thus respects – without touching on the foundations of the monistic concept laying stress on the primacy of international law – the fact that in the sphere of the legal regulation of cases with an international element, states have a very extensive jurisdiction; the failure to respect this jurisdiction in the doctrine uncovers the weak points of every monistic theory. Scelle compares the situation currently existing in this field to the situation which existed in every feudal unit in the Middle Ages when power had not yet been centralized in larger units. This historical parallel is naturally used as basis for developing the theory of the future world, state, world federation, etc.

Scelle's idea of a "law of functional duplication", formulated for the sphere of international law in general, was developed in the sphere of private international law in particular by H. Wiebringhaus.[15] His whole work is devoted to the effort to bridge the contradiction between the internationality or the international character of the cases governed by private international law and reality, manifested in the extensive activity of individual states in formulating and applying this law. This construction, whose necessity may be doubted, is also in keeping with the old tendency of the doctrine of private international law, which points almost constantly to the need of such solutions, whose acceptability rests, among other factors, in the essential respect that must be paid to the interests of other states.

Wiebringhaus points out that in the sphere of private inter-

---

[15] *Das Gesetz*, pp. 39 ff. and 93 ff.

national law (in the sense of Scelle's doctrine a part of international law as a whole), much more than in the sphere of public international law, the law of functional duplication manifests itself quite frequently, and he even asserts that the whole sphere of private international law is subjected to this regime.[16] Most authors do not realize this state of affairs and consequently do not consider the rules of private international law as being a part of international law in general. The theory of functional duplication applies in this sphere the more so, as here individual states, as a rule, themselves create private international law by their own legislation, their courts apply it, and their decisions are again executed by state agencies, which facts meet all the conditions required by Scelle's theory for the validity of functional duplication.

Relations governed by private international law are relations which are international in their character; although they arise between individuals, they are realized within an international framework. According to Scelles's theory, which Wiebringhaus has taken over, international law is superior to municipal laws. The non-existence of supranational organizations or institutions, which is a typical feature of the chaos prevailing in the sphere of international law, is an even more prominent phenomenon in the sphere of international relations between individuals than it is in relations between states. As a result, relation arising between individuals on the international level must be regulated almost exclusively by legislation or by judicial or executive organs on the level of individual states. Therefore, this, too, is a sphere which is subject to the theory of functional duplication.[17] According to Wiebringhaus, a chaotic and untenable situation prevails in the sphere of private international law for the time being, in particular as a result of the fact that there do not exist international – or supranational – institutions which should and could correct the situation.

In the final part of his study,[18] Wiebringhaus tries to project

---

[16] *Ibid.*, p. 39.

[17] *Ibid.*, pp. 43 and 44.

his basic theoretical premises into the individual spheres of activity of the state, which are related to private international law, and deduces that the whole legal regulation of international relations (and therefore also of international relations between individuals) must be uniform, and the existing, undesirable situation, characterized by the well-known assertion that there are as many private international laws as there are states in the world, must be eliminated.

What is remarkable about the Wiebringhaus theory is the fact that it does not try to ignore the problems we come across in private international law and which the proponents of the universalistic trends and theories usually do not solve. However, in view of the dualistic theories we have already mentioned, we must ask whether it does not involve merely a "transposition" of dualism into the monistic theory, which respects to a considerable degree the existing social reality in the sphere of private international law but which, at the same time, abandons it and thereby ventures into utilitarian and *a priori* speculation which cannot attain the intended goals precisely because of the aforesaid conflict with reality. That is also why it cannot be evaluated in any other way but as a theory which, guided by wishful thinking, tries to eliminate and negate the existing state of affairs of whose unsatisfactory nature there is, of course, no doubt.[19]

## (8) Conclusion

Another, and much more serious question, which arises in connection with the above internationalist theories, is the question whether it is possible to renounce the seemingly integral and,

---

[18] *Ibid*, pp. 93 ff.

[19] When we speak here of Wiebringhaus' views and their confrontation with dualistic theories, we must bear in mind that some dualists, such as Anzilotti, hold a very similar opinion when speaking of the functional division of private international law into the two spheres of law.

from the viewpoint of the doctrinal trends, seemingly unequivocal concepts which represent, on the one hand, an extreme internationalist universalism and, on the other hand, various "etatistic" or "nationalist" trends, and try to find a common path which is necessary for the development and progress of private international law. We realize that it would be absurd to talk in this respect about a convergence of universalist and nationalist trends, or their reconciliation. Nevertheless, we have tried already in the introduction to this chapter to show that the future progress of private international law does not rest in a stubborn insistence on and promotion of individual doctrinal tendencies and concepts, which meet with a no less vehement opposition and criticism, but in the endeavour to find acceptable solution of individual situations, which is one of the specific tasks of the science of private international law. It seems that the reality of international legal life is much more in keeping with the dualistic views, which are prepared to admit that public international law contains certain rules which limit the activity of states in the sphere of private international law, while the overwhelming majority of its rules is contained in the rules of municipal law.

The social purpose of private international law thus conceived is to facilitate the co-existence of the laws of individual states with respect to relations between non-sovereign subjects with a foreign element, and to make possible their coordination to a certain degree. Under the current situation of the plurality of legal systems, every state must proceed from the fact that by failing to pay some fundamental respect to other states or other laws, it cannot achieve the objectives which it follows in the sphere of private international law. Unilaterally defined jurisdiction, arbitrary application of substantive law, failure to respect the fact that there exist other laws than the law of the forum, all these cannot but result in failure to have decisions of the courts of such a state recognized or executed in other states, and in rejection of the application of its law with reference to the fact that such law violates public order. Of course, this can be prevented, if states, when formulating and applying private international law, strive – precisely with regard to the existence of other states and other laws, and the need of coordination between them – for as suitable solutions as possible, which would also secure the recognition of their decisions in other states.

There is certainly no doubt that the current situation in the sphere of private international law is unsatisfactory and is far from the ideal state of affairs. This does not mean, however, that legal theory should react towards this situation with idealistically blind, *a priori* concepts, which may perhaps be "pure" from the viewpoint of theoretical – often only conjectural – dogmas that cannot solve the situation or influence the development of private international law.

Although there exist considerable differences on whether international law contains certain principles or rules which would generally predestine or limit the activity of states in the sphere of private international law (these principles include the rules *locus regit actum* or *lex rei sitae,* or the application of the law chosen by the parties in the field of conflict rules governing obligations), it seems that it is indeed possible to deduce from international law certain fundamental premises concerning the activity of states in this sphere. It is, of course, difficult to prove that public international law contains, for example, a rule which instructs states to apply to the form of legal acts the law of the place (or places) where the parties had manifested their will, or a rule that the legal status of immovables (or movables as well) is governed by the law of the place where the respective thing is located. This gives rise to the question whether such rules exist at all in public international law, whether they are a part of customary international law, or whether they are merely "general principles of law, recognized by civilized nations" in the sense of Article 38 (c) of the Statute of the International Court of Justice. We feel that the latter view should be accepted; we have been led to this conclusion by the thought that these rules have such a different impact, scope, formulation and importance in individual laws, that it is impossible to speak of them as of uniform principles or of customary rules of public international law. Thus, as regards the principle *locus regit actum,* it is not clear whether it should be applied as a mandatory rule or a subsidiary one, while the principal rule governing also the form of a legal act is the *lex causae.*[20] Just as vague is the interpretation of seemingly such an indisputable principle as the application of the law of the place where the contested thing is located *(lex rei sitae);* does it apply to immovables only or to movables as well? The situation is still more complex in the field of conflict rules governing obligations as regards the autonomy of the will of the parties in determining the applicable law. As it is well known, this principle is expressed in many different and mostly contradictory forms.[21] The author feels that we should not speak here of the existence of such rules of customary international law, which could be concretely specified as conflict rules binding states in the field of private international law but only with respect to the "general principles of law, recognized by civilized nations", as formulated in Article 38 (c) of the Statute of the International Court of Justice. A similar situation prevails in other spheres of law as well; for example, in the case of the definition of the basic types of contracts in the field of the law of obligations (such as contracts of sale, of donation, etc.).

In this connection it is necessary to view the aforesaid rules as a part of the legal culture of society which secures thereby some homogeneity; at the same time, of course, such rules transposed by various formulas (*lex rei sitae, locus regit actum,* etc.) into a common denominator acquire in their concrete shape different forms. This situation does not mean, of course, that the laws of different states do not have much in common in the sphere of private international law.

In spite of the fact that the existence of conflict rules of customary international law, binding states as subjects of internatio-

---

[20] See P. Kalenský, "Ke kolizní problematice vzniku obligačních smluv" ("Some Problems of the Conflict of Laws Concerning the Formation of Contracts"), *Studie z mezinárodního práva (Studies in International Law),* No. 6, pp. 191 ff.

[21] See the author's monograph *Obligační statut (Conflict of Laws),* pp. 70 ff.

nal law, cannot be proven in our opinion, we feel that the obligation of states to cooperate and co-exist peacefully with each other imposes on them certain obligations also in the sphere of private international law. We therefore hold that although states have considerable freedom in this respect, it would be contrary to the aforesaid principles of international law, if some state were to reject completely the application of a foreign law and applied only its own law. This means that, in our opinion, every state must have its private international law which should not, of course, lead to an unrestricted application of the *lex fori.* We consider these defined obligations of states to constitute a certain minimum degree of obligations. The natural interests of individual states then lead in the sphere of private international law to concrete efforts to have decisions of the courts of the respective state, which settle relationships containing an international element, recognized in other states as well; these efforts are made with the awareness that an arbitrary procedure in this sphere could frustrate the recognition and execution of such decisions, and could result in a rejection to apply the law of that state on the grounds that the law disturbs public order.

Naturally, this state of affairs and interest in mutual cooperation also spur individual states to govern growing sectors of private international law in mutual agreement in the form of international treaties, which, the author feels, is the most appropriate form of recognizing the international character of private international law.

# CHAPTER 3
# The Main Concepts of the Doctrine of Private International Law

## (9) The Controversy Between "Universalist" and "Nationalist" Trends

The doctrine of private international law, too, is basically divided into two major groups of opinion, namely a universalist trend and a trend which may be defined as one of a "national" private international law. Both these groups can be, naturally, subdivided, but, on the whole, we may say that in the proper doctrine of private international law the opinion has prevailed, that contemporary private international law is independent in every state and that, therefore, there are as many private international laws in the world, as there are individual states. The majority of this opinion represents a reaction to the weak points of the internationalist and universalist concepts we have partly discussed when dealing with the doctrine of public international law and which we shall yet discuss in connection with the doctrine of private international law. The opinion, which is critical of the universalism of some of the doctrinal trends in public international law, proceeds from the fact that the sphere of public international law as that branch of law, which governs relations between sovereign states, is separate from the sphere of private international law, which governs relationships between non-sovereign subjects involving a foreign element. There is yet the additional fact that the overwhelming majority of the rules of private international law is to be found among the rules of municipal law. Thus we must distinguish between the two categories both on the basis of the differences in the social relationships they govern and on the basis of the differences in their formal sources; this is an argument which has been used in particular after private international law had been made positive. According to the majority of the opinion underlining that private international law is inseparable from the whole body of law of the individual state, the law of every state constitutes a closed set of rules; this opinion is manifested especially with respect to the fundamental questions of the application of the foreign element in the law, which takes place on the basis of the rules governing conflict of laws.[1] Thus, when speaking of the doctrine of private international law, we may justly speak of a latent controversy or conflict between "universalists" and "nationalists". However, this controversy does not mean that some "nationalists" have not tried to give the solutions they recommend for individual types of cases as much of a universal character as posible.

Nevertheless, both trends in the doctrine of private international law are essentially in agreement in their criticism of that part of the doctrine of public international law, which presents the solution of conflicts between state sovereignties as the principal object of private international law. They point out that the term "conflict of sovereignties" is contradictory within itself because under the classical concept of international law, sovereignty, as an original, supreme and unlimited category, is strictly set and, in the given connections, can hardly find itself in conflict with other sovereignties; conflicts of laws governing differing relationships between non-sovereign subjects, which involve a foreign element, are, of course, something quite different. The criticism and critics of monism in international law are also supported by the fact that the reality of the contemporary world is far removed from postulates of an identical solution of the same cases under different legal systems in accordance with one and the same law.

When we speak of universalists and particularists in the doctrine of private international law, this does not mean to say that these trends unequivocally reject the links and interaction

---

[1] See Part Six of the present study and the author's study "Podstata a povaha aplikace cizího práva" ("The Substance and Nature of the Application of Foreign Law"), *Studie z mezinárodního práva (Studies in International Law)*, Vol. 13, pp. 41–66.

which exist between private and public international law. One of the examples frequently quoted to point to the divergence of views and arguments used in this respect are two German authors, Zitelmann and Frankenstein, who are generally viewed as universalists; while Zitelmann based his theory on the impact of public international law on private international law, Frankenstein denied such an influence, and yet both promoted the idea of universalism of private international law. (For more on the two authors see below.)

Nevertheless, a historical view of private international law seems to indicate that irrespective of its once universality, based on the heritage of the statutory theory, it has always formed a part of municipal law in its individual units. The universalist trends in private international law did not begin to assert themselves until the 19th century in connection with the growth of the influence of public international law in the theory and practical politics of individual states. The link between public and private international law, explained by the idealistic postulates prevailing at the end of the 19th and the beginning of the 20th centruries, served as the basis primarily for the older universalistic school of thought, represented by such authors as von Bar, Weiss or Pillet, whose opinion is quite frequently also used by more modern universalists.

## (10) "Universalism" in the Doctrine of Private International Law

A universalistic view of private international law appears as early as in the case of Savigny, who refers in many parts of the eighth volume of his *System des heutigen römischen Rechts* – when localizing individual legal relationships – to the existence of a "community of nations" *(Völkergemeinschaft)*, which serves him – among other reasons – for trying to find universalistic solutions by determining the "site" of every relationship.[2]

---

[2] See Part Two of the present study, Chapter 4, sub-chapters 19 and 20. Also Gutzwiller, *Einfluss Savignys*, p. 12.

The main advocate of universalism in private international law at the end of the 19th century, and the author whose work strongly influenced all the subsequent proponents of the universalist trend, was Ludwig von Bar.[3] Typical of this author, who concerned himself with both public and private international law, is the link he makes between the two when settling individual problems. We may generally describe von Bar's theory as an attempt to make a synthesis of Savigny's doctrine and Mancini's national school of law. He procceded from the conviction that public international law nd private international law were two parts of a broader international law;[4] this also made it possible for him to distinguish between the two according to the object of the respective rules. Von Bar modified the basic division of international law into two parallel and equal branches in the sense that he proceeded from the premise that the legislative activity of states in the sphere of private international law was determined by public international law, while taking it for granted that the foundations of private international law were determined by public international law since what was basically involved was the limitation of the sphere covered by one sovereignty with respect to another sovereignty.[5]

In his study of private international law, von Bar was, on the whole, quite subservient to Savigny's doctrine of localization according to the nature of the case, laying special stress on the activity of the judge in finding this localization on the basis of principles and directives laid down by the legislator; in this respect von Bar's theory shows a marked influence of the school

---

[3] L. von Bar, *Das internationale Privat- und Strafrecht*, Hannover, 1862, *Internationales Privatrecht*, Leipzig, 1882, *Lehrbuch des internationalen Privat- und Strafrechts*, Stuttgart, 1892, and *Theorie und Praxis des internationalen Privatrechts*, Hannover, 1889.

[4] L. von Bar, *Theorie und Praxis des internationalen Privatrechts*, p. 4: "*Völkerrecht und internationales Privatrecht sind Teile des internationalen Rechts; beide beruhen auf der gemeinsamen Grundlage des Verkehrs der Staaten und es gibt Materien, welche man ebenso gut diesem wie jenem zuweisen könnte . . .*".

[5] *Ibid.*

of natural law. Von Bar also raised certain principles in the form of postulates regarding private international law; he believed that the purpose of private international law was to create conditions favourable to co-existence between individual municipal laws; he considered as esential the existence of private international law in every state; for him, the decisive factor in the sphere of private international law was an equilibrium in the application of municipal and foreign law, and he rejected the doctrine of international comity as a basis for the application of foreign law, proceeding from the premise that this application was a legal obligation of the state, arising from social and legal necessity, as well as a binding, consuetudinary rule of international law. According to von Bar, in the legislative sphere states were authorized to issue rules of private international law, but these municipal systems were determined by their appurtenance to the international community, which gave private international law its international character. Although von Bar had a respect for reality, he opposed the inclusion of private international law in the municipal law of individual states. His doctrine is thus characterized by the parallel existence of public and private international law as two branches of international law in general, as well as by the fact that private international law is restricted within limits set by public international law. Von Bar's doctrine dates from a period when Germany had still not codified her private international law, as she did later in the Intruductory Act to the Civil Code. This fact forced von Bar to resort quite frequently to solutions based on natural law, and, in doing so, to place in his methodology special stress also on the use of the comparative method.

In the French doctrine of private international law of the first half of the 20th century, the leading representative of the universalist trend is A. Pillet;[6] his whole work is marked, not only in its basic theoretical premises but also in the proposed solutions, by an opposition to the concept of the "disintegration" of

---

6 A. Pillet, *Principes du droit international privé*, Paris, 1903; *Traité pratique du droit international privé*, 2 vol., Paris, 1923, 1924.

private international law into parts of the municipal laws of individual states, as well as by a link between the construction of the rules governing conflict of laws and the basic premise that private international law is, in Pillet's opinion, a solution for conflicting sovereignties.[7] Pillet holds that private international law, as a branch of law governing relations between individuals, derives its rules from rules governing relations between individual state sovereignties, that is from public international law; for this reason, he argues, it is inadmissible to separate private international law from public international law, because the former is derived from the latter and originally grows therefrom.

As regards his method of work, Pillet – just as von Bar – proceeded mostly from Savigny. He was fully aware of the great influence the theory of private international law had on the formation of this law; he considered international consuetudinary rules to be the true source of private international law, which had an international character. However, Pillet was somewhat critical of Savigny's attempt at localizing individual legal relations. He felt that questions of private international law could be solved primarily on the basis of the true nature of the laws, depending on whether rules of "personal" or "territorial" character were involved; in doing so, he quite realistically viewed the problems of private international law as a whole, as problems of co-existence between territoriality and personality.[8] The choice between the permanent and general laws, in Pillet's opi-

---

[7] Pillet, *Traité pratique,* p. 20, where the author stresses that all conflict rules of private international law represent conflicts of sovereignties.

[8] We cannot, in this connection, reproduce all of Pillet's rather complex theory. Pillet considered some laws to be personal (permanent), others territorial (general, universal). The solution of conflict of laws rested in distinguishing whether one or the other group of rules was involved; it is noteworthy that Pillet chose as the distinguishing criterion the social purpose of the law, which was to be determined with the help of an analysis of the intent of the legislator, the character of the respective rule, etc.

nion, was to be made on the basis of the social purpose of the rule with a view to the principle of lesser sacrifice.[9]

Another French author from the first half of this century, André Weiss, also proceeds in his theory from a link between private and public international law;[10] he considers the two to constitute a law of the same nature because the purpose both follow is to govern relations between states; both develop as two branches sprouting from the same trunk. However, Weiss, as his writings reflect, is very strongly influenced by Mancini's theory of the personal character of law.[11]

A special type of universalism may be found in the case of the Dutch jurist Jitta;[12] although this author proceeds from universalistic positions, his theory does not rest on a link between private and public international law as in the case of von Bar or Pillet, but on the belief that private international law should be used to help individuals, as members of the human community, live in universal surroundings; thus, in his case, we may speak of strong anthropocentrism. Also interesting is Jitta's endeavour to formulate the principles governing not only the law of conflict of laws (as it was in keeping with the then usual definition of the concept of private international law) but also of substantive law in view of the growing internationalization of the human community and its life.

A feature common to many of the universalistic views we have mentioned is the continued acceptance and introduction of Savigny's idea of a community of nations *(Völkergemeinschaft)* which then makes them re-assert the existence of an identical root of both public and private international law. Some of them

---

[9] The speculative nature of this procedure naturally evoked sharp criticism by later French authors, especially Henri Batiffol, which is undoubtedly – at least in part – justified.

[10] A. Weiss, *Traité théoretique, 6 vols,* 2nd ed., Paris, 1907–1913; *Manuel de droit international privé,* 9th ed., Paris, 1925.

[11] This is also true of other French and Belgian authors of the same period, such as Surville, Audinet or Laurent.

[12] See his *La méthode du droit international privé,* the Hague, 1890.

(André Weiss, for example) are obviously trying to synthetize the theories of Savigny and Mancini.

The universalistic trends in private international law, which are based on the theoretical presumption of a link between private and public international law, undoubtedly found their culmination in the doctrine of the German jurist Ernst Zitelmann,[13] who argued that it was the international obligation of all states to respect each other and guarantee on their own territory an unobstructed exercise and assertion of the rights of foreign nationals as well. In Zitelmann's opinion, private international law is influenced by public international law to the extent, that a judge is obliged – unless he is prevented from doing so by provisions of positive law – to apply *das völkerrechtliche International-Privatrecht*[14] on the basis of the assumed will of his own state as substantive municipal law. Here, Zitelmann is obviously under the influence of Triepel's dualism which, however he still surpasses by the just mentioned construction. Methodologically Zitelmann's theory is characterized by an extensive use of the deductive method proceeding from several *a priori* assumed principles. If it were to be accepted as a comprehensive theoretical construction, Zitelmann's universalism had to keep up with the progress made since Savigny's early universalism by both public and private international law. This could not be done otherwise than by the acceptance of Triepel's dualism as starting point and, at the same time, by the endeavour to bridge the dualistic separation of international law from municipal law.

Zitelmann proceeds from Savigny's idea of limitation of the validity of laws in space and from the ensuing necessity of localizing individual legal relationships. In his opinion, the necessity of the existence of private international law arises from the co-existence of states and their legal systems in such a way, that their effect is mutually defined in a comprehensive system.

---

[13] E. Zitelmann, *Internationales Privatrecht,* 2 vols., Leipzig, 1897, 1912.

[14] It is practically impossible to find a corresponding English term and I have therefore used the original German term. *Ibid.,* Vol. I, p. 73.

Zitelmann based his theory on the fiction that a rule of private international law was binding because the state had the authority to proclaim it; since the individual rules are the prerequisite of the existence of subjective rights, the question arises at the same time, whether the state does or does not have the authority to issue and proclaim a rule establishing the subjective righs whose assertion is involved in each individual case.

This dualistic solution also made Zitelmann basically recognize the existence of dualism in private international law.[15] He therefore distinguishes between an "international" private international law and a municipal private international law; this distinction was essential at the time of advancing codification of private international law in municipal legislation. In Zitelmann's opinion, the "international" private international law is a set of rules governing the authority of individual states to issue regulations wherein the individual, subjective rights are to be asserted; thus, once again, we meet with a solution of conflicts of sovereignties.

As regards conflicts between personality and territoriality arising from the sovereignty of individual states, Zitelmann gives a preference to the territorial principle in view of the fact that a state is primarily a territorial entity.

It is on this basis that Zitelmann then develops his system of private international law as a body of rules determining the law from which ensue individual subjective rights. He divides the individual statutes into three categories:

(a) personal statutes (including the law of obligations, personal law and family law);
(b) statutes *in rem* (rights *in rem*);
(c) territorial or special statutes (personal and immaterial rights).

Respect for these solutions, together with the definition of jurisdiction, have brought Zitelmann to the advocacy of universalism wherein, however, the municipal private international law, applied by the judge, represents a far from perfect state of affairs. Of course, the advanced progress of the "imperfect"

---

[15] See, e.g., the above quotation.

category forced Zitelmann to assign a basically subsidiary role to the category of the higher, "international" private international law.

A renaissance of universalism in the doctrine of Continental private international law is how we might describe the theory developed by yet another German author, Ernst Frankenstein.[16] Although Frankenstein's approach to the problem was basically affected by universalism, it is typical of this theory, that it rejects Zitelmann's universalistic concept, in particular his arguments concerning the connection between private and public international law. In the proper sphere of private international law, Frankenstein tries to formulate universal rules (see his draft of a European Code of Private International Law) deduced from certain *a priori* set principles. Frankenstein holds that the universality and supranationality of the solutions proposed by him represent the ultimate stage of the past development of private international law, which is gradually overcoming the fragmentation of this law in individual municipal bodies of law. However Frankenstein, unfortunately, assigns practically no role to comparative law and is guided mainly by speculative deductions. Frankenstein's sociologico-psychological method creates from the link existing between the law and the respective social group a special system of points of contact, which are used to determine the applicable law. Frankenstein distinguishes primary points of contact established by territoriality (localization) with respect to things and by personality with respect to persons. These primary points of contact are deduced in Frankenstein's theory from the very substance of law and are objectively valid. On their basis the respective state may apply either its own law (substantive law) or refer to another law with the help of what in called secondary points of contact. Frankenstein recognizes yet what he defines as pseudo-points of contact which arise when a state, acting in contradiction to the primary points of

---

[16] E. Frankenstein, *Internationales Privatrecht (Grenzrecht)*, 4 vols., Berlin, 1926—1936; "Projet d'un Code Européen de droit international privé", *Biblioteca Visseriana,* 1950, Vol. XVI, etc.

contact, arbitrarily refers to a law of its choice; this, under his concept, constitutes a negation of private international law. This construction – presented with great consistency and thoroughness in his aforesaid draft of a European Code of Private International Law – has helped Frankenstein devise, by the deductive method, a system of universal private international law, which is unique as a comprehensive system but which has utterly failed when confronted with the substantive private international law of individual states. If we are to characterize Frankenstein's opinion regarding the relationship between private international law and public international law, we can do so by noting that in spite of his clear-cut universalism, Frankenstein rejects the existence of a link between the two, which is used by most advocates of the universalistic trend as a basis for their arguments; he, on the other hand, proceeds from the assertion that there is no need for a special construction of the dependence of private international law on public international law because private international law is universal in its own right and therefore its universal character is original.

This shows that the universalistic trend in private international law can be based on different arguments. Besides the theory of the dependence of private international law on public international law, or the doctrine of "two branches of the same trunk", and their numerous modifications, of which the principal ones have been outlined above, Frankenstein's theory represents a noteworthy attempt at arriving at a universalistic concept of private international law, which would ensue directly from the original character of this law.

Of the other authors advocating universalistic trends in private international law we may list, for example, Neuner,[17] who argues that in spite of the existence of "municipal" universal private international laws, private international law is international because it proceeds from the existence of different muni-

---

[17] Neuner, *Der Sinn der internationalprivatrechtlichen Norm,* Brno, 1932.

cipal laws whose effect it defines, whereby the national legislator assumes a role which should appertain to an international legislator.[18] Generally speaking, this is just another variation on Scelle's theory of functional duplication. Niederer, too,[19] bases his theory on the dependence of private international law on public international law.

## (11) The Main Trends of the "Nationalist" Doctrine

As already noted, universalistic trends are essentially a minority opinion in the modern doctrine of private international law. Parallel to the abandonment of universalistic illusions in the successive stages of modern political development in the international sphere, a trend prevailed in the theory of private international law, which we might call "nationalist" (quite naturally, without the derogatory connotation sometimes being given to the terms "nationalism" and "nationalistic"), whose essence lies in the facts that it views private international law as a branch of "national" or municipal law, and whose difference from public international law rests in the differences existing both in their formal sources and in the character of the relationships and the subjects the two laws govern. Some authors even deny the possibility of the relationships governed by private international law being transposed onto the level of public international law – e.g. because of a violation of some principles of public international law – in view of the differences existing between the two laws. The list of authors following the "nationalist" trend includes a whole galaxy of well-known German, French, English, American and Italian authors, such as Kahn, Bartin, Niboyet,

---

18 *Ibid.*, p. 28.

19 See his *Einführung in die allgemeinen Lehren des internationalen Privatrechts*, Zurich, 1956, pp. 134 ff.

Nussbaum, Lerebours-Pigeonnière, Schnitzer, Melchior, Lewald, Raape, Martin Wolff, Maury, Arminjon, Louis-Lucas, Savatier, Batiffol, Franceskakis, Albert Ehrenzweig, Currie, Cheshire, Graveson, Falconbridge, Schmitthoff, Ago, Quadri, Neuhaus, and many others.

It is obviously quite difficult to survey the theories of all these (and many other) authors on such a theoretically important problem as their basic, synthetising view of private international law; therefore, we can only point to the very fundamental problems.

Although the views held by the representatives of this extensive doctrinal trend are based on their common belief in the substantial difference between private international law and public international law, we may distinguish among them several groups which are quite apparently subservient in their opinion primarily to their common legal tradition influenced by the development of the systems of law to which the individual (especially national) groups appertain.

A leading position among these national groups is held by a large number of German authors. Although German jurisprudence prides itself on Savigny as the founder of the modern doctrine of private international law, whose universalistic leanings are beyond any doubt — in spite of his fundamental belief in the historical school of law and his opposition to the theory of natural law — it is, on the whole, marked by rejection of universalism. German theory viewed private international law — mainly under the impact of German legal positivism — as an integral part of German law; this opinion was strengthened by the codification of this law in the form of a system of unilateral conflict rules contained in the Introductory Act to the German Civil Code.

We should, of course, bear in mind that in spite of this character, German doctrine was essentially aware of the mutual links existing between individual states and their laws, without which there could be no modern private international law. Thus the classic of German theory, Franz Kahn, underlines the regard individual states must pay to each other in the sphere of private international law,[20] but this regard was due to the moral strength of legal conviction rather than to a legal obligation. This is, basically, the source of the realistic approach of the German doctrine of private international law. Similarly, another classic of German theory, Niemeyer,[21] proceeds from the leading role of the municipal legislator in formulating his own private international law.

The apex of the German school of private international law in the period between the two World Wars was undoubtedly reached in the works of Melchior, Lewald and Nussbaum. Having proceeded from an analysis of the sources of law, Melchior,[22] became a leading proponent of German positivism, who used the thesis that "the private international law valid in Germany is a part of German law" to deny any connections between private international law and public international law; this he also substantiated by the argument that there existed no case of diplomatic intervention, which would be based on an improper application of a municipal conflict rule. His opinion that any ties between private and public international law are not predetermined by the rules of private international law is shared, among other authors, by Schnitzer.[23] Lewald's greatest work, beside his

---

[20] See F. Kahn, *Über Inhalt, Natur und Methode des internationalen Privatrechts. Abhandlungen zum internationalen Privatrecht,* Munich–Leipzig, 1928, Vol. 1, pp. 268 ff.: *"Wir erkennen ... dass der Staat bei Festsetzung seines internationalen Privatrechts nicht mit unbegrenzter Willkür verfahren darf, dass gewisse Schranken existieren müssen an welcher er ... international gebunden ist. Offenbar sind diese völkerrechtlichen Schranken sehr weiter Natur. Sie sind nicht aus allgemeinen Prinzipien abzuleiten, sondern der internationaler Übung und Rechtsüberzeugung zu entnehmen. Sie bestehen aus dem Komplex derjenigen Regeln, welche im Gemeinschaftsinteresse der Kulturstaaten bei Aufstellung von Kollisionsnormen übereinstimmend beobachtet würden, und auf deren Beihaltung die Staatengemeinschaft ein Recht erworben hat ...".*

[21] T. Niemeyer, *Das internationale Privatrecht des bürgerlichen Gesetzbuches,* Berlin, 1901.

[22] Melchior, *Die Grundlagen,* Berlin–Leipzig, 1932.

[23] Lewald, *Handbuch des internationalen Privatrechts,* Vol. I, Basel, 1950, p. 29: *"Das geltende Völkerrecht enthält weder materiallrechtliche Bestimmungen noch Normen, die auch nur die Staaten anweisen, ihren*

textbook,[24] is his general course of private international law, published in the collection of lectures of the Academy of International Law in the Hague,[25] which, in addition to a thorough discussion on the general problems of private international law, is characterized in particular by a detailed analysis of the "technique" of the law of conflict of laws, and a thorough knowledge of the then judicial practice, which appeared as an escape to details in the period preceding the Second World War, when the "great ideas" of the doctrine of private international law had receded completely into the background under the presure exerted by the political consequences of an overextended étatism.

This "technical" tendency of the German doctrine gradually became its characteristic feature. Nevertheless, in spite of the legal positivism permeating German theory,[26] the German authors made some major contributions especially as regards the general problems of conflict law. The most important among these contributions (especially when confronted with its nationalist character) are the postulate of the harmonious nature of conflict solutions, the endeavour to achieve uniformity of judicial decisions in the same category of cases, the orientation towards the comparative method, as well as the unequivocally accepted conclusion that foreign law is applied "as law" rather than as a fact,[27] wherein lie the main results of the effort of the German authors to approach realistically the general problems of private international law.

The nationalist trend also found some very prominent advocates among today already classical French authors concerned

---

*Gesetzen in der Materie einen bestimmten Inhalt zu geben ... demnach ist jedes internationales Privatrecht oder richtiger gesagt jedes einzelne internationale Privatrecht Teil der einzelstaatlichen Rechtsordnung ...".*

24 L e w a l d, *Das deutsche internationale Privatrecht,* Leipzig, 1931.

25 See *Recueil des Cours,* 1939, Vol. 69.

26 This is true of such prominent authors as M. Wolff, Nussbaum, Raape, Schnitzer, Wengler, or Neuhaus.

27 This problem is discussed in the author's study "Podstata a povaha aplikace cizího práva" ("The Substance and Nature of the Application of Foreign Law"), *Studie z mezinárodního práva (Studies in International Law),* Vol. 13, and Part Six of the present book.

with private international law. The most prominent author of the older school, who reacted to the French idealistic humanism was Bartin,[28] who stressed the municipal nature of the rules governing conflict problems as some kind of a "natural obligation".[29] Bartin was therefore essentially a nationalist, but at the same time he was aware of the existence of the international legal community which demanded some application of foreign law. However, his concept of the law of conflict of laws was characterized by the stress he laid on its appurtenance to the municipal law, which also made him ignore comparative jurisprudence even as a method. In contrast to his fellow-countryman and universalistic contemporary Pillet, who, as we have already noted, concentrated on the social purpose of the respective rules, Bartin proceeded from the link between conflict law and the whole system of municipal law, which was reflected in particular in his well-known postulate that conflicts of qualification should be settled in principle on the basis of the *lex fori.* In the sphere of the general problems of private international law Bartin's nationalism made this French author – beside stressing the necessity of qualification according to the *lex fori* – also reject *renvoi* as a matter of principle.

The basic opinion held by the leading French author of the interwar period, J. P. Niboyet,[30] is also marked by radical natiolism which introduces into the sphere of private international law a number of considerations of an extremely political nature. Niboyet, just like Bartin, proceeds from the premise of the appurtenance of private international law to municipal law, and it is interesting that he considers private international law to be a part of municipal public law. His theory is in utter contradiction to the universalistic doctrine of his contemporary, G. Scelle. Niboyet's nationalism results in serious consequences, of which we should, perhaps, underline his views that conflict rules should

---

[28] See, in particular, E. Bartin, *Principes de droit international privé,* 3 vols., Paris, 1930–1935.

[29] *Ibid.,* Vol. I, p. 112.

[30] See, in particular, his *Traité de droit international privé français,* Paris, 5 vols., *Cours de droit international privé,* Paris, 1949, et al.

be formulated primarily as unilateral conflict rules, that the *lex fori* ranks first among all the methods of testing legal relationships, as well as his demand that the foreign law applied, which he views in principle as a fact, should have, as a prerequiste of its application, at least some identity with the municipal law; it was especially this last demand, which was reactionary with respect to the application of Soviet law (in cases involving the recognition of the extraterritorial effects of nationalization) in France.

Nationalism also essentially constitutes the basis of the theory promoted by Lerebours-Pigeonnière,[31] who, quite naturally, also considers private international law to be a part of French municipal law. A major part is played in his theory by the idea that private international law involves state interests rather than mutual respect for individual state sovereignties, state interests including the interest of every state in international commercial relations. His awareness of these elements led Lerebours-Pigeonnière to certain eclecticism which helped him to overcome the one-sided nature of the narrowly nationalistic approach of Bartin or Niboyet; in spite of his nationalistic leanings, Lerebours-Pigeonnière greatly respects the comparative method and its impact on the development of private international law.

Another leading French author, Jacques Maury, may be described as the foremost representative of realism in the French doctrine. His work is characterized by a sociological and philosophical approach encouraging Maury to attempt making a synthesis of the interests of society and the individual in the spere of relations governed by private international law. He greatly modified the nationalism underlying the French doctrine in that he called for a mutual definition of state jurisdiction on basis of reciprocity. According to Maury, the application of foreign law was not the outcome of a unilateral consideration of the domestic legislator or judge, but an imperative rule of in-

---

[31] See in particular, his *Précis de droit international privé,* 5th ed., 1948, and the 8th edition of this work, published in 1962 in revised form by Y. Loussouarn.

ternational justice; quite obviously, Maury was in this respect under the influence of the theory of natural law.

While the leading representative of the French doctrine after 1930 and especially after the Second World War, Henri Batiffol,[32] proceeds in his work from positions of nationalism and territoriality, his pragmatic approach to judicial precedents and legal doctrine, quite obviously influenced by the Anglo-American doctrine, helps him bypass the weak spots of the French nationalism and try to make a certain convergence of nationalism and universalism. Batiffol takes up the ideas of Savigny as regards localization of individual types of contracts, and goes so far in this endeavour, as to consider also the choice of the applicable law by the parties to be one of the means of such localization. The central idea of Batiffol's philosophy of private international law, influenced by neo-tomism, is the role of private international law as a co-ordinator of individual systems of law.

Batiffol's disciple and continuator of his work is the Greek author living in France, P. Franceskakis,[33] who embraced Batiffol's idea of co-ordination of individual systems of law with the help of international private law; typical of Franceskakis is his endeavour to take a critical approach to French judicial decisions, often in contradiction to his teacher whose opinion was frequently marked by the effort to reach a rapprochement between the doctrine and the courts. Franceskakis advocates the theory that private international law also includes rules of substantive law, governing relationship characterized by the existence of a foreign element.

As appears from this brief and necessarily incomplete survey of the French theory of private international law, this theory has been characterized in recent years by a retreat from the positions of Bartin's and Niboyet's integral nationalism towards

---

32 See, in particular, his *Les conflicts des lois en matière de contrats,* Paris, 1938, *Traité élémentaire de droit international privé,* 1st ed., 1948, *Aspects philosophiques du droit international privé,* Paris, 1956, "Principes de droit international privé", *Recueil des Cours,* 1959, Vol. 97, etc.

33 See, in particular, his monograph *La théorie du renvoi en droit international privé,* Paris, 1958.

the endeavour to find space for the assertion of a modified territorial approach, influenced by the effort to achieve a mutual co-ordination of individual systems of law in the sphere of private international law, which is typical of the doctrine promoted by Batiffol and Franceskakis; the broad use of the comparative method in French private international law makes then possible a rapprochement with the universalistic postulates of the older French doctrine.

A quite special place is held in the doctrine of private international law by Anglo-American theory, which has been deeply affected by the specific features of the Anglo-American system of law and legal thought. However, as regards the question of universalism v. nationalism in the doctrine of private international law, English-American theory, based on the heritage of the Dutch advocates of the territorial principle, the doctrine of comity, acquired rights and the force of judicial precedent, stands almost without exception among the nationalist trends. Quite naturally, it is marked, especially as regards American authors, by some specific features. They arise from the fact that American theory and practice do not proceed from international but rather inter-regional conflicts, which frequently differ from the traditional Continental doctrine; nevertheless, some authors have tried to take their own, new approach to the solution of conflict problems.

While in the older English doctrine especially Westlake tried to transplant Savigny's theory into the English system of law, since Dicey's times (i.e. the end of the last century), a purely positivistic and casuistic approach has prevailed in England, based, in particular on the analysis of individual judicial decisions or of passages from the opinions expressed by individual judges. For many years, this theory was ideologically based on the doctrine of comity, which called for the application of foreign law not as a legal obligation but merely as an expression of international comity supplemented, especially in the United States, by Beales's doctrine of acquired rights. However, parallel with the formulation of this doctrine in Beale's system and in the North American Restatement of the Law of Conflict of

Laws opposition arose against it primarily in legal theory. Nevertheless, the whole American doctrine of private international law is dominated by the common tendency to overestimate the validity of the *lex fori* to the detriment of the application of foreign law.

Another common feature of this doctrine is the tendency to consider private international law as a part of the municipal law.

Beale centered his doctrine on the demand that the subjective rights acquired by an individual on the basis of a particular law should also be recognized abroad, not, of course, as law but as any other fact, which corresponds to the argument that law is created by the courts; on the other hand, the advocates of the local-law theory, especially Cook and Lorenzen, proceeded from a denial of the concepts promoted in Beale's doctrine. They considered them wrong because their speculative character made them contradictory to the reality of judicial decisions, which was characterized especially in the United States by a considerable lack of uniformity and by a failure to make any effort to achieve some unity or harmony of decision-making (not mentioning, of course, an utter aversion towards universalism). This preference for the *lex fori* to the detriment of the allegedly too broad application of foreign law was being "explained" by what is being called the homeward trend.[34] This tendency goes as far as trying to asert (and has done so in practice) the application of the *lex fori* to the final consideration of the question whether a true recognition of a right acquired abroad is involved on the basis of the existing law.

A certain opposition to the local law theory is represented by Yntema's sociology-minded approach, which calls for a rapprochement between this theory and international interests; this is to be achieved with the help of the comparative method. Professor Currie also proceeds from sociological considerations

---

[34] It is a transposition of Nussbaum's term *Heimwärtsstreben,* explaining the tendency of every court to apply primarily its own substantive law, into American terminology.

especially when he underlines the role played by state interests and views as the main purpose of private international law service to these state interests.

The centre of the considerations of the American and partly also English authors regarding universalistic and nationalist tendencies rests in their theory concerning the character of foreign law, which we have discussed elsewhere;[35] this, as we have already noted, is a strongly nationalist theory. It cannot be otherwise when we realize that this system of law of conflict of laws is based on the territorial principle which tries to subjects the largest possible number of legal relationships to the *lex fori*, the doctrine of comity, which denies the legal obligation of a state to apply foreign law, and to the principle under which the application of foreign law is interpreted only as meaning that subjective rights acquired under a foreign law are recognized as any other fact, which means that the foreign law is not being applied as an objective law or that the judge creates the foreign law "according to the example of the foreign judge". The territorial principle was, quite naturally, most suitable in the period of British world domination and the resulting expansion of foreign law; in the United States this principle was modified to fit the settlement of inter-regional conflicts between the laws of the individual States of the Union. Nevertheless, a certain universalistic trend begins to emerge within this system of law of conflict of laws, which disturbs the territorial character of the older Anglo-American conflict law. Under this trend, American and English courts – which create the law – are trying, with the help of a more intensive use of the comparative method, especially in the past twenty years, to arrive at solutions – from the viewpoint of substantive law – which would be appropriate to the conflicting laws. What we have here is, therefore, certain influence exerted on the municipal law through comparison with the conflicting foreign law.

---

[35] A detailed analysis of their doctrine in this respect is to be found in Part Six of the present book and in the author's article quoted in footnote 27 of this chapter.

A basic feature of all universalistic doctrines is their attempt to demonstrate that there exists (or should exist, as the case may be) a single, uniform and universally binding private international law. However, contrary to these postulates, which are all trying to deduce that every legal relation can be uniformly and rationally localized in space, any analytical view of positive private international law will show that there actually exists a plurality of localization and points of contact, which applies as a rule with only a few exceptions, such as the principles *locus regit actum* or *lex rei sitae*, or autonomy of will in the sphere of conflict regulations governing the law of contracts. The postulates of the universalistic doctrines thus find themselves in conflict with the undeniable reality of private international law, which has made a number of prominent authors negate all, even the slightest, universalistic trends. The doctrine of private international law therefore quite frequently points to the impossibility of achieving universal solutions, due to the plurality of municipal laws which also include private international law, as well as to the contradictory interests of individual states as regards the adoption of this or that solution.[36]

But even the opinion of those authors, who proceed from the plurality of "national" private international laws, is not devoid of elements we might describe as universalistic. For while it is true that the concept of separate, national private international laws is a reality, it is also true, on the other hand, that there is a growing differentiation between legal relationships characterized by the existence of a foreign element and internal, domestic legal relationships which have no foreign element. This, of course, leads to certain parallels in the sphere of individual private international laws, which are necessarily aware of the existence of the foreign element just as they are of the fact that

---

[36] For example, states with large-scale immigration have an interest in subjecting the legal relationships of the immigrants to the law of their new domicil or place of residence, while the states from which these people emigrate are interested in subjecting their relationships to the law of their citizenship which they usually keep although they have changed their domicil.

this existence is a common feature of all private international laws. At the same time there is the endeavour to obtain reasonable and generally acceptable solutions. Even though we proceed from the parallel existence of individual private international laws, it remains an open (and mostly unanswered) question, whether the purpose of private international law is not something more important than a mere definition of the scope of validity and applicability of individual municipal laws made by individual, national legislators. For an ever growing number of authors come to realize that one of the essential components of private international law is also the endeavour to co-ordinate the individual systems of law, which is done by rather complex technique particular to this branch of law. The basic elements of this co-ordination are to be seen in the mutual dependence objectively existing in the plural system of individual private international laws between the choice of the applicable law, the determination of the jurisdiction of one's own courts with respect to other countries, the application of foreign law, and also the executability of the decisions of local courts in other states. This tendency towards universalism is even manifested in the legal technique used in the law of conflict of laws. While, for example, the strictly nationalistic concept of the Introductory Act to the German Civil Code, which contains the German private international law, had made its authors choose a system of unilateral conflict rules defining the scope of applicability of German law, in the more recent period, the technique of bilateral conflict rules has become the standard; these rules seek the applicable law *in abstracto,* irrespective of whether that law is the local, municipal law, or the law of a foreign state. This technique has quite logically and unavoidably resulted in the endeavour to co-ordinate the conflict rules contained in the laws of individual states.

These then are some of the fundamental questions which authors, who would want to deny any universalism of private international law, find very difficult to answer. The common, characteristic features of the private international law of different states must be therefore always respected, if we are to observe the objective reality existing in this sphere.

All this underlines the fact that in the modern period we can very rarely come across an author who would try to persit in developing his initial premise into all its detailed consequences. The overwhelming majority of those authors, who proceed from the parallel existence of individual private international laws in different states, respect to the necessary extent the reality of the common problems of these private international laws and try to deal with such problems through a realistic approach, as we have already noted.

The dispute between universalism and nationalism in private international law and its doctrine may be viewed as a latent dispute between the general and the specific. While, by underlining the elements of the general, we wanted to point to the impossibility of an integral nationalism, we cannot overlook, on the other hand, the elements which promote the principal features of any nationalistic concept.

These elements include primarily the territorial principle and the territorial applicability of every legal system, including its private international law; another such element is the positivistic trend affecting private international law, which has resulted in the existence of quite a number of separate private international laws in force in individual countries. To this we must add the natural resistance of any court or judge to apply foreign law. The principle of the validity of the *lex fori* in procedural law is closely related with the endeavour to assert the initial applicability of the *lex fori* also in the sphere of conflict law, of which some authors made the fundamental principle of their particular system of private international law.[37]

---

[37] See in particular A. Ehrenzweig, "The Lex Fori — the Basic Rule in the Conflict of Laws", *Michigan Law Review*, 1960 (58, No. 5, pp. 637 ff.; "The Lex Fori in the Conflict of Laws — Exception or Rule?", *Rocky Mountain Law Review*, Vol. 32, No. 1.

## CHAPTER 4
## The Comparative Trend in Private International Law

Every concept of private international law, irrespective of whether it is universalistic or "nationalist", is influenced in its substance and manifestations by a number of factors; among the primary factors in this respect we find those, which ensue from the contemporary economic and political organization of society, both national and international.[1] Quite naturally, this also applies to phenomena we have encountered in the recent period in particular the years following the end of the Second World War. If we are to characterize this period, we may say that it is one of a steadily progressing internationalization of human society, manifested in the legal sphere in far-reaching changes in public international law which has been growing in both extent and depth in particular under the impact of the activities of the United Nations and its bodies; questions are being raised, which only recently had been considered as falling within the domestic jurisdiction of states, classical doctrines on the exclusive character of states as the sole subjects of international law are being revised, attention is centering on problems directly related with the status of the individual within society, such as his human, political and social rights, numerous questions relating to the activity and relations of non-sovereign subjects have become – especially in the sphere of international economic in-

---

[1] See Part One of the present work and the author's article "K některým soudobým aspektům mezinárodního práva soukromého, jako společenského jevu" ("Some Contemporary Aspects of Private International Law as a Social Phenomenon"), *Časopis pro mezinárodní právo (Czechoslovak Journal of International Law)*, 1968, No. 2. pp. 119 ff.

tegration – the backbone of such organizations as the European Economic Community, etc.

If we bear in mind all these phenomena in their specific details and as a whole in the light of the preceding analysis of universalistic and nationalistic tendencies in private international law, we may state that these are phenomena which cannot but have very serious consequences for the whole concept of private international law, profoundly marked by the development and influences which had shaped it in the past. We could therefore rightly speak of the present stage of development of private international law as of a transitional and temporary stage which, it appears, marks the beginning of changes which the contemporary private international law cannot avoid. If we are to assess and characterize this development trend, we may say that it seems to lead towards greater internationalization of private international law, which will probably take place both on a universal basis and in smaller units created on a regional as well as economic and political basis, all in connection with the needs and the progress of international economic integration. This development has almost organically given rise to trends aiming at the unification, harmonization or at least a rapprochement of individual legal systems, as we have witnessed this process in the West European communities, in particular the EEC, but also in other organizations; there seems to be no doubt that if the socialist states are to develop their economic co-operation, especialy through the Council of Mutual Economic Assistance, it will be necessary that a similar process (although different in the substance of its individual manifestations) and phenomena take place in connection with such co-operation.

We therefore believe that in the long run this tendency will aim at the formation of certain communities within greater or smaller territorial units, and it is only natural that private international law may considerably spur this trend. One of its manifestations has been the substantialization of private international law in the past decades; what has happened is that relations under substantive law, characterized by the existence of a foreign element, are being governed – usually in the form of internationally unified rules (unified either by treaty or by model statutes) — differently from purely municipal relationships devoid of any foreign element.

This overall atmosphere spurs the growth of a modern trend in the doctrine of private international law, which we may describe as comparative. In a different part of the present work we have pointed to the link that has existed ever since the beginnings of private international law between that law and comparative jurisprudence without which the former could simply not do.[2] However, here we are not concerned only with this particular aspect of the matter, which is manifested primarily in the field of the "technique" of private international law, but rather with the impact of this problem on the overall concept of private international law.

Private international law is a branch of law which (in contrast to other branches) must daily deal with foreign systems of law and this, quite naturally, presupposes their knowledge and comparison either with the local law or the law of another foreign state. However, this is true not only of the application of the substantive law which is to be applied under the respective conflict rule, but also of the whole sphere of the law of conflict of laws, which involves the same process, a process that also asserts itself in connection with the fact that sometimes it is necessary to proceed not only from the local but also from a foreign conflict rule as in the case of *renvoi*, qualification, preliminary questions, evasion, etc.

However, the problems of private international law must not be confused or interchanged with the problems of comparative jurisprudence,[3] which have their own, specific character at the

---

[2] See Part Five, Chapter 3, and the author's article "Mezinárodní právo soukromé a srovnávací právověda" ("Private International Law and Comparative Jurisprudence"), *Časopis pro mezinárodní právo (The Czechoslovak Journal of International Law)*, 1968, No. 1, pp. 20 ff.

[3] On this point see Part Five of the present work and the author's study "K soudobým teoretickým problémům srovnávací právovědy" ("Contemporary Theoretical Problems of Comparative Jurisprudence"), *Právník (The Lawyer)*, 1968, No. 4, pp. 289 ff.

legal, philosophical, methodological,[4] as well as sociological levels. But a doctrinal tendency has arisen in connection with the development trends of private international law we have mentioned and, in particular, in connection with the process of its substantiation, which we might call the "comparative trend of private international law";[5] this trend differs markedly from both universalistic and "nationalistic" trends, whose theoretical analysis we have attempted in the present study.

While the universalistic tendencies in private international law, as a rule, stress the dependence of private international law on public international law and thereby try to deduce its universal nature, the nationalistic trends proceed from the connections between the private international law of every state and the systems of law of such state; in contrast, the comparative trend in private international law tries to grasp private international law as a phenomenon in its whole by stressing the common elements of the individual private international laws on the basis of their mutual comparison and, in some cases, by attempting to formulate the knowledge thus obtained in the form of new rules of law. This objective is also promoted by the activity of a number of governmental and non-governmental organizations striving for the unification of rules in different spheres of private international law. Naturally, the comparative school of private international law, which at first unwittingly, automatically, and then purposefully, has been trying to achieve coordination and rapprochement of positions in the given sphere, is not separated from either the universalistic or "nationalistic" tendencies by a Chinese Wall. These tendencies, too, have been making use of the comparative method, but it is not typical of them; in contrast, the comparative doctrine of private international law is characterized by the broad application of this

---

[4] See Knapp, "Některé metodologické problémy srovnávací právni vědy", ("Some Methodological Problems of Comparative Jurisprudence"), *Právník (The Lawyer)*, 1968, No. 2.

[5] See K. Zweigert, "Die dritte Schule im internationalen Privatrecht", *Festschrift für Leo Raape zu seinem 70. Geburtstag*, Hamburg, 1948.

method as a dominant feature which is international and manifests itself in a number of legal spheres.

The comparative trend in private international law has its roots in both the methodology and history of private international law. Since also a number of authors proceeding from "nationalist" trends have been making use especially in the recent period of the comparative method to a greater or lesser degree, we may say that this method of work has apparently become a corrective feature of a "nationalistically" orientated approach to the problems of private international law even in the case of tendencies which are based on the extremely territorial Anglo-American concepts.

The comparative trend in private international law views the whole field and phenomenon of private international law synthetically, which facilitates the understanding of its nature and social purpose, and it is only on this basis that we can speak of private international law as a separate branch of law. The comparative orientation is, of course, also helpful in the quest for a proper methodological approach and for the attainment of a just and reasonable solution of problems of law of conflict of laws as well as of problems relating to substantive law. Of course, the comparative method as such is not a cure-all in private international law, which would solve all its problems, and although its use is very broad, it is, nevertheless, not unlimited. This limitation of its use arises from the fact that, *de lege lata,* private international law cannot extricate itself from its subordination to the legal systems of individual states and operate in the vaccum of abstract speculation. It must be seen that while the comparative school or orientation in private international law should help raise this law to a qualitatively new and higher level, this objective can be attained only on the realistic basis of the validity of the individual systems of law.

The comparative school of private international law, whose true founder is undoubtedly Rabel, naturally has its predecessors in history. It is generally known that the comparative approach to the problems of private international law saw its beginnings with Savigny and Mancini and that it considerably developed in connection with the solution of such general problems as, for example, the conflict rule and its structure, individual methods of testing legal relationships, qualification and conflict of qualifications, *renvoi,* the application of foreign law, as well as of individual, specific problems. But only Rabel began to develop a comprehensive, synthetic view of private international law, which in its conclusions has led to the proclamation of the autonomous nature of private international law as an independent branch of law.

The comparative approach to the individual problems of private international law is extremely valuable and useful also because it helps to overcome the narrow solutions offered by individual authors and individual systems of law, which it orientates towards a broader view. The comparative school of private international law may, of course, be criticized – from the viewpoint of individual municipal laws – for the fact that it must be linked with eclecticism both as regards the overall approach and the solution of problems of a general nature, such as the conflict of qualifications or concrete, special problems.

As may be seen, the comparative trend in private international law draws its arguments from this branch of law alone rather than borrowing them from public international law as is done (with some minor exceptions) by the universalists, or from municipal civil law, which is the approach chosen by authors (especially the older ones) belonging to the nationalist school. This fact, too, supports the conclusion regarding the autonomous nature of private international law. This is also why we may list among the supporters of this school many of the more recent authors who are considered as proponents of the national character of private international law, such as Martin Wolff, Batiffol, Franceskakis, Lerebours-Pigeonnière, Kahn-Freund, Neuhaus, and others, who develop their theories in principle on the postulate of harmonization and co-ordination of conflict solutions. Quite naturally, this is also true of the authors who proceed from the sociological point of view and for whom the use of the comparative method is also a necessity, as indicated by a whole group of German authors, such as Wengler, Zweigert or Kegel, or such French authors as Louis-Lucas and Lerebours-Pigeonnière, who want to find a solution throught the assessment of the prevailing interest, either national or international.

Thus, we may say in conclusion, that both the universalistic theories and the "nationalist" trends, which wanted to settle the theoretical problems of the concept of private international law through arguments drawn from outside private international law, could not cover the complex nature and the individual manifestations of this branch of law, whose objective existence creates quite a number of doctrinal and practical problems. On the other hand, coming much closer to the true understanding and promotion of this hybrid phenomenon is what is known as the comparative or autonomist trend in private international law which is trying to overcome the weak points of the "nationalist" school, based on the dogma of the supremacy of the municipal law of the decision-making forum, whereby it greatly spurs the international trends in private international law. Although classical private international law is concretely concerned with the localization of legal relations within a certain municipal law (which exists paralel with other laws), no progress can be achieved in this field except through the application of the autonomous methods based of the comparative approach, which are common to private international law as an independent branch of law.

# PART FOUR

# The Object and Character of Private International Law and its Place in the System of Law

## CHAPTER 1

## Introduction

As we have already pointed out, the question of the object and character of private international law, and the question of the place it occupies in the system of law, have not yet been satisfactorily settled and are the topic of discussion in the literature of both the capitalist and the socialist states.

In this part of the present work, we should like to take up these questions without claiming, of course, that the problems involved will be completely exhausted; what we are merely attempting to do is to outline the solutions offered thus far, to assess these solutions critically, and to determine whether we can accept them or whether we offer solutions of our own.

Private international law is a branch of law characterized by its hybrid nature; its very name and the doubts arising therefrom indicate that fighting contradictions is typical of private international law. The task of defining the object and character of this branch of law, which may be viewed from the systematic aspect as a transitional and secondary phenomenon,[1] is not, of course, a simple matter and the results we arrive at will probably not be accepted without reservation.

The task we have set ourselves is not made easier by the fact that private international law is a branch of law that has undergone intensive development since the beginning of the last century and has considerably changed in the recent period, a branch whose connections and scope are not stable and fixed as compared with such rather firmly established and defined

---

[1] On this point see Knapp, *Předmět a systém československého socialistického práva občanského (The Object and System of Czechoslovak Socialist Civil Law)*, Prague, 1959, p. 73.

branches as public international law, civil law, or the law of civil procedure, which are most closely in contact with private international law. To this we must add the fact that private international law, which is not in substance a truly international, or rather inter-state, law, i.e. a law common to all sovereign states, but primarily a municipal law which is, however, marked by a specifically international nature, has much in common in different states; since Savigny's days we have met in practically all systems and textbooks with assertions, originated and repeated doubtlessly under the impact of Kant's philosophy, that the proper task of the law of conflict of laws is to create a harmonious and identical solution of conflict problems in all states. This tendency in the doctrine of private international law has naturally resulted in the situation where a common solution is also sought for the questions we have raised in the heading of this part of the present work.

In the preceding part we already had the opportunity of pointing to the fact that the views of different authors on the scope of private international law are far from identical. Besides views which consider private international law as a part or even the basis of international law, there are views underlining its municipal character. While some authors (especially the French) include in private international law also questions of public law, such as those of citizenship, other authors (especially German) have tried to reduce private international law only to the law of conflict of laws; to this we must yet add the original views of the American and English lawyers who, proceeding from the "jurisdictional" concept, precede the usual question of which law is applicable to the given relationship, by the question, which state will have the jurisdiction to apply the law to the given relationships. Problems of including what is known as international law of civil procedure and international penal law in private international law are the cause of still more difficulties.

Even today we can find in literature dealing with private international law a multitude of views on the character of this law; while some of these views are still based on arguments proceeding from natural law, others seek the theoretical explanation of the existence of private international law in the concept of the *comitas gentium;* still other authors try to prove that municipal law is competent to decide the given question only on the basis of some allegedly existing rules concerning the applicability and choice of the decisive law, which, they say, form a part of a universal and supranational system of law; there are also authors who admit that private international law has a municipal character but that besides this municipal law there exist "supranational" and "universally acceptable" conflict criteria, such as the principle of the applicability of the *lex rei sitae* to matters of substantive law, the applicability of the rule *locus regit actum* to consideration of the form of legal act, or the principle of the "autonomy of the will of the parties", which is to govern the determination of the applicable law in the sphere of conflict of laws of obligations, etc.

Soviet literature and the literature of the socialist countries have not unequivocally settled the problem of the object and character of private international law either. While Professor Pereterski holds (just as he did, at the time he wrote his study, with respect to labour law or agricultural co-operative law) that private internatioal law is a part of what he calls civil jurisprudence, wherein, however, it is a quite independent field, his opinion was subsequently reduced by Professor Lunts to the assertion that private international law was a part of civil law.

On the other hand, the advocates of the internationalist trend, led by Professor Krylov, have been stressing the international character of private international law, and are of the opinion that this law is a part of "international law in the broader sense". These differences between Soviet jurists were not bridged even at a conference on the object of private international law they held in 1955.[2] The discussion on the object of private international law continued among jurists from the socialist coutries also on the international level. Beside additional studies

---

[2] A report on this conference was published in *Sovietskoye gosudarstvo i pravo,* 1955, No. 8, pp. 121 ff.

by Lunts,[3] it was joined, in particular, by Horst Wiemann from the German Democratic Republic and Professor L. Réczei of Hungary, who discussed especially the question whether so-called direct rules, i.e. rules which govern civil-law relationships without the intermediary aid of a conflict rule, belong into private international law.[4] The fact that the topic of this part of the present work is closely related with and is being solved within the framework of a broad debate on what is called "economic law", which has been going on among jurists in the Soviet Union and the other socialist countries, is also indicated by Wiemann's opinion which eventually has come to call for the abandonment of all previous concepts of private international law and for the adoption of the concept of a "law of international economic relations".[5]

The views of Czechoslovak jurists are not identical either. A textbook on civil and family law, dating from the 1950's,[6] claims that "under the prevailing opinion, private international law is in its substance a part of civil law because it, too, is concerned with civil-law rather than inter-state relations", but at the same time stresses the specific features of private international law, which resulted in the situation where "private international law separated as an independent field of jurisprudence, which is being most often taught in connection with public international law". The textbook thereby apparently

---

[3] "O predmete mezhdunarodnogo chastnogo prava i nyekotorykh osobyenostyakh mezhdunarodnogo chastnogo prava v otnosheniyakh mezhdustranami socializma", *Voprossy mezhdunarodnogo chastnogo prava,* Moscow, 1956, pp. 5—17.

[4] See Wiemann, "Die Bedeutung des internationalen Privatrechts in der Deutschen Demokratischen Republik", *Staat und Recht*, 1954, pp. 743 ff.; "Zur Frage des Gegenstandes des internationalen Privatrechts", *Staat und Recht,* 1955, pp. 988 ff.; Réczei, "Zur Frage des Gegenstandes des internationalen Privatrechts", *Staat und Recht,* 1955, pp. 488 ff.

[5] Wiemann, "Gedanken zur Gestaltung der neuen Vorlesung", "Recht der internationalen Wirtschaftsbeziehungen der DDR", *Staat und Recht,* 1958, No. 10, pp. 1033 ff. However, we do not want to settle this question in the present study because it forms only a part of the general debate on "economic law".

[6] Vol. I, 2nd ed., p. 72.

wanted to distinguish between the inclusion of private international law in the system of law and its inclusion in the system of jurisprudence as a set of scientific findings about law. Bystrický, too, comes to the conclusion that "private international law must be viewed as a separate field of study, which has its own problems and system, but which is also greatly dependent on and connected with substantive and procedural civil law as well as public international law".[7] On the other hand, Professor Knapp, who thinks primarily of the place of private international law within the system of law – which, of course, substantially influences the placement of a particular field of study within the system of jurisprudence – reached the conclusion that private international law was a part of civil law, with the exception of the rules governing family relationships, which appertain to the Czechoslovak family law.[8] In his book on the object and system of Czechoslovakia's socialist civil law, Professor Knapp reduced the question of the place of private international law as a whole only to a study of where conflict rules should be located; referring to the arguments raised by Professor Lunts, with whose opinion he fully identified himself, he then reached the conclusion that conflict rules formed a part of civil law.[9]

As this brief introduction indicates, the subject of this part of the present work requires a more detailed analysis. Somebody might object that it involves an academic dispute between authors, which is of very little practical value; however, to accept such an objection would mean, in my opinion, an *a priori* negation of a healthy trend that has appeared in a discussion which aims at exploring and explaining the character of private international law, and at defining its relationships to other branches of law which are important for the practical solution of different problems.

---

[7] R. Bystrický, *Základy (Principles)*, p. 23.

[8] V. Knapp, "K otázce systému československého socialistického práva" ("On the System of Czechoslovak Socialist Law"), *Stát a právo (State and Law)*, IV, pp. 215 and 217.

[9] V. Knapp, *Předmět a systém (The Object and System)*, p. 255.

# CHAPTER 2
## The General Characteristics of Private International Law and the Question of Its Object

The general characteristic of a specific branch of law may be carried out only on the basis of an analysis of its object. The marxist-leninist science of state and law has proceeded either from the finding that the object of law is human behaviour in certain social relationships[1] or from the premise that the object of legal regulation are the social relationships themselves, which opinion seems to have prevailed in the recent period.[2] However, Knapp pointed out still at the time when he felt that the object of law was human behaviour in certain social relationships, that this definition did not fully exhaust the object of legal regulations, and reached the conclusion, that the answer to the basic question concerning the object of law, i.e. the question what the law governs (in a specific society and at a specific time), is fourfold: human behaviour in certain social relations, the subjects of this behaviour, its object, and certain facts.[3]

Socialist jurisprudence usually defines private international law as "that branch of jurisprudence, which is concerned with questions arising in connection with civil-law and family relationships containing some foreign (international) element, and

---

[1] *Ibid.*, pp. 67 ff.

[2] This was also recognized by Knapp in his textbook on Czechoslovak civil law, published in 1965 (Vol. I, Chapter 1), which proceeds from this premise; this opinion has been held from the very beginning of the discussion on the object of law in Czechoslovak literature by Š. Luby.

[3] *Ibid.*, p. 69.

with the principles and rules being applied to the solution of these questions in a specific state. The set of rules issued by a given state to govern civil-law and family relationships with an international element constitutes private international law". Other socialist authors define private international law, or its object, as the law governing civil-law relationships arising under conditions of struggle and co-operation between states,[4] or as the law containing rules that govern civil-law relationships with an international element, which arise under conditions of struggle and co-operation among states.[5]

We may use any one of these definitions for the purpose of our analysis, because they all proceed from the fact that the fundamental and necessary criteria for differentiating the system of law must be sought in human behaviour in certain social relationships, governed by law,[6] and that we must therefore proceed from the principle that the system of law must be created according to the specific features of the legally governed human behaviour in these relations.[7]

Let us try once more and quite briefly confront the marxist characterization and definition of private international law with the considerable number of characterizations and definitions of this law, offered by non-marxist jurisprudence.

It is, of course, impossible to reproduce here all the definitions, whose number corresponds to the notorious quest for originality, common to all authors; after all, each author wants to be original and "new" in his characterization and definition.

Some of these definitions proceed from the fact that the core of private international law is the law governing conflict of

---

[4] Lunts, *Mezinárodní právo soukromé (Private International Law)*, p. 1.

[5] Kutikov, *Mezhdunarodno chastno pravo na N. R. Bulgaria*, 2nd ed., Sofia, 1958, p. 12.

[6] Knapp, *Předmět a systém (The Object and System)*, p. 73.

[7] Knapp, "K otázce systému československého socialistického práva" ("On the System of Czechoslovak Socialist Law), *Stát a právo (State and Law)*, IV, p. 209.

laws; a representative of this group of authors may well be Nussbaum, for example.[8]

Another group of definitions lays stress on relationships between subjects of different citizenship as the main and typical feature characteristic of private international law.[9]

Another typical group is made up of authors who proceed from the concept that private international law deals with conflicts of the sovereign legislative competences of individual states in space, and who, in their majority, then claim that every conflict of laws therefore at the same time constitutes a conflict of sovereignties.[10]

We may note as a sideline of this brief survey, that among definitions and characterizations there occasionally appear some, which deduce with a certain sense of reality, that private international law is based on "life relations which have a contact with other countries", and thereby come close to the definitions

---

[8] *Deutsches internationales Privatrecht,* p. 1: *"Das internationale Privatrecht (IPR) bestimmt, welche unter mehreren gleichzeitigen bestehenden Privatrechtsordnungen auf einem gegebenen Sachverhalt anzuwenden ist; es bildet den Inbegriff der Normen, die eine solche Regelung enthalten."* However, in his later work, *Grundzüge des internationalen Privatrechts,* Nussbaum abandoned this narrow definition and defines private international law broadly as that branch of private law, which deals with relationships to other countries. Nussbaum's original definition quite obviously proceeds from the older definition drawn up by von Bar.

[9] Here belong most definitions promoted by authors of the Italian school of "national" law, i.e. by Mancini's disciples.

[10] See, e.g., Pillet, *Traité pratique de droit international privé,* Paris, 1923, Vol. 1, p. 20, or Weiss, *Traité théorique,* Vol. 1, No. 1; according to the latter author, private international law constitutes *"l'ensemble des règles applicables à la solution des conflicts qui peuvent surgir entre les souverainetés à l'occasion de leurs lois respectives ou des intérêts privés de leurs nationaux."* Similarly, Bustamante claims that the purpose of private international law is to *"délimiter la compétence législative et jurisdictionelle de chaque État".* (See *Revue de droit international privé,* 1927, p. 375.) It is natural that Pillet's or Weiss's definitions express the concept of private international law upheld by these authors, which asserts that all principles of private international law must be deduced from public international law. On this point see the author's arguments in this part of his work as well as in Part Three.

coined by socialist authors, but it is sometimes not quite clear whether these relations are those falling under civil law, or some others.[11]

The differences of concept, which have already been quite sufficiently demonstrated, are, naturally, also manifested in the definition of the scope of what constitutes, according to the individual views, the object of private international law. In this connection it would serve no useful purpose, if we pointed once more to the well-known differences between the German concept of private international law, which limits the object of this law only to rules governing conflict of laws, the French concept, which divides private international law into questions of citizenship, questions of the legal status of aliens, conflicts of jurisdictions, and the law of conflict of laws, and the prevailing English opinion, which defines the object of private international law as questions of domicil, questions of jurisdiction with respect to other coutries, and questions concerning the application of the decisive law.[12] All these questions create considerable problems in the theory of private international law.

Another question which remains disputable is that of where to place matters regarding civil procedure, which include an international element.[13] The practical links existing between these matters and the law of conflict of laws, which are manifested especially in questions regarding the definition of the scope of court jurisdiction with respect to cases with a foreign element, which in most instances determines what conflict law (and thus

---

[11] See, e.g., M. Wolff, *Das internationale Privatrecht Deutschlands*, p. 1. Roughly corresponding to the definitions put forward by the socialist authors is the definition presented by Valéry, namely that private international law is a branch of law, which deals with relations of private law with a foreign element. See Valéry, *Manuel de droit international privé*, No. 3, Paris, 1914.

[12] On these differences see, e.g., Bystrický, *Základy (Principles)*, p. 20, Lunts, *Mezinárodní právo soukromé (Private International Law)*, p. 22, and in detail also Niederer, *Einführung in die allgemeinen Lehren des internationalen Privatrechts*, Zurich, 1954, pp. 81—84.

[13] A survey of opinion on this question can be found in I. Szászy, *International Civil Procedure*, Budapest, 1967, pp. 20 ff.

also what substantive law) would be applied in the respective case, exert pressure on having these matters included within private international law. Their mutual links and impact are so strong that under the pressure of this practical necessity, jurisprudence was forced, for example in Germany, to abandon the theory which otherwise placed procedural law in the category of public law and which would therefore logically exclude procedural relations with a foreign element from private international law. However, this problem does not arise in this form in the sphere of French law and the law of the Romanesque states; the jurisprudence of these states mostly holds the opinion that procedural law is a part of private law, so that no objections are usually raised against the inclusion of the aforesaid relationships in private international law.

On the other hand, legal theory has almost universally abandoned the practice of linking what is known as international penal law with private international law, a practice quite common at the end of the last century. A remnant of this old opinion is to be found in the Code of Bustamante, where it is the subject of a special chapter.

Yet another question that has not been cleared up in literature is the question of whether what is known as international fiscal or financial law should not be considered as a part of private international law. Questions of this type appear in the works of some authors, whose definition of the scope of private international law is sufficiently broad.[14] Other authors, on the other hand, consider so-called international labour law as a part of private international law; this is nothing out of the ordinary especially in those countries, where under the prevailing opinion labour law still constitutes a part of civil law.

The characterization of private international law and the definition of its object (and, as we shall see later, also the definition of its place in the system of Czechoslovak socialist law) are determined by a number of facts.

---

[14] See Beale, *A Treatise on the Conflict of Laws*, Vol. 3, who also discusses international fiscal law.

According to the concurrent opinion of authors from the socialist states, the object of private international law are civil-law relations with a foreign or international element.

The present study is not the proper place to discuss the concept of civil-law relationship. This was successfully done elsewhere, and we therefore refer to the arguments of Professor Knapp.[15]

We should rather discuss that specific feature of civil-law relations, which resulted in the specialization and differentiation of these relations from the other human relations governed by civil law. This specific feature is the presence of a foreign element in the respective relation. The foreign element appears in a legal relation usually as a result of the fact that the subjects, or at least one subject, of the given relation are related to a foreign state, that the object of the legal relation is located abroad, or that certain legal circumstance, which have caused the establishment, change or extinction of the legal relation took place abroad.[16]

In the opinion of Professor Pereterski, the occurrence of an international element in a given legal relationship is characterized either by the fact that the legal relation has been established and is being realized in a specific state, but the subject of this relation is a person who is not a citizen of that state, or by the fact the the legal relation was established in one state and is realized in a different state.[17]

All these circumstances, which lead to the definition that a legal relation has a foreign element, have one, common feature, namely the fact that every relation containing an international element is international in the sense that relation exceeds the limits of one state sovereignty, or rather the limits of the law of one sovereign state, and enters an area where the legislation of at least two, or more, sovereign states is in

---

[15] Knapp, *Předmět a systém (The Object and System)*, in particular pp. 88 ff., and 146 ff.

[16] Bystrický, *Základy (Principles)*, pp. 12 and 13.

[17] *Sovietskoe gosudarstvo i pravo*, 1946, No. 8, p. 26.

operation.[18] It is precisely this common, characteristic feature of the existence of a foreign element in a given legal relation, that makes this relationship an international one, which, of course, does not mean to say that it is an inter-state relation; it is precisely this fact, which is the specific feature that has led to the differentiation of private international law from civil law. If this specification of private international law did not lead to the aforesaid differentiation, all the subject-matter which constitutes its object would have to be a mere component of the general part of civil law.[19] The question of whether this differentiation has already progressed to the point where private international law occupies its own, special place in the system of law, will be discussed below.

Now, after we have defined in general that the object of private international law are civil-law relations with a foreign element, we must specify this object in more concrete terms. In connection with the already mentioned fourfold answer to the question concerning the object of law, and with reference to the results of the Soviet debate on the object of international law, held in 1955, we may concretely specify that the object of private international law are:

(a) the law of conflict of laws, which undoubtedly forms the basis and core of private international law; its existence is the outcome of the fact that identical legal relationships are governed differently in the law of different countries, which leads, in the case of relationships with a foreign element, to the ne-

---

[18] See Kutikov, *Mezhdunarodno chastno pravo na N. R. Bulgaria*, p. 9. Kutikov speaks only of an "excess" of the sovereignty of a state. However, his definition lacks precision in that in many cases the "excess of sovereignty", which Kutikov considers typical, is only illusory; it would probably mean embracing the views of the advocates of the supranational character of private international law, if we believed, for example, that in the case of a contract made between a local citizen and a foreigner in the former's country where it is also to be performed, the sovereignty of two states has been affected.

[19] For a discussion on this solution as regards conflict rules see Knapp, *Předmět a systém (The Object and System)*, p. 265.

cessity of deciding the question, what substantive law is to govern these relationships;

(b) questions of the legal status of subjects of civil-law relationships with a foreign element, which means primarily questions of the civil-law status of foreign natural and legal persons in this country and questions of the legal status of subjects who are citizens of this country abroad;

(c) questions of civil procedure with a foreign element, which undoubtedly form a unity with the other component parts of private international law;

(d) what is known as direct rules of substantive law, either internationally unified, or issued by individual states for the purpose of governing relations characterized by the existence of a foreign element, such as the Czechoslovak Code of International Trade.

While socialist authors concerned with private international law are, on the whole, unanimous as regards the inclusion of the relationships listed under (a) to (c) in private international law, the inclusion in that law of the direct rules became the subject of the already mentioned discussion, conducted mainly between H. Wiemann and L. Réczei. The discussion centered on the question whether beside the direct rules, drawn up on the basis of an international unification of a particular branch of law, which makes the application of a conflict rule to the given relationships unnecessary, the object of private international law should not also include rules which, while governing civil-law relationships with a foreign element, proceed from the sovereign legislative authority of one state alone. The inclusion of these rules in private international law has sometimes been rejected, usually with the explanation that these relations are not governed by an internationally unified rule which would eliminate the possibility of conflict of laws in the given sphere, and that, on the contrary, their use presupposes the existence and application of a conflict rule.[20] However, the arguments put forward by

[20] See Lunts, "O predmete mezhdunarodnogo chastnogo prava", *Voprossy mezhdunarodnogo chastnogo prava,* Moscow, 1956, p. 13; also Bystrický, *Základy (Principles),* p. 20.

the above-quoted authors do not seem convincing. We should bear in mind that the inclusion of a particular rule in a specific branch of law should not be determined by the fact that such rule is to be found in this or another formal source of law, but by the question, what social relations the given rule governs. It is then beyond any doubt, that in the case of the disputed direct rules we are faced with civil-law relations with a foreign element, which are the object of private international law. Thus, in our opinion, the question of where all such rules should be included should be decided in favour of their inclusion in private international law; Lunts's argument that the inclusion of these direct rules in private international law would substantially reduce the subject-matter of civil law, does not seem convincing either.[21] In this connection we should also point to the undeniable fact that the importance of these direct rules has been steadily growing, irrespective of whether they are internationally unified and therefore proceed from the concurrent will of two or more sovereign states, or have been issued by an individual state to govern relations with a foreign element. This is true in particular of the internationally unified rules which are trying to eliminate in the most exposed and busiest sectors of international relations, namely the international exchange of goods, almost completely the possibility of conflicts between the laws of individual countries. The multilateral General Conditions of Delivery applicable to trade between the foreign trade organizations of the member-countries of the Council of Mutual Economic Assistance, or the Hague Uniform Laws on the International Sales Contract offer a clear evidence of this fact.

As already indicated, there also exists the view that, in addition to claiming that conflict rules form a part of civil law, at the same time asserts that those conflict rules, which provide for the application of the family law of a particular state, are a part of the family law;[22] this conclusion was reached on the basis of the

---

[21] Lunts, *Voprossy mezhdunarodnogo chastnogo prava.*

[22] Knapp, *Stát a právo IV (State and Law)*, pp. 215, 217,

differences between civil-law relations and relations governed by family law, which are characterized in a socialist society by the fact that they are not property relationships and therefore are quite distinct from the relationships governed by civil law. We cannot agree that this type of conflict rules form a part of family law, for there is no doubt that besides the rules of substantive law and procedural law, conflict rules represent a special type of rules concerned with the question, what system of law should be applied. In our opinion, it is not warranted to divide them between different branches of law according to whether they provide for the application of civil, family (or labour) law, as the case may be. Moreover, we must also bear in mind that just as the provisions of the general part of civil law are valid for family law, the law of conflict of laws is common for the spheres of both civil and family law. And then, there is still the fact that some property aspects of family law must not be underestimated as regards relations with a foreign element, for we are often faced with the application of foreign family law where property aspects are still prevalent. Although in a socialist society family relationships do not have a property character and involve only personal matters, we cannot ignore the fact that the regulation of family relations has, as a rule, property reflections which must not be overlooked. Thus, in our opinion, it is not proper to separate conflict rules concerned with family relationships from the body of the law of conflict of laws a substantial part of private international law, and to include them in family law. This solution is also supported by the fact that conflict rules concerned with family relation, as well as other conflict rules, are governed by certain principles and universally valid tenets, which form the general part of the law of conflict of laws, which, in turn, is quite distinct from the general part of civil law.

In conclusion we should yet add a few notes to support our opinion that questions of civil procedure with a foreign element form a part of private international law as defined above. Views were raised in a polemic discussion with the author of the present work, that this subject-matter was a part of public international law,[23] or that it constituted a separate branch of law.[24] Our opinion that the rules of civil procedure governing relationships with a foreign element form a part of private international law is based on the narrow link existing between this subject-matter and the law of conflict of laws. This link stands out quite clearly when we recall the importance, in private international law, of the definition of the scope of jurisdiction to apply the law of conflict of laws and substantive law, and of the parallel existing with respect to the solution of the conflict question and jurisdiction with respect to other countries, as well as the influence the solution of both these questions has on the problem of the possible execution of judicial decisions abroad.

While in French law and the law of most Romanesque countries the prevailing opinion places rules of civil procedure in the category of private law, so that the inclusion of relationships with a foreign element in private international law has raised no objections, in German law the already mentioned link was viewed as a very strong argument which led to the abandonment, as regards international rules of procedure, of the theory which includes procedural law as a whole in the category of public law, and the opinion has prevailed, that procedural law forms a part of private international law. Since, in the English opinion private international law as a whole proceeds from the jurisdictional concept, and for reasons due to the historical development of common law, which led to differences in the understanding of the question of the system of law and its division into individual branches of law, the above problem did not arise in English law as it did in the law of the states of the European Continent.

There is no doubt that any study of the problems of private international law, which would ignore questions of procedural law and their connection with the problem of legal provisions go-

---

[23] See Donner in *Časopis pro mezinárodní právo (Czechoslovak Journal of International Law)*, 1960, pp. 357 ff.

[24] See Steiner in the same journal, pp. 344 ff. Steiner's views are, in turn, debated by Ledrer, again in the same journal, issue No. 4, 1961.

verning relations with a foreign element on the level of the law of conflict of laws would be incomplete and open to justified criticism; similarly, it is practically impossible to make a separate study and analysis of international law of procedure in isolation from private international law. Here we may only underline the links and interaction between the two; these links are quite correctly stressed by Szászy in his recent book where the Hungarian author at the same time points to the differences existing in the opinion of individual authors.[25]

[25] I. Szászy, *International Civil Procedure*, pp. 20 ff.

## CHAPTER 3
# Links Between Private International Law and Other Branches of Law and the Question of the Place Private International Law Occupies in the System of Law

In the introduction to this part of the present work mention has already been made of the wealth of conflicting opinion on and explanations of the existence of private international law, as well as of views whether private international law was a part of international law in the broader sense, or whether its nature showed that it was a part of municipal law, specifically civil law. We shall now take up these views and opinion systematically and critically, and shall try to find the links and define the differences between private international law and public international law on the one hand, and civil law on the other hand, and after we have ascertained these links and differences, we shall also try to answer the question as to the place occupied by private international law in the system of law.

## (1) Theories Considering Private International Law as a Part of Public International Law and Their Evaluation

The opinion which argues that private international law is (as a whole or, at least, in part) a component part of public international law mostly proceeds from the assumed supranational character of international law which is wrongly also being assigned the task of drawing the line between the legislative competence of individual states and thereby between individual municipal systems of law as well. Private international law, on the other hand, this opinion claims, is only derived from these supranational rules of international law or, in other words, it only implements these rules and thereby becomes a part of public international law.

Although the proponents of this opinion do not constitute in their theories a monolithic unity which could be derived from their central thesis, they have much in common. A whole galaxy of well-known older authors concerned with private international law, beginning with Savigny and Mancini, and their disciples Félix, Despagnet, Weiss and others, proceeded unwittingly from concepts of natural law and believed that the existing private international law in force was only a weak reflection of a true, natural private international law, and motivated the existence of this "superior", "natural" private international law in a most varied manner.

It is rather strange and curious that of all people it was precisely Savigny, that great opponent of natural law, who promoted a basically natural-law dependence of private international law on public international law, when he argued that conflict of laws had to be settled uniformly in all states as a demand of the community of nations which were in mutual contact. The theory of Savigny's great rival, P. S. Mancini, contains strong universalistic elements on which still draw even the modern advocates of the unity of private and public international law. For Mancini viewed private and public international law as two branches of international law in the broader sense, which, in turn, he considered to be a superior part of a universal law of all makind. After Savigny's and Mancini's disciples merged in a single internationalist school of law, their doctrine of the unity of private and public international law prevailed for many years.

These older theories, all motivated by the concept of natural law, which claimed that private international law was a subordinate part of public international law, became – after a temporary retreat caused by their conflict with dualistic and positivistic concepts, in which they lost – the basis on which the latest proponents of universalistic theories are trying to prove the existence of a universal unity of all law, with international law standing highest, in other words, what is usually being described as the doctrine of primacy of international law.[1]

This universalism of all law and the doctrine of the primacy of international law may, of course, be based on different grounds – psychological, biological, sociological or normativistic. But the conclusions reached on these grounds are the same and basically assert that there exists no division between municipal law and international law, and that, therefore, they are both only component parts of a universal system of law in which international law, quite naturally, plays the dominant role. This universalism, no matter how it is presented, is essentially but a resurrection of the old concepts of natural law. This also applies to the advocates of the normativistic theory, for whom universalism is a normological necessity.

In this universal system of law, where the supreme position is held by international law, from which the laws of individual states are derived and to which they are subordinated, private international law is a part of international law as the highest category in the universalistic hierarchy. As a rule, universalistic theories assert that private international law is a part of public international law because both define the spheres of competence of individual systems of law.

This, according to many authors, who take a somewhat more realistic view and try to cope with the fact that private international law is not essentially an inter-state law, does not, of course, preclude the existence of a municipal international law which must, however, also be derived from international law.

An extreme representative of the "integral internationalist" character of private international law, derived from an internationalistic attitude motivated by international solidarity, is –

---

[1] We cannot concern ourselves in this place with a general critique and analysis of the foundations of these theories which represent an attack against the concepts of state sovereignty as the basis on which the existing international law has been built. These theories have been discussed in Czech literature by Žourek, "Kritika učení o tzv. primátu mezinárodního práva" ("Critique of the Doctrine of Primacy of International Law"), *Studie z mezinárodního práva (Studies in International Law)*, I, pp. 68 ff.; also see Part Three of the present work.

beside the proponents of normativism – Scelle, who argues, proceeding from the principle of unity of the international community and international law,[2] that the differences existing between public international law and private international law are only the outcome of a fictitious systematization of law and should therefore be rejected. Other advocates of the theory that private international law is a part of public international law argue – in the sense of natural law – that private international law exists as a rational law given by nature, and stands above all individual systems of law which are but its more or less imperfect image.

However, when confronted with reality, which manifests itself primarily by the existence of a highly developed and technically perfect municipal law of conflict of laws, the aforesaid views had to fail, and their *a priori* nature and speculative character are quite obvious. This has led to a different, but for the concept of state sovereignty as the basis of international law no less dangerous theory, which wants to preserve the alleged existence of a supranational private international law. This theory, usually known as the delegation theory, concludes that the scope of the effect of individual municipal laws, existing parallel with each other and being equal, is determined by international law. Conflicts between these individual systems of law must be settled according to that law of conflict of laws, which has been delegated for this purpose under the principles of international law. This means, therefore, that the supranational private international law allegedly contains conflict rules which delegate the competence to settle conflicts of laws to individual municipal laws of conflict of laws. One of the advocates of this theory is Frankenstein,[3] who argues that what is known as primary testing, i.e. finding the applicable conflict law on whose basis the applicable substantive law is then determined, is done on the basis of the competence rules of public international law.

---

[2] Scelle, "La société est une et le droit international est un", *Précis de droit des gens,* Vol. 1, p. 45, Vol. 2, pp. 348 and 349.

[3] Frankenstein, *Internationales Privatrecht,* Vol. 1, p. 3.

The state, whose conflict rules are competent under the conflict rules of public international law, can then further delegate its thus established competence.

As may be seen, the advocates of the theory that private international law is a part of public international law admit at the most that besides a supranational law of conflict of laws there also exists municipal law of conflict of laws, which, however, must be called to competence only by international law.[4]

Beside these theories there also exist, of course, dualistically based concepts which assert that private international law has a dual substance and that it forms a part of the separate spheres of law, i.e. international law and municipal law. This theory usually proceeds from Triepel's dualism,[5] which makes a clear distinction between municipal and international laws; the two laws have different subjects and different sources, and Triepel concludes that there can be both an international and a municipal private international law. If we view private international law as a set of rules addressed to states which are to settle conflicts between their municipal laws, it may be considered to be a part of international law. However, if we view the law of conflict of laws as rules designed to govern relations between individuals and addressed to such individuals, then, Triepel claims, it is a part of municipal law.

While many proponents of the dualistic trend share their opinion on the primacy of municipal private international law, Zitelmann,[6] who advocates the primacy of the international character of the law of conflict of laws, argues that this conflict

---

[4] One of the leading contemporary advocates of this theory is Wiebringhaus, *Das Gesetz*; he concludes that the municipal legislator, who issues rules of private international law, governing international relationships, fulfils the role of an international legislative organ. This author views private and public international law as two component parts of a single branch of law, namely international law, which has a supranational character. See more about this author in Part Three, Chapter 2, No. 7, of the present work.

[5] Triepel, *Völkerrecht und Landesrecht,* especially, p. 23.

[6] Zitelmann, *Internationales Privatrecht,* Vol. 1.

law exists as a complete unit and thus constitutes a true private international law; thereby he comes in his conclusions (but not in his grounds of them) very close to Frankenstein's concept which is, of course, more recent.

Among the representatives of the dualistic trends we should also list Franz Kahn,[7] who argued that beside several basic conflict principles contained in public international law, binding upon all states as the subjects of international law in the formulation of their own law of conflict of laws, there existed basically only municipal private international law. First among these principles, which Kahn considered to be a part of public international law, was the principle that every state had to have its private international law and should not act arbitrarily in applying a foreign law. Another such principle was the validity of the *lex rei sitae* as regards rights *in rem* to movables, etc. If we acquaint ourselves with the varying form of these alleged principles in the laws of individual states, we find that Kahn's principles are at the most abstractions of existing rules, but lack any normative force of their own.

On the other hand, when studying the views of English and American authors on private international law, we find that their basic concept, for example in Dicey's classical form, was very little or, we may say, not at all, influenced by the speculative views of the authors writing in the bourgeois states of continental Europe, who believed that private international law was a part of public international law. But this does not mean that these views had found no response at all in Anglo-American theory. For example, the theory, so fervently advocated by Professor Beale, that private international law is based on the recognition of "vested rights" has some substantial links with the internationalist school of the European continent; these links stand out more clearly, if we supplement Beale's original proclamation of vested rights with his other postulate, namely

---

[7] F. Kahn, *Abhandlungen zum internationalen Privatrecht,* Vol. I, pp. 286 ff.

that the state, the recognition of whose right is involved, should have "legislative competence" to establish that right.[8]

Thus, Beale's territorial concept is, in fact, quite close to the speculation of those authors, who promote the supranational character of private international law. For in practice, the consequence of Beale's theory are such that, for example, the court of A would have the jurisdiction to investigate whether the court of B, on whose territory and under whose law the right to be recognized originated, had the "legislative competence" to establish the respective right. On what basis should such investigation take place? On the basis of the court's own views as to what constitutes the legislative competence of states, or on the basis of international law? No matter what would turn out to be the criterion of such legislative competence in Beale's views, which, unfortunately lack in concrete detail, it is quite obvious that Beale's opinion comes very close to the already mentioned trends in the literature of the capitalist states of Europe.

After this brief enumeration and analysis of the main doctrinal trends, which consider private international law, in its whole or in part, to be a component part of public international law, let us concentrate on their critical evaluation.

As we have already pointed out, many of the allegations concerning the supranational character of private international law essentially proceed from the doctrine of natural law which is currently being activated by the tendency to assert the need of a "world" state and a "supranational" or "world", "timeless" or "eternal" law, which ignores the social substance of law in general and private international law in particular. This doctrine therefore runs counter to the fact that private international law, just as law in general, is an expression of the will of the ruling class. Most of the aforesaid views moreover ignore the substance of the legal relationship covered by private international law

---

8 Beale, "The Jurisdiction of a Sovereign State", *Harvard Law Review*, 1923, p. 241; also the criticism contained in Nussbaum, *Grundzüge*, pp. 26 and 27.

and constituting its object. It is obviously a mistake in logic, if the above-quoted authors in their great majority replace a study of the substance of the relations, which are the object of private international law, by assertions and assumptions of its supranational character which, of course, they deduce from their subjective views on the form of the sources of private international law rather than from the substance of the legal relations involved.

But we must deal not only with shortcomings resting in the *a priori* character of the approach used by most authors to the subject of our study. What is more serious, is their ignoring the fact that private international law is a law whose object are civil-law or private-law relationships (even though with a foreign element) and which is undoubtedly reserved to the domestic jurisdiction of states under the valid international law. The fact that some of the sources of private international law have the character of sources of international law, primarily in the form of the international law of contracts, is of no consequence in this respect. The efforts of these authors to deduce rules of a supranational private international law from mostly quite doubtful "principles" that in all states the *lex rei sitae* is applied to rights *in rem* regarding immovables, or the rule *locus regit actum* to the form of legal acts, or that it is up to the autonomous will of the parties to determine the applicable substantive law of obligations, etc., are doomed to failure after a somewhat more detailed investigation. After all, it is, for example, quite obvious that the rule *locus regit actum* does not exist in all systems of law in an identical form. Beside states which consider this principle to be an obligatory and unconditionally valid one, there are also those – and they are in the majority – who consider it only as optional or (as in the case of Czechoslovakia) only subsidiary to the law of the place, which governs the given relations as a whole *(lex causae)*. Each of these possibilities means either the validity or invalidity of the aforesaid principles and a completely different application of the substantive law. The same is true of the other alleged rules of international law, which states are supposedly obliged to observe (as Kahn still maintained), such as the *lex rei sitae* or autonomy of will. And yet, nobody would dare to assert or try to obtain a judgement from an international court, that, e.g., a state which would replace the rule *locus regit actum* in its obligatory form by its optional form or by the *lex causae,* or which would not permit the contracting parties to determine the law to govern their contractual relationship by their free choice, has thereby violated international law. The similarity existing between certain basic forms appearing in the laws of different states cannot be used as an argument to prove that all law, irrespective of the substance of the social relations involved, governed by international law.[9]

## (2) Theories Which Consider Private International Law as Part of Municipal Law and Their Evaluation

We have already mentioned those views – mostly influenced by the dualistic theories regarding the relationship between international and municipal laws – which claim that private international law is, in a certain sense, a part of public international law and, otherwise, a part of municipal law, but differ as to what belongs under which law; these views range from Zitelmann's assumption of the existence of a comprehensive system of private international law, which forms as a whole a part of international law, to Kahn's most careful formulations, asserting that except for a few very general principles, which fall under public international law, private international law belongs basically into the sphere of municipal law.

---

[9] It would go beyond the scope of the present study, if we were to deal in this connection critically with the question whether the general principles of law, recognized by civilized nations, in the sense of Article 38 (c) of the Statute of the International Court of Justice are a source of international law. We must simply note that in spite of the fact that the Court may use these principles as a basis for its decisions, they do not constitute international law in the strict sense.

In this connection we must bear in mind that Kahn's opinion served as the basis for the views held by a whole group of essentially positivistic authors dealing with private international law, who claimed – except for a rather vague admission of the existence of some principles of "public-international law" character – that private international law in general and the law of conflict of laws in particular were a part of municipal law, and sharply opposed all "internationalist" theories. This group includes many, especially German, authors, such as Nussbaum, Martin Wolff, Raape and Melchior, as well as the Frenchmen Bartin, Lerebours-Pigeonnière, Batiffol, Arminjon and also Niboyet, who, after having abandoned Pillet's internationalist opinion, eventually reached the conclusion that private international law was a part of municipal public law. Among the authors favouring the "municipal" concept we may, of course, find some extreme views which completely deny the claim that there exist some principles or rules of public international law, determining or limiting in any way the jurisdiction of states in formulating private international law. In addition to most English and American authors, like Westlake, Dicey, or Becket,[10] who upheld this concept, we can list a number of Continental authors who (on different grounds) reached the same conclusion. These include, for example, Fedozzi and Ago[11] in Italy, who, of course, did not proceed from the vague and hardly definable concept of comity of nations, which serves as the basis for the theoretical views held by the English and American authors.[12]

---

[10] A recent denial of any limitations placed on states by a supranational law in formulating private international law was made, e.g. by Brierly in the German translation of his book *Die Zukunft des Völkerrechts,* 1947, p. 30.

[11] Ago, "Règles générales des conflicts des lois", *Recueils des Cours,* 1936, Vol. IV, p. 256; Fedozzi, *Il diritto internazionale privato,* Padua, 1939, p. 115.

[12] In this connection we should perhaps mention the fact that essentially the same result has also been obtained by the strict positivists who take a negative opinion on the existence of international law. These are views of extreme state monism.

The doctrine asserting that private international law is exclusively a part of municipal law has, quite naturally, also certain consequences as regards the consideration of conflicts between the rules of private international law and rules of international law. Such a conflict, if it can occur at all in view of the already mentioned theories of state monism, must be settled in a manner which will be in keeping with the exclusive validity of the municipal rule.

Countering arguments raised by the advocates of the theory that private international law forms a part of international law, which usually point to the great number of rules of private international law contained in different international treaties, the proponents of the municipal character of private international law assert that an international treaty, too, due to its necessary transformations, acquires its municipal validity only under the order of the municipal legislator and that – if they admitted at all the existence of a supranational rule of private international law – such a rule would also have to be transformed into the municipal law.

While under the universalistic concept, not only international law and municipal law, but also all individual systems of municipal law form parts of a single, universal, world system of law, according to the aforementioned views, individual spheres of law and systems of municipal law are strictly isolated from each other. This isolation serves as the basis of what is known as the incorporation theory under which the foreign substantive law which is being applied on the basis of a municipal conflict rule is valid under the manifestation of the will of the state of the forum as an incorporated part of its own law.[13]

However, it would mean going too far beyond the scope of this part of the present work, if we were to continue describing the differences between the proponents of the two trends and the consequences of these differences for the concept of the general part of private international law, especially since we have partly discussed them also in the preceding part.

---

[13] See Part Six of the present work.

If we are to evaluate the views held by the advocates of an exclusively municipal character of private international law, we see that beside the fact that their views do not directly attack state sovereignty as the basis of international law, these authors have not avoided the errors made by their opponents. It is obvious that even they do not proceed from the substance of the social relations governed by law, which constitute the decisive factor, but rather from the fact – partly correct, but viewed presumptively – that private international law had been created in the historical process of its formation from municipal sources of law. If we disregard the fact that this is only partially true, we can see again that these views are once more characterized by the endeavour to deduce the nature of a branch of law from the forms of the sources of law. This endeavour also seems to be wrong as regards its approach to reality. For both the fundamental internationalists and the fundamental proponents of the municipal character of private international law quite ignore the second half of the truth, which does not fit their theories and which they refuse to see, namely that there is no doubt about the dual nature of the sources of private international law. In making this distinction we must not, in our opinion, proceed from the assumption that one category of sources of private international law might have precedence over another category; this would again be an *a priori* approach to the given question, which also ignores the fact that the question of formation of law, or the choice of this or that form of law, is a question determined historically and, primarily, by the existence of social classes, that essentially every ruling class chooses that form of law, which suits best its interests and better expresses its class substance, and that by laying abstract stress on the assumed superiority of one category of sources over another category one cannot arrive at real truth.

### (3) The Soviet Discussion on the Object and Character of Private International Law

Also Soviet literature, which proceeds from the correct tenet that the character of a particular branch of law can be determined only on the basis of the character of the social relations governed by that law, or the behaviour of people involved in these relationships, contains on one hand views that private international law is a part of international law in the broader sense, and, on the other hand, views that it forms a part of civil law.

The views of the "internationalists", i.e. those authors, who claim that private international law is a part of international law and whose main representative is S. B. Krylov (and, partly, also A. M. Ladyzhenski and Tille), essentially proceed from the international character of the relations governed by private international law which Krylov views as one of the branches of international law in the broader sense, the other branch being public international law.[14] In doing so, Krylov fully recognized that the object of private international law were civil-law relations with a foreign element, but he argued — pointing to the specific feature of internationality, manifested in the fact that the said civil-law relations exceeded the frontiers of a single state — that relations governed by public international law and private international law were inseparable; this was due to the fact that "behind every individual firm, behind every individual in international contacts stands the state of his domicil, and every dispute and conflict in this sphere of civil law, and even a divorce case under family law, may eventually grow into an international conflict". Krylov also points to the erro-

---

[14] Durdenevski—Krylov, *Mezhdunarodnoye pravo,* Moscow, 1947, pp. 28 ff.; Krylov, *Mezhdunorodnoye pravo,* Leningrad, 1930; also see Krylov's opinion presented in the discussion sponsored by the Institute of Law of the Academy of Sciences and the All-Union Institute of Jurisprudence in 1955 (a report on this discussion was published in *Sovetskoye gosudarstvo i pravo,* 1955, No. 9, pp. 121 ff.).

neousness of the views denying private international law the character of internationality and asserting that it is a part of municipal law, but he himself, on the other hand, stresses that many of the sources of private international law, including the principles *locus regit actum* and *lex rei sitae* as an international custom, have the character of sources of international law. In a discussion between Soviet jurists on the character and object of private international law, held by the departments of civil law and procedure of the All-Union Institute of Jurisprudence of the Soviet Ministry of Justice and the Institute of Law of the Soviet Academy of Sciences, Krylov raised similar arguments, basing them primarily on the alleged link between public and private international law, and on assertions that the main source of private international law were international treaties.

The original opinion held by Professor A. M. Ladyzhenski[15] also had a purely internationalistic character; Ladyzhenski argued that it was necessary to denounce "nihilistic" theories which considered private international law to be a branch of municipal law. He even asserted that there existed rules of private international law with a supranational character, which determined the jurisdiction of individual states in matters of application of law, that states could not modify.

However, Ladyzhenski apparently did not insist on the opinion he held in 1948; in the aforesaid discussion between Soviet jurists in 1955 he went on record against the object of private international law being defined only according to the object of the matter governed by that law (i.e. property relations), and asserted that private international law was neither international nor civil law, but rather a special branch of law which had to be defined according to its sources.

Tille, too, was essentially in favour of the thesis that private international law was a part of international law in the broader sense because, as he claimed, it was wrong to include it within

---

[15] A. M. Ladyzhenski, "K voprosu o yuridicheskoi prirode norm tak nazyvayemogo mezhdunarodnogo chastnogo prava", *Vestnik Moskovskogo universiteta*, 1948, No. 5.

civil law only on the grounds that states alone could be the subjects of international law; he asserted that while in one branch of international law only a state could be the subject, in another branch of this law the subjects could be different (i.e. natural and legal persons).

If we are to assess the views of those Soviet jurists, who hold that private international law and public international law form a unity, we must see that this unity is primarily deduced from the partial identity of the sources of both laws, which, in our opinion, is not a convincing argument on the one hand because it is wrong to distinguish law according to its sources, since the criterion must be the character of the human behaviour governed by the law, and, on the other hand, because the existence of the customs quoted by Krylov, or their validity, may be quite effectively denied on the basis of the actual practice of states. While it is true, as Krylov claims, that behind every individual stands the state of his domicil, this does not mean that diplomatic protection in which is manifested this interest of states in legal matters of individuals or legal persons, containing a foreign element, alters the character of the law which is otherwise the object of a private international claim; the provision of diplomatic protection does not change even the subject of the original claim, which is not, after all, transferred to the state.

But the main argument against the above views is offered by the fact that in spite of the indisputable element of internationalism (in the broader sense), civil-law relationships with a foreign element are, by their nature, completely different from relations between states, whose subjects are states as the carriers of state sovereignty. On the other hand, it is typical of relations governed by private international law, that their content quite differs from the relations into which enter states as carriers of state sovereignty, and we may say that these are relations where the sovereignty of states — which can, of course, become in exceptional cases also subjects of these relationships — is not manifested.

The viewpoint that private international law is a part of civil law is held primarily by Professor L. A. Lunts,[16] who, according to his own words, proceeds from the opinion formulated by I. S. Pereterski, which he further develops. Therefore, we should first outline the essence of Professor Pereterski's opinion which is to be found in his already quoted article on the system of private international law.

Pereterski reached the conclusion that private international law formed a separate branch of civil law in which he also included labour law and agricultural co-operative law. He first pointed to the fact that the division of law into individual branches was based on the relations the law governed. In spite of the undeniable fact that the object of private international law were civil-law relations, Pereterski stressed that private international law had the right to a quite separate existence. He explained this independence by the specific feature of private international law, namely the existence of an international element in the relations that law governs. If this specific feature did not exist in private international law and did not distinguish it from civil law, the subject-matter covered by private international law would mostly have to be included in the general part of civil law. According to Pereterski, the relations governed by private international law have their inner unity which makes them a special, characteristic group of legal relations requiring special study. After having analyzed the circumstances which give rise to the foreign element as a specific feature of private international law, Pereterski reached the conclusion that the separation of private international law from civil law was of special importance precisely in view of its specific character distinguishing it from civil law, which, in his

---

16 L. A. Lunts, *Mezinárodní právo soukromé (Private International Law)*, p. 15; "Niekotorye voprossy mezhdunarodnogo chastnogo prava", *Uchennyie zapisky VIJUN*, 1955, pp. 70 ff.; "O predmete mezhdunarodnogo chastnogo prava i nekotorykh osobyenostyakh mezhdunarodnogo chastnogo prava v otnosheniyakh mezhdu stranami socializma", *Voprossy mezhdunarodnogo chastnogo prava*, Moscow, 1956, pp. 5 ff. In the aforesaid discussion, this character of private international law was also advocated by P. O. Khalfina, M. M. Magidson and D. M. Genkin.

opinion, was especially important for Soviet law. Pereterski quite correctly pointed to the fact that while Soviet civil law was concerned with municipal relationships, based on the uniform, monolithic legislation of the socialist state, the fact could not be ignored, that private international law dealt with different systems of law with a different class substance and, in particular with laying the dividing line between Soviet socialist law and the law of the capitalist states. This function of private international law is different from the function of civil law and rested primarily in the protection of Soviet interests abroad, which gave it a special political significance. All this prevented private international law from being restricted to the bounds of civil law.

Pereterski concerns himself in his article with questions of the separation of agricultural co-operative law and labour law, which constitute a unique mixture of principles of civil law and administrative law, acting simultaneously and inseparably, into distinct, independent branches of law; the content of these independent branches are indisputably civil-law property relations between autonomous subjects, a characteristic feature of these relationships being their establishment by the manifestation of will of the respective subjects. Pereterski called this group of legal doctrines together with that of civil law "civil-law sciences" or rather "civil jurisprudence". The existence of this category of jurisprudence leads to two conclusions with regard to private international law: (1) private international law is to study relations with an international element, concerning all the branches of civil law as defined above, and (2) private international law, too, must be characterized as a branch of civil law. In fact, however, it represents a unique mixture of principles of civil law and international law, which act simultaneously and inseparably.

In this connection, the opinion of Professor L. A. Lunts, as expressed in his works quoted above and referring to Pereterski, only represents a reduction of Pereterski's arguments to the assertion that private international law is civil law, even though Lunts proceeds from the fact that the object of private international law are civil-law relations with a foreign element which, as Pereterski noted, distinguish private international law from civil law. Nor does Lunts attach the same importance as Pereterski to the fact that private international law is not concerned only with the monolithic legislation of the socialist state but also with foreign laws and their distinction with respect to the municipal law, and that its main function is the protection of Soviet interests abroad; thus, as regards the theoretical definition of the object and character of private international law, or the definition of the differences existing between private international law and other branches of law, this fact does not, in our opinion, stand out prominently.

CHAPTER 4

# The Place of Private International Law in the System of Law

Before we attempt to give a final answer as to the true place of private international law in the system of law (and thus also the system of jurisprudence), let us yet briefly outline some of the links and the differences existing between private international law and civil law on the one hand, and private international law and public international law on the other hand;[1] in doing so, we shall not repeat the arguments regularly raised in socialist literature, but shall concentrate on some findings which we consider of special importance for determining the place private international law occupies in the system of law.

It would be quite wrong, in our opinion, to deny the existence of a link between private international law and public international law. This link undoubtedly exists, but this does not mean that private international law and public international law form a unity or, at least, two branches of an international law in the broader sense, as frequently asserted by the proponents of the internationalistic concept.

Although the object of both public international law and private international law are social relations arising from contacts with other countries, which cannot be fitted within the framework of the sovereignty of one state,[2] or rather its system of law, we cannot but see that these relations differ and that there is also a difference between the behaviour of individuals in the

---

[1] On this points see, in particular, the arguments of I. S. Peretersk i in the quoted article, of L. A. Lunts, Bystrický, *Základy (Principles)*, pp. 21 ff., and Kutikov, *Mezhdunarodno*, pp. 31 ff.

[2] This question may create some doubts in the case of private international law; see above the criticism of the opinion of Prof. Kutikov.

relations governed by private international law and those governed by public international law. Private international law governs relations under civil or private law, characterized by the presence of a foreign element, while public international law basically governs the activities of states in their political, economic and legal relations with other sovereign states.[3]

The scope of subjects and their nature differ in public international law and private international law, and it would be doubtlessly wrong, if this scope of subjects were reduced to a common denominator; in private international law the subjects are individual natural and juristic persons, while in public international law sovereign states.

There is a similarity of sources of both private international law and public international law, but this similarity is not, in our opinion, quite complete. While in public international law an important role is still played by customary law, which still governs very important questions of contacts between sovereign states, the role of the custom as a source of private international law is most doubtful and disputable, as already shown on the example of the alleged "principles" of private international law, such as the rules of *locus regit actum*, "autonomy of will", etc. This does not mean, of course, that we underestimate the role played by such consuetudinary rules of public international law, as the principle *par in parem non habet imperium,* in relations with a foreign element. But we must see that these are principles of public international law. Also the fact that the international treaty is a source of private international law besides municipal law, either formed by legislation or by judicial precedents, is not decisive in our opinion.

Private and public international law quite frequently use terms and categories which are common to them both, such as citizenship, reciprocity, etc., but this, we feel, in no way alters the fact that the substance of the relations governed by the two laws, differs.

Nor does the fact that in formulating its own private inter-

---

[3] See Knapp, ***Stát a právo (State and Law),*** IV, 1957, p. 217.

national law, a state is bound by such principles of public international law, as the principle of equality of states and their laws, favour the conclusion that private international law is a part of public international law. For no state may violate the rules of public international law even when formulating other branches of its system of law.

Nor is the fact that both public international law and private international law are to promote peaceful co-existence and the struggle for peace in any way decisive for the conclusion that both branches of law cover identical relations. The same function appertains to other spheres of social relations as well, which are not identical with either public or private international law.

Thus, none of these reasons warrants the assertion that private international law is identical with public international law.

There are also links as well as differences between private international law and civil law; and it is precisely these differences, primarily the already mentioned specific feature of the international element, which is an essential condition for the establishment of a relation governed by private international law, that prevent private international law from being considered a part of civil law, even when in this case the mutual links are closer than those between private international law and public international law.

A common feature of both civil law and private international law is the fact that both branches govern civil-law relations. This gives rise to a number of additional links, beginning with the connection existing between the institutions and concepts with which both branches operate, a connection usually manifested in the setting of the scope of the conflict rules and, eventually, in the application of the substantive law. Moreover, private international law, or rather its core represented by the law of conflict of laws, takes over a considerable measure of the system of civil law of the respective state, and when studying private international law it is necessary to proceed from a knowledge of civil law and the law of civil procedure. No less obvious is also the very important link existing between private international law and civil law (as well as other branches of the law of the respective state), namely the fact that they both express the will of the same ruling class. This all may seem to offer sufficient support for the assertion that private international law is a part or, at least, a subsidiary branch, of civil law.

But the matter is not all that simple. We cannot, on one hand, stress the above-mentioned links, and, on the other hand, ignore or underestimate the specific feature of the international element, whose importance for private international law we have already mentioned. If we bear in mind the existence of this specific feature, we find that private international law governs not merely civil-law relations, but *special* civil-law relations which acquire their inner unity precisely as a result of the existence of the international element.

However, there still remains the question, whether the typical human behaviour in social relations, which, as we know, provides the basis for a systematic classification of law and which also provides sufficient grounds for the creation of a branch of law,[4] is identical in the relations governed by civil law and those governed by private international law. We feel that although both private international law (if we disregard cases coming under family law, involving a foreign element) and civil law are concerned with property relationships, the content of the concrete behaviour of every subject in every sphere, both municipal and international, characterized by the presence of a foreign element in the given relationship, is different.

We must yet consider the question whether the relation between civil law and private international law is not a relation in which the main branch (i.e. civil law) also attracts the regulation of human behaviour in relations which are similar to or are connected with the typical relations.[5] On this point, Knapp uses as an example the relationship between civil law and copyright law. But in our case, where the presence of an

---

[4] See Knapp, *Stát a právo (State and Law)*, IV, p. 210, and *Předmět a systém (The Object and System)*, p. 74.

[5] See Knapp, *Předmět a systém (The Object and System)*, p. 75.

international element in the relations governed by private international law gives these relations inner unity and harmony, and at the same time distinguishes them from municipal civil-law relations, there is no such relationship.

Besides the already quoted views of Professor Knapp, also Professor Luby expressed in Czechoslovak literature on civil law the view that private international law was not a special branch of law but primarily a part of civil law and possibly of other branches with which the individual conflict rules are concerned, such as, for example, family law or labour law.[6]

Personally, I believe that the Czechoslovak literature on civil law failed when it discussed the object and the place of private international law in the system of law only on the sidelines of the discussion whether it was proper to separate economic law from civil law as a separate branch. This has made the authors more or less ignore the specific problem of private international law, arising from the existence of the international element in the social relations governed by private international law.

In quite general terms, law has the tendency to govern social relations and the behaviour of individuals comprehensively, which applies not only to the content but also the forms representing the method of its existence. We feel this finding to be of importance also for the definition of the place private international law occupies in the system of law.

When determining the object of a branch of law and its place in the system of law, we proceed from the economic relation which exists in the base and belongs in the category of existence. At the same time, of course, it exists in the consciousness of the subjects of this relation, as well as in the consciousness of

---

[6] Š. Luby, "K otázkám učenia o systéme socialistického práva" ("Doctrinal Approaches to the System of Socialist Law"), *Právny obzor (Legal Review)*, 1966, 1, p. 53; "Vznik a vývoj a stav sústavy socialistického občianského práva" ("Origin, Development and Present State of the System of Socialist Civil Law"), *Právnické štúdie (Legal Studies)*, 1967, No. 3, pp. 527—580; "Systematika jednotlivých častí socialistického občianského práva" ("Systematic Arrangement of the Parts of Socialist Civil Law"), *Právnické štúdie (Legal Studies)*, 1967, No. 4, pp. 743—800.

other people, as a relation which is simultaneously moral, political, etc. These forms of relations, too, belong in the category of existence; we therefore believe that the content of a legal relation is primarily the economic relationship, but at the same time its forms which are the method of its existence. These forms, it should be noted, are forms in view of the economic content, but may also be the content in view of their legal form.

We therefore believe that law governs certains social relations but that these relations must not be viewed only from the economic point of view; instead, they should be understood in the complexity of the social content and social form.

The social content and form of the relations governed by private international law are characterized by the existence of a foreign element, that is, basically, by contact with more than a single system of law. This is what is essential, in our opinion, and these specific features of social relations governed by private international law must not be ignored and simply identified with municipal civil-law relationships, when we realize the special problems arising from the fact that they are linked with more than just one system of law. This shows that we cannot proceed only from an economic characterization because law develops from all the factors which constitute social relationships as a whole.

Nor can the behaviour of individuals in relations governed by law be understood, in our opininon, only on the basis of an economic characterization, but from a comprehensive viewpoint. On this basis then appears the difference in the behaviour of people in purely municipal relationships and in relationships with a foreign element, which are determined by the parallel existence of more states and by the fact that the given relation concerns more than one state and its system of law.

In our opinion, private international law then constitutes an independent branch of the law of every state, which in spite of considerable connections with civil law and public international law, is distinct from both these branches of law.[7] The fact that

---

[7] On this opinion also see Kutikov, *Mezhdunarodno*, p. 30.

the private international laws of all states have much in common has already been discussed especially in the first part of the present work.

There seems to be no dispute in Czechoslovak literature as to the fact that private international law has its specific place in the system of jurisprudence, as a system of findings about law. Since it is generally recognized that the criterion for classifying jurisprudence may be found only in the object of learning, i.e. in the law proper, rather than in the subject of learning,[8] we believe that the general acceptance of the independent place of private international law in the system of jurisprudence, too,[9] offers another proof of the independence of this branch of law in the system of law.

---

[8] See Knapp, *Předmět a systém (The Object and System)*, p. 77.

[9] See, e.g., *Učebnice občanského a rodinného práva (Textbook of the Civil and Family Law)*, Prague, 1955, Vol. I, p. 72; Bystrický, *Základy (Principles)*, p. 23.

# PART FIVE
# Comparative Jurisprudence, Private International Law and the Law of International Trade

## CHAPTER 1
## General Survey

The rather obvious fact that both comparative jurisprudence and private international law (as well as the law of international trade) owe their existence and continuation to the plurality of the systems of law has made us discuss in this part of the work their nature and their relation. It is quite clear that both private international law and comparative jurisprudence would disappear as a branch of law, or as a branch of jurisprudence, if there were no differences in the systems of law; the attainment of this state of affaires in the sphere of the legal regulation of the international exchange of goods is the very purpose of a unified law of international trade, which wants to replace the diversity of the laws, especially in the sphere of the law of obligations in international commercial contacts, as a new and, by its substance and character, most disputable category.

We deem it, of course, necessary to stress already at this point, that the character of comparative law and comparative jurisprudence – the latter being our topic of discussion – is highly debatable, and that, for the time being, we do not wish – by using such terms as "branch of law" or "branch of jurisprudence" – to prejudice in any way the results we shall reach further on. At the same time, we must also bear in mind that very few branches of law are connected with such doubts as to the definition of its object and character, as private international law.[1] However, these doubts and differences of opinion are

---

[1] On this point see Parts Three and Four of the present book and the author's article (in Czech) "K předmětu a povaze mezinárodního práva soukromého a k otázce jeho místa v systému práva" ("The Object and

still further intensified when it comes to the definition of the object and character of comparative jurisprudence and the law of international trade.

While the substance and character of private international law, as well as the question of its object, have been the topics of a number of works in juristic literature – works that have mostly reached different conclusions – the question of the character and object of the law of international trade and of its place in the system of law is a relatively new one. And, as regards comparative law, or rather comparative jurisprudence, it is obvious that it does not constitute an independent branch of law in the objective sense; while some authors point to the fact that comparative law is only a method of studying law and its institutions which are of importance for practically all branches of law, other authors hold that comparative jurisprudence alone can give us a comprehensive and reliable picture of law as a social phenomenon, asserting that comparative jurisprudence is a social science in the true sense rather than just a method. Although we do not wish to formulate already in the very introduction our opinion on the character of comparative jurisprudence, we deem it necessary to point to the fact that comparative jurisprudence has a quite specific and primary importance precisely for private international law as a branch of law whose task it is not only to solve conflicts of laws clinically by the choice of the applicable substantive law, but also – and, we feel, primarily – to try to eliminate preventively the occurrence of such conflicts in appropriate spheres. When we underline already at this place the preventive social function of private international law as a branch of law governing civil-law (or private-law) relations with a foreign or international element and including within this scope not only conflict rules but also substantive or procedural rules, we do so in order to assess properly the importance of the law of international trade, where

---

Nature of Private International Law and Its Place in the System of Law"), *Časopis pro mezinárodni právo (Czechoslovak Journal of International Law)*, 1960, No. 2, pp. 81–102.

the endeavour to remove the causes of conflict of laws is especially marked. If the objectives of the law of international trade are to be achieved, it can happen only through the full utilization of the findings and methods of comparative jurisprudence.

Naturally, this work does not want to be a mere academic affair or a theoretical treatise. Its topical character and urgency would clearly show, if we compared statistical data concerning the civil-law relations of the subjects of rights and obligations in different states today and some decades past, i.e. in the period when the views on the object and character of private international law, which are still considered to be standard, were being formulated. Under the present situation, which reflects the initial, far-reaching consequences of the scientific and technical revolution, the very number and increased intensity of civil-law relations between subjects from different states, expressed, e.g., in the numerical manifestation of the price of goods which are the object of international commercial contracts concluded every year, place great demands on the legal regulation of these relations, whose importace for society therefore greatly increases. Although this fact is generally recognized, there exist quite differing concepts as regards the legal solution of the current social needs in the spheres under study. These concepts and views are almost always, even though in a different degree, affected by the underlying politico-legal positions which, naturally, we cannot discuss. It should, however, be sufficient, if we point out that the very fact of plurality of the systems of law, which is the essential condition of the existence of both private international law and comparative jurisprudence, and which is based on the plurality of individual state sovereignties – is sometimes being viewed as a very harmful and dangerous state for the development of civil-law relations with an international element. A radical solution that is being recommended – often motivated by political purposes – is to abandon the concept of state sovereignty and the ensuing plurality of system of law, and to replace it with a concept of a world-wide, supranational and universally valid law. Some authors even assert – wrongly, in our opinion – that such law already exists, and interpret its alleged existence as a criterion of the legality of the legislation of individual states. This concept is opposed by views which realistically bear in mind the contemporary political and legal situation, and assert that only increased and intensive co-operation among states may be — even in the sphere of law — an adequate means meeting the increased demands placed on the legal regulation of the international life in the present situation, and which consider as such means the growth of both public and private international law.

Bearing this situation in mind, we must see that it is impossible to exhaust fully the whole set of problems related with the existence and inter-relationships of such complex categories as comparative law, private international law, and the law of international trade. Much of what should deserve a more thorough explanation will have to be, therefore, simply outlined or summed up, and many of the questions which we only touch upon in the present work deserve separate and independent treatment. Although, when considering the fundamental questions of some branches of law or jurisprudence, marked by the indisputably hybrid nature which is typical of private international law, the law of international trade and comparative jurisprudence, we must proceed from the natural endeavour of every scholarly study to define the object of such study, as well as the method used, as exactly and comprehensively as possible, we cannot at the same time but see that neither the system of law nor the system of jurisprudence are permanently fixed and that they are subject to a certain development, mostly dictated by the needs of social life. While only a few decades ago, private international law — then, of course, viewed only as the law of conflict of laws — could be considered a part of civil law (or — in the opinion of other authors — as a part of public international law), such views today evoke a justified reaction from those, who consider private international law to be a separate branch of law characterized by the fact that it not only governs the solution of conflicts of law, but that it also represents the complex of all rules governing civil-law relations with a foreign element, for which the existence of this element is specific because it results in such relations being distinguished from relations of purely municipal nature. The purpose of this part of our work is not, of course, to discuss private international law, the law of international trade and comparative jurisprudence from the viewpoint of dividing the system of law or system of jurisprudence into individual categories or branches. Although such study is important and interesting, we consider it more topical to discuss the interdependence and interaction of these individual fields, because they can greatly help us in tracing their social functions, which differ in many respects from the past in today's context of international social need. In doing so, we feel that a rigid systemization of law would be an obstacle rather than an aid in this study, especially if it obstructed the trends of development, dictated by the needs of the contemporary development of society. This does not mean, of course, that we want to renounce what we consider to form in our area a part of legal culture and to be the outcome of past and present development; we do not want to force arbitrarily the adoption of unwarranted changes in the system of law, but are interested in a study of the interaction of the individual branches, which, we feel, is of extreme importance today.

This process of thought has led us first to discussing comparative law and its role in jurisprudence from the viewpoint of its methods and functions, and then we shall concentrate on explaining the tasks and possibilities of comparative law as regards private international law in general and the law of international trade in particular.

## CHAPTER 2

**(Excursus)**

# Some Problems of Comparative Jurisprudence

### (1) The Development of Comparative Law

Comparison as such is one of the essential parts of the process of human thinking and learning[1] not only as regards acquiring knowledge of the strange but also, and perhaps primarily, as regards learning of one's own.[2] If we trace the growth and development of individual branches of science especially in the 19th and 20th centuries, we can easily see, what major role comparison and the comparative method had played there.[3] It is only natural, that comparison has also played a major role in the process of learning law and in jurisprudence in general. It had do undergo a long and difficult process which we cannot discuss in this work in its individual stages; perhaps it will suffice, if we point to Cicero's well-known statement on the perfection of Roman law, which he based on a comparison with foreign laws *(incredibile est quam sit omne ius civile praeter hoc nostrum inconditum ac paene ridiculum)*[4] which he considered to be im-

---

[1] K. Zweigert, "Méthodologie du droit comparé", *Mélanges offerts à Jacques Maury,* Vol. I, pp. 579 and 580, and 580, and the quotations made therein, e.g. Novalis: *"Il semble que toute connaissance repose sur une comparaison ...".*

[2] Goethe once said: *"Wer fremde Sprachen nicht kennt, weiss nichts von seiner eigenen ...",* Quoted from Zweigert's work.

[3] Jerome Hall, *Comparative Law and Social Theory,* Louisiana State University Press, 1963, pp. 3–5. Hall points in this connection to a number of basic works in the field of natural sciences (e.g. Darwin's Origin of Species or Cuvier's Leçons d'anatomie comparée) but also in the field of linguistics, ethnology, etc. Also see Schnitzer, *Vergleichende Rechtslehre,* 2nd ed., Basel, 1961, Vol. I, pp. 7 ff.

[4] Cicero, *De oratore,* Lib. I, cap. 44, § 197; quoted from M. Wolff, *Private International Law,* p. 20.

perfect and almost ridiculous, to the *collatio legum Mosaicarum et Romanorum,* as perhaps the oldest systematic comparative work,[5] and to contemporary problems of comparative law — or, better said, comparative jurisprudence – which we want to consider in this part of the present work. Since, beside the general problems of comparative law, the present study is also concerned with the clarification of the relation between comparative law and private international law, we deem it necessary to stress already at this point that comparative law, which could have been on occasions more or less ignored by some branches of law, has been of special significance for private international law from the very beginning of its existence. As evidence let us quote the opinion voiced by Magister Aldric, who asserted at the very birth of the problem of conflict of laws in the 12th century, that the judge should apply the law which he found more useful and better,[6] for which purpose it is, of course, necessary to compare the conflicting laws.

Leaving aside the details of the historical development of comparative law,[7] we may, perhaps, point to Montesquieu as the founder of modern comparative jurisprudence.[8] It was he, who wrote in the sense of his concept of natural law that *"la loi en général est la raison humaine en tant qu'elle gouverne tous les*

---

[5] See Schnitzer, *Vergleichende Rechtslehre,* p. 8, and the literature quoted therein.

[6] *"...quaeritur si homines diversarum provinciarum quae diversas habent consuetudines, sub uno eodemque iudice litigant, utrum earum iudex qui iudicandum suscepit sequi debeat? respondeo eam: Quae potior et utilior videtur* (debet enim iudicare secundum) quod melius ei visum fuerit" (underlined by the author). Quoted from Gutzwiller, *Recueil des Cours,* 1929, Vol. IV, p. 301; also see Krčmář, *Základy (Bases),* p. 117.

[7] See Mario Sarfatti, "Les premièrs pas du droit comparé", *Mélanges Maury,* Vol. II, 1960, p. 238; Walter Hug, "The History of Comparative Law", *Harvard Law Review,* 1952, pp. 1027–1070; Schnitzer, *Vergleichende Rechtslehre,* pp. 7 ff.; H. C. Gutteridge, *Comparative Law (An Introduction to the Comparative Method of Legal Study and Research),* Cambridge, University Press, 1946, pp. 11 ff.

[8] Montesquieu, *De l'Esprit des Lois,* Vol. I, Chapter III.

*peuples de la terre; et les lois politiques et civiles de chaque nation ne doivent être que les cas particuliers où s'applique cette raison humaine".*[9] However, already before the French Engligh-teners, Leibniz drew up a complete survey of the law of the then civilized world;[10] others date the founding of modern comparative law from Anselm Feuerbach,[11] and still others from as far back as Bodin or even Aristotle whose Constitution of Athens or Politics are being quoted as examples of the ancient use of the comparative method.[12] However, the question of the origin of comparative law is certainly not of major importance for our purposes. When we consider the questions of the historical development of comparative law from the viewpoint of its overall connection within the history of law, we find that isolated, usually utilitarian, attempts at learning foreign laws and comparing them with local law, can hardly be described as the beginnings of comparative jurisprudence in the modern sense. For we should bear in mind that until the 18th century, the law of the European Continent had existed under the impact of the tradition of a common, universal and general law represented by Roman law;[13] in English law, which had mostly passed through a different development than Continental law, the need of comparing the former with the latter did not arise, especially in view of the fact that in relationships with a foreign element, a major role was played by general law of merchants *(lex mercatoria)*. This *lex mercatoria* was in its substance a universally valid customary law which originated in the Italian city states in the 12th to 15th centuries, and from there spread to Spain,

---

[9] *Ibid.*, the importance of this thinker for comparative law is discussed in Niboyet, "Montesquieu et le droit comparé", *La pensée politique et constitutionelle de Montesquieu*, 1952, pp. 255 ff.

[10] See Gutteridge, *Comparative Law*, p. 12.

[11] E.g., Gustav Radbruch, "Anselme Feuerbach, précurseur du droit comparé", *Mélanges Lambert*, Vol. I, Paris, 1938, p. 284; for more details on this point see Hall, *Comparative Law*, p. 16, footnote No. 38.

[12] Hall, *Comparative Law*.

[13] On this points see M. Ancel, "Valeur actuelle des études de droit comparé", *XXth Century Comparative and Conflicts Law* (Legal Essays in Honor of Hessel Y. Yntema), pp. 15 ff., in particular, p. 17.

France, Germany and England, as a special merchant law, promoted by organizations of merchants and by the special jurisdiction of mercantile courts applying the rules of international trade custom. In England, this law became at the end of the 17th century a part of common law, after the judgment in Woodward v. Rowe, issued in 1666, had stated that "the law of merchants is the law of the land and the custom is good enough for any man without naming him merchant". It is this fact, too, which underlies the very late formation of conflict rules governing obligations in England.[14]

On the Continent, Roman law provided the basis of legal thought, studied and interpreted by jurists who spoke the same legal language; it was a perfect cultural heritage whose value rose even higher, spurred by the admiration the Renaissance felt for all that was Roman. How this cultural heritage served as a perfect, ready-made tool securing the needs of the bourgeoisie, which was born in the womb of feudal society, was masterfully decribed by Engels.[15]

The Roman law concept of legal though remained unaltered until the era of the great thinkers of natural law, who gradually replaced Roman law as the universal criterion of all law, by the ideal categories of natural law, which was to be ascertained and interpreted by jurisprudence so that it might become a part of individual municipal laws in written form.[16] This law, as the supreme product of human reason, in the sense of the above quotation from the *Esprit des lois,* had – similarly as Roman law – a universal character, although its individual manifestations could differ according to the specific situation of individual countries, their climate, degree of freedom, wealth, etc.[17] Under

---

[14] On this points see, e.g., the first decision made in this sphere (Robinson v. Bland) in 1760.

[15] F. Engels, *O rozkladu feudalismu (The Disintegration of Feudalism),* p. 14.

[16] See Ancel, "Valeur actuelle des études de droit comparé", ***XXth Century, Comparative and Conflict Laws,*** Leiden, 1961.

[17] Montesquieu, *De l'Esprit des Lois.* It should also be noted in this connection, that Montesquieu is frequently considered to be the founder of the sociology of law as well.

the concepts of natural law, the individual manifestations of law were to be studied and compared so that this study and comparison could help the legislators grasp and express the true and comprehensive character and manifestations of rationality as its source, and incorporate this natural law as fully as possible in written rules of law. This rationalistic universalism found its expression in the Declaration of the Rights of Man and the Citizen of 1789, and the study of foreign laws, promoted by Napoleon in the period of the legislative preparation of the French Civil Code, which was to have provided the best solutions of individual questions, was undoubtedly influenced by considerations based on natural law;[18] we may say, on the whole, that since the preparation of the *Code civil,* every major codification has been preceded, with greater or lesser intensity, by a study of foreign laws and by their comparison.[19] The development of comparative law orientated on natural law at its beginnings, was also parallelled by another trend – also orientated towards natural law – which, proceeding from Grotius, wanted to reduce, through the creation of international law based on and derived from natural law, the importance of the legal regulations in force in individual territorial units.[20]

In the 19th century, bourgeois comparative law developed at a relatively rapid pace; its utilitarian objectives, which initially predominated, gradually changed, and the tendency asserted

---

[18] On this point see Grunebaum–Ballin, "Comment Bonaparte, Premier Consul, fonda la premiède organisation d'études des législations étrangères et du droit comparé", *Revue internationale de droit comparé,* 1953, pp. 267 ff.; M. Ancel, "Politique législative et le droit comparé", *Mélanges Maury,* Vol. I, 1960, pp. 9 ff.

[19] A similar objective is pursued by some associations active in the sphere of comparative law. Thus, e.g. the statutes of the French *Société de législation comparée,* founded in 1869, which proceeded from the tradition of French comparative law (in France, the first university department of comparative law was founded as early as in 1832) proclaim, i.a., as one of the society's purposes, *"... étudier les lois des différents pays et la recherche des moyens pratiques d'améliorer des diverses branches de la législation".*

[20] See Gutteridge, *Comparative Law,* p. 12.

itself rather strongly, to make comparative law a separate branch of study. In 1829, Mittenmaier founded his journal *Kritische Zeitschrift für Rechtswissenschaft und Gesetzgebung des Auslandes,* in 1832 the Collège de France established a department of comparative law, in 1846 the Sorbonne in Paris began to offer courses in comparative criminal law, in 1869 the French *Société de législation comparée* was established, followed somewhat later by similar associations in England and Germany, in 1890 two professorships of comparative civil law were founded at the Sorbonne, the study of comparative constitutional law was beginning to be promoted, and in 1900, the first international congress of comparative law was held in Paris, to be followed by a number of others.[21] The importance of this first congress lay especially in the fact that the delegates urged the consideration of comparative law as an independent branch of scholarly study; the congress raised a number of scientific and methodological problems, beginning with the question of what comparative law was and what was its purpose, which is a question still being debated today and which may be expected to recur with varying intenstity at different stages of development of comparative law.

In the early 20th century (and we may, in fact, say until the period just preceding the Second World War), comparative law was strongly affected by both its natural-law heritage and idealistic universalism. The extent of the latter stands out clearly when we recall that the founder of modern French comparative jurisprudence, Raymond Saleilles viewed as the purpose of comparative jurisprudence the finding of *"droit commun de l'humanité"* – a common law of makind – that the rapporteur general of the 1900 congress, Edouard Lambert wanted to find a *"droit commun législatif",* which, however, he did not view as a return (direct or indirect) to natural law, or that the continuator

[21] The list of these congresses is given in Bystrický, "Za marxistickou srovnávací právovědu" ("For a Marxist Comparative Jurisprudence"), *Právník (The Lawyer),* 1962, No. 8, pp. 625 ff. The last but one, Seventh Congress of Comparative Law was held in Uppsala in 1966 and the last one met in Pescara in 1970.

of the work of both these authors, Henri Lévy-Ullmann even tried to construe in the period between the two World Wars a "world law of the 20th century" *(droit mondial du XXème siècle)*.[22]

Saleilles did not understand the purpose of comparative jurisprudence as a mere juxtaposition of individual rules of law, as had been the custom in the 19th century, but from a comparative study of the German Civil Code and the French *Code civil* tried to arrive by critical analysis at an understanding not only of the rules of substantive law, but also at their overall inspiration and trend, so as to deduce therefrom a law common for all mankind as a directive for the future law of the legislator.[23] His dependence on the 18th century doctrine of natural law is quite obvious.

The rapporteur general of the first international congress in 1900, Lambert, no longer sought the purpose of comparative jurisprudence in the renaissance of the doctrine of natural law. He rejected the vagueness of the objectives pursued by his predecessor and wanted to reduce comparative jurisprudence to narrower groups of nations linked by traditions of common upbringing, history and economy, proclaiming as the basic rule comparative jurisprudence that "only the comparable could be compared". Lambert wanted to deduce from individual substantive rules of the compared systems of law "legal constants" which he no longer assumed to be reflections of natural law, but rather solutions adopted by systems of laws standing on the same level of civilization. In contrast to earlier views on comparative jurisprudence, Lambert's opinion reflects an influence of legal positivism. For him comparative jurisprudence was an autonomous branch of jurisprudence aiming at an objective study of substantive law, which had to have regard for sociological reality. His *"droit commun législatif"* was to be studied

---

22 A description of the basic concepts of these authors may be found in M. Ancel, "La tendance universaliste dans la doctrine comparative française au début du XXème siècle", *Festschrift für Ernst Rabel*, pp. 17 ff.

23 *Ibid.*

just as individual municipal laws, while the value of scholarly investigation in the sphere of thus conceived comparative jurisprudence was to rest in a rapprochement of the individual systems of law.

The work of Henri Lévy-Ullmann, who was intensively active in the period between the two World Wars, was characterized by the endeavour to create a universally valid "world law of the 20th century" on the basis of the results obtained by comparative jurisprudence. This law was to be deduced, in his opinion, from the common trends to be found in the studied legal institutions and in the form of rules of substantive law which were identical with, or at least similar to, the rules existing in the systems of law which were in force. As we can see, Lévy-Ullmann's endeavour to create a world law of the 20th century was marked by a very active universalistic tendency, combined with strong overtones of the natural-law heritage; both these elements were clearly expressed in his postulate that law thus formed should become a universal *ius inter gentes*.[24]

The French school of comparative law of the first third of the 20th century was characterized by the effort to create an independent branch of jurisprudence, but, as we have seen, its disciples failed to reach the desirable unity on its purpose. Even if we were to accept these views, we could not overlook the fact that comparative jurisprudence is basically a new and relatively young branch of study, which becomes quite clear when we bear in mind that the other branches of jurisprudence, derived from the objective existence of the individual branches of law are mostly very old and have a very long tradition.

However, the conclusions reached on the character of comparative jurisprudence as an autonomous field of study were not accepted unanimously. German and English authors in particular claimed that comparative jurisprudence was not a science

---

[24] See Lévy-Ullmann, "Vers le droit mondial de XXème siècle", the introduction to the first volume of his *Collection d'études théorétiques et pratiques de droit étranger, de droit comparé et de droit international*, Paris.

but merely a method, although one that could be applied in almost all branches of jurisprudence. Thus, the English author Sir Frederick Pollock pointed out already at the First Congress of Comparative Law in Paris, in 1900, that *"le droit comparé n'est pas une science propre mais il n'est que l'introduction de la méthode comparée dans le droit"*.[25] Similarly, Kaden states in the encyclopedia of comparative law, the greatest work of its kind in the period between the two World Wars, that comparative law "is merely a method of juridical scientific research. The purpose of comparative law is only to compare the rules of different systems of law; it points directly only to the similarities and differences in the solution of individual problems under different systems of law. It cannot be considered a science".[26]

In his already classical book on comparative law,[27] Professor Gutteridge holds that "comparative law is an unfortunate but generally accepted label for the comparative method of legal study and research which has come to be recognized as the best means of promoting a community of thought and interest between the lawyers of different nations and as an invaluable auxiliary to the development and reform of our own and other systems of law". In support of his opinion, Gutteridge also proceeds from terminological doubts ("comparative law" in contrast to the German term *Rechtsvergleichung* and the French *droit comparé)* and concludes already in the opening passages of his work,[28] that much of the atmosphere of doubts and suspicions surrounding comparative law and hostile to its development would disappear if there were a general recognition that the term "comparative law" decribes a method of study and research rather than a separate branch of law; he believes that

---

[25] *Procès verbaux,* Paris, 1905, I, p. 60, quoted in J. Hall, *Comparative Law,* p. 7. Hall points out that in their three-volume work on the system of comparative law, Arminjon–Nolde–Wolff ascribe this theory to De Francisci and Kaden.

[26] Kaden, *Rechtsvergleichendes Handwörterbuch, Berlin,* 1938, Vol. VI, p. 11.

[27] Gutteridge, *Comparative Law,* p. VII.

[28] *Ibid.*, p. 1.

the process of comparing the rules of different systems of law does not lead to the formulation of any independent rules governing human relations and action. Although greatly criticized,[29] Gutteridge's opinion is shared by other highly reputed authors.[30] Nevertheless, his reaction to the French idealistic universalism of the first decades of this century has not been received unequivocally. The views that comparative jurisprudence is not a separate branch of jurisprudence but only a method of research (which, however, even according to Gutteridge, is to study laws in the light of their political, social or economic purpose)[31] is paralleled by the opinion that comparative jurisprudence is a certain conglomerate or type of knowledge and that as such, it is a social science in the true sense of the term.[32] Arminjon, Nolde and Wolff, as the authors of a three-volume book or the system of comparative law, even go as far as to accept the older French heritage of natural law, when they claim that *"le droit comparé étant une branche de droit, sa fin est la même: règler et améliorer la conduite des hommes"*.[33]

## (2) The Theoretical Discussion on the Nature of Comparative Jurisprudence

In all these speculative theories, we see coming to the fore a basic dispute between authors concerned with the substance of comparing different laws, which we could briefly describe as

---

[29] E.g. Hall, *Comparative Law*, pp. 3—15 in particular.

[30] E.g. René David, *Traité élémentaire de droit civil comparé*, Paris, 1950, pp. 4 and 8; C. J. Hamson, *The Law, its Study and Comparison*, Cambridge, 1955, pp. 21—22.

[31] David, *Traité*, pp. 10, 15, etc., where the author stresses as essential for comparative jurisprudence knowledge on the whole social and cultural complex.

[32] Hall, *Comparative Law*, and the literature quoted there on pp. 10 ff.

[33] Arminjon—Nolde—Wolff, *Traité de droi comparé*, Paris, 1950, Vol. I, p. 32.

a dispute on whether comparative jurisprudence is a true science or whether it is but a method of study. Some authors are trying to bridge this difference in a pragmatic way,[34] whereby, of course, they cannot find the truth.

We must ask to what we are to ascribe such differences of opinion between authors who are concerned with the concept and purpose of comparative jurisprudence and who are at the same time trying to outline its method.

We believe that the French idealistic universalism, whose main points we have already outlined, failed to strike a balance with legal positivism which had deeply influenced comparative jurisprudence and considerably disturbed the idealistically motivated search for a "universal law of all mankind" or a "world law of the 20th century", as conducted by Saleilles or Lévy-Ullmann. A natural reaction to this fact was the setting aside of the idealistic postulates of the French authors and the prevalence of views that comparative jurisprudence is only a method of comparing different systems of law and their individual rules. This may be illustrated by the opinion of Kaden,[35] who, proceeding from the initial premise that comparative law was nothing but a method of scientific legal research, restricted it to a formal comparison of laws *(formelle Rechtsvergleichung),* i.e. to the study of individual forms or formal sources of law and a dogmatic comparison *(dogmatische Rechtsvergleichung),* which is concerned with the different solutions of the same problem in different systems of law. Another advocate of the opinion that comparative law is only a method, Professor Gutteridge, divides comparative law into "descriptive comparative law", which differs from "applied comparative law" by being limited

---

[34] Schmitthoff writes in the *Cambridge Law Journal,* 1939, p. 5 (quoted from Gutteridge, *Comparative Law,* p. 5), about this difference: "How vague these expressions (i.e. "science" and "method") are, so far as legal terminology is concerned, may be seen from the fact that there exists an essay entitled "the method of legal science" as well as a book styled "the science of legal method". It may well be left to philology to disentangle this problem ...".

[35] *Rechtsvergleichendes Handwörterbuch,* Vol. VI, p. 17.

only to an analysis of the differences existing between individual systems and by not wanting to solve any abstract or concrete problem, its purpose being only informative. Applied comparative law, as Gutteridge distinguishes it,[36] has a different purpose than just information, but the purpose must not be of a practical nature and may serve, for example, legal philosophy in developing abstract theories, or a historian of law in tracing the beginnings and the development of individual legal institutions. At the same time, of course, these are not to be just descriptions of the individual differences, but a deeper investigation undertaken for the purpose of determining whether the differences are fundamental or chance ones, what their causes are, and what their relationship is to the general structure of the system of law wherein they arise; also to be ascertained is the effect of legal rules in practice with a view to the whole medium wherein the studied system of law operates. According to Gutteridge, the success of such a study depends on a thorough analysis which is to lead to a synthesis made for either abstract or utilitarian purposes (e.g. a reform or unification of the system of law). Gutteridge at the same time blames Rabel for trying to warrant the existence of a third trend in comparative jurisprudence, namely abstract, pure or speculative comparative study which, according to Gutteridge, may be imagined, but which, as a comparative study *in vacuo,* practically does not exist and has no justification.[37] Thus defined comparative jurisprudence (descriptive or applied) is then usable as a method, according to Gutteridge, in all forms of juridical theorical work in the spheres of both public and private law, and its results are important for both economics and sociology; such comparative study makes it possible to compare individual systems of law and helps uncover aspects which do not emerge when municipal systems of law are studied in isolation.

There is no doubt that it was primarily Gutteridge's realistic position on the problem of the existence of comparative juris-

[36] *Comparative Law,* pp. 8, 9.
[37] *Comparative Law,* p. 10.

prudence as a science or a method, which represented a reaction to the obvious failure of the French idealistic theories of Saleilles, Lambert or Lévy-Ullmann — failure which could not manifest itself at a time when each of the newly founded states in different parts of the world was building its own system of law as the sovereign legislator — that helped correct a number of views common in the early stage of development of comparative jurisprudence, characteristic of the era preceeding the Second World War. However, already at that time, contrasting with the speculative search for the "world law of the 20th century", legal positivism began to assert itself in comparative jurisprudence (especially in Germany), which meant in its consequences, that the object of jurisprudence was only the law in force, namely the valid law of one's own state; under such situation, comparative jurisprudence and, in general, the attention sometimes paid to foreign law was considered to be a basically harmful phenomenon for the current stage of one's own, valid law. To this we must add the fact that legal positivism was directed against the quest for and deduction of universal legal principles, that it was inherently opposed to any consideration whether this or that legal rule was in keeping with the requirements of justice, with the existing economic and social conditions, etc. None of this offered fertile soil for the development of comparative jurisprudence.

On top of all this there was frequently an extreme legal nationalism manifested in the overestimation of its own solutions of substantive law and underestimation of the value of foreign systems of law, which had dire consequences especially as regards the realization of certain unification efforts, which necessarily ran counter to the solutions adopted by the individual systems of municipal law, particularly in the sphere of private international law and the legal regulation of international commerce. However, already in the course of the consideration of a number of unification proposals, the endeavour often manifested itself, as a result of legal nationalism, to find a compromise (frequently inorganic) between the solution offered by individual municipal laws, which on many occasions suppressed the effort to make a functional analysis of individual institutions, that could have been reached on the basis of the comparative method. While, therefore, the idealistic search for a "world law of the 20th century" and similar trends meant, on the one hand, that the vagueness of this objective expanded the scope of comparative studies, Gutteridge's empirical approach to comparative jurisprudence, undoubtedly influenced by legal positivism, led on the other hand, to the situation where what had been once viewed as a separate branch of jurisprudence, became a mere method – often only a suffered one – applicable to the study of the individual branches of the municipal systems of law in force.

We may say in general, that even in the positivistically orientated comparative jurisprudence of the prewar years there occasionally – and timidly – occurred trends to take also into account broader aspects of the material conditions of the life of society, provided they manifested themselves in the compared rules and systems of law. Gutteridge's doctrine, too, stated – although to a limited extent – that it was necessary to study law in the light of its social or economic purpose, and that its dynamic nature rather than its static or doctrinal aspects had to be borne in mind.[38] Also Rabel stressed – especially in the postwar period – the necessity of a broader approach to the compared legal rules, and called it the "social aproach".[39] Another American author (also of German origin), Max Rheinstein,[40] asserted that "comparative law", as a special term, should cover such scientific instruction, which goes beyond a mere analytical description of the compared rules or the application of one or more existing systems of law. He felt that comparative jurisprudence should cover two fields, namely the field of a functional comparison of legal rules, and the field of the social function of law in general; as for the latter, comparative law blended in his concept with the sociology of law. Because at the same time he believed that

---

[38] A similar opinion was held by René David, *Traité,* pp. 10 and 15–25.

[39] On this point see Hall, *Comparative Law,* p. 10.

[40] "Teaching Comparative Law", *University of Chicago Law Review,* 1938, pp. 617, 619, 622, quoted in Hall, *Comparative Law,* p. 11.

the existence of legal sociology was doubtful, he recommended that the study and teaching of comparative law should be limited to the functional comparison of legal rules and institutions. However, at a later date, the trend towards sociology re-emerged in Rheinstein's works;[41] he claimed that comparative jurisprudence should seek those laws, which, according to him, existed in the legal sphere just as they did in nature; thus conceived comparative jurisprudence parallels the natural sciences. This sociologically orientated approach is sometimes promoted by generally humanistic tendencies which frequently appear in idealistically accented comparative jurisprudence. Thus, for example, Yntema speaks in connection with comparative law about a community of justice,[42] and wants to use comparative jurisprudence for finding a "humanistic concept of universal justice", etc.[43]

Similar considerations led Schnitzer[44] to formulating the eclectically substantiated view that comparative studies were a separate branch of jurisprudence, while Hall[45] tried to settle the existing doubts by demonstrating the erroneousness of those views (Gutteridge's in particular), which wanted to identify a set of findings with the method of study, and saw the main difficulty in the problem of finding the results of the comparative method applied to law. He argued that even in the natural sciences, every science had its own special methods (e.g. physics

---

[41] In his article "Teaching Tools of Comparative Law", *American Journal of Comparative Law,* 1952, p. 98, he wrote: "Comparative law is the observation and exactitude seeking science of law in general ... it searches for laws in the sense in which the word is used in "sciences", laws in the kind of Newton's laws of gravitation ... laws ... in that sense in which the word is understood in modern natural science ...". Quoted from Hall, *Comparative Law.*

[42] "Le droit comparé et l'humanisme", *Revue internationale de droit comparé,* 1958, p. 698.

[43] Similar arguments may be found in his article "Comparative Legal Research", *Michigan Law Review,* 1956, pp. 899 ff.; quoted in Hall, *Comparative Law,* p. 12.

[44] *Vergleichende Rechtslehre,* Vol. I, p. 19.

[45] *Comparative Law,* pp. 12–15.

or biology), but that nobody asserted there that method and science could be made identical; his arguments led to the conclusion that comparative jurisprudence was a social science in its own right.

The dispute whether comparative jurisprudence is a separate branch of science or just a method of comparison usable in different branches of jurisprudence, is therefore a scientific and methodological dispute which has been latently accompanying every discussion on comparative law from the beginning of this century until today. A great variety of views has been put forward in this discussion, based on different school of legal philosophy (ranging from natural law and positivism to pragmatism and sociological trends). However, the basic question to be answered is how to distinguish comparative jurisprudence from the standard branches of jurisprudence and how to solve the inseparably linked methodological problem. In the endeavour to make this distinction convincing enough, many authors have run the risk that comparative jurisprudence, if it wants to deal with legal life and manifestations of law in their whole, is often identified with legal sociology,[46] as indicated by Hall's conclusions, or with bourgeois legal philosophy.[47] Attempts are also being made to clarify the methodological problems,[48] etc.

---

[46] The relationship between comparative jurisprudence and legal sociology is very thoroughly discussed by Drobning, "Rechtsvergleichung und Rechtssoziologie," *Rabels Z.*, 1953, No. 2–3, pp. 295 ff.; for other literature see Schnitzer, *Vergleichende Rechtslehre,* Vol. 1, p. 30. Although Drobnig favours the independence of comparative jurisprudence as well as of legal sociology, the difference of the meeting points of the two, which he tries to clarify in detail as being common to both categories, shows the problem he has run into in his endeavour to draw up exact definitions.

[47] On the relationship between comparative jurisprudence and legal philosophy see Schnitzer, *Vergleichende Rechtslehre,* Vol. I, pp. 27 ff. Vol. I, pp. 27 ff.

[48] See Zweigert, *Mélanges Maury,* Vol. I, 1960, pp. 579 ff.; also Knapp, "Některé metodologické problémy srovnávací právní vědy" ("Some Methodological Problems of Comparative Jurisprudence"), *Právník (The Lawyer),* 1968, No. 2, pp. 91 ff.

### (3) The Contemporary Problems, Character and Some Tasks of Comparative Jurisprudence

The doctrinal dispute about the character of comparative jurisprudence as a branch of legal science or as a "mere" method, however, pays little respect to the fact that comparing of laws as such has become common in a number of branches of law, and it is remarkable that this is true not only of private law in the traditional sense, but also of a number of branches of public law, such as penal, contitutional or administrative law. This phenomenon should be ascribed to the influence of the general internationalization of the life of society, which cannot but also manifest itself in the sphere of jurisprudence and legal theory. Comparing of law has become essential in practically all the spheres and branches of jurisprudence, occuring mostly in a spontaneous manner and outside the theoretical or methodological dispute about the character of comparative jurisprudence; however, this fact does not mean that legal theory should not concern itself with the widespread growth of comparative jurisprudence that has taken place especially in the recent period, search for its causes, help solve the methodological problems, or study the social function of comparative jurisprudence in general and in the individual branches of law in particular. For it is obvious that comparative jurisprudence, or the use of the comparative method in the theoretical study of the individual branches of law, has ceased to be a tolerated "luxury" of theoreticians, and has become a social necessity just as other branches of the social sciences. This fact will not be altered in any way, if we view comparative jurisprudence as a separate branch of legal science or merely as a method applicable to a greater or lesser degree.

The motives for comparing systems of law are very broad and varied. They range from the traditional study of foreign systems of law, undertaken, as a rule, within the framework of the preparation of individual legislative measures or complete codifications[49] to a greater or lesser extent, when we can witness

[49] Thus, for example, the explanatory report on the Czechoslovak Code

a relatively frequent spontaneous or intentional reception of the provisions of foreign systems of law or of their fundamental principles,[50] and thereby also a certain rapprochement between individual systems of law. Going much farther is the endeavour to unify legal regulations in a particular sphere, becoming more frequent in the recent period, which is absolutely impossible without preliminary comparative studies.[51]

Although a preliminary comparative study is quite essential for some types of legislative work (e.g. in the spheres of civil law, the law of international trade, patent law, copyright, family law, labour law, etc.), while elsewhere its need is not so pronounced (e.g. in administrative law), we may assert today,

---

of International Trade expressly states that the authors of the draft had taken full account of the experiences gained in Czechoslovak foreign trade as well as of international experience; an expression of this experience are, on the one hand, the General Conditions of Delivery of the Council of Mutual Economic Assistance, and, on the other hand, the Hague Draft of uniform laws concerning the conclusion of international sales contracts and the international sales contract. In order that the draft of the Code be sufficiently in keeping with the demands raised internationally on the regulation of international commerce, an assessment was also made of the rules governing these questions in modern foreign civil and commercial codes (e.g. the Swiss Act Concerning the Law of Obligations, the Civil Code of the Russian Soviet Federal Socialist Republic of 1922, the Greek Civil Code, the Italian Civil Code, the 1948 Egyptian Civil Code, the Ethiopian Civil Code of 1960, the Uniform Commercial Code of the United States (the Pennsylvania Act of 1953), the Principles of the Civil Legislation of the USSR of 1961, and the Ghana Sales of Goods Act of 1962).

[50] For the solutions contained in the Czechoslovak Code of International Trade and the Uniform Hague Laws see the author's works "Poznámky k haagským návrhům právní úpravy mezinárodní kupní smlouvy" ("Remarks on the Hague Projects for a Legal Regulation of the International Sale of Goods"), *Časopis pro mezinárodní právo (Czechoslovak Journal of International Law")*, 1965, No. 1, pp. 41 ff., and "Die Grundzüge des tschechoslowakischen Gesetztes über den internationalen Handeln", *Rabels Zeitschrift*, 1966, No. 2, pp. 296—323.

[51] A survey of these efforts was given in the general report submitted to the Seventh International Congress of Comparative Law at Uppsala in 1966 by Jean Limpens, "Le problème de la coordination des mouvements d'unification du droit".

that the success of any legislative regulation depends in many aspects — although, most certainly, not completely — on knowledge gained (directly or indirectly) from foreign systems of law and their mutual comparison, as well as from comparison between these systems and one's own.

However, we are concerned with more than just legislative regulations of a municipal character or a discussion on the international influences and interrelationships, which must manifest themselves in the sphere of municipal regulations, seemingly determined only by the needs of the material life of the society of the given state (e.g. the influence of international trade or the international division of labour in the sphere of what is known as economic law). In this connection we deem it necessary to underline the universal phenomenon of economic integration which manifests itself in different forms and with varying intensity not only in almost all parts of the world, but also in both the capitalist and the socialist economic systems; integration is the direct economic consequence and form of the internationalization of economic life, which realized the necessity of the rapprochement or unification of law sometimes quite clearly, while at other times it only seems to sense it; nevertheless, it is quite obvious that sooner or later every integration effort will have to deal with this matter. Thus far, the longest step in this direction has been taken by the European Economic Community[52] which raised as one of its objectives also the "rapprochement of the legislation of the member-states in order to facilitate the functioning of the Common Market", for which purpose the EEC Council is to issue special directives on the recommendation of the Commission. But also in the Council of Mutual Economic Assistance, which operates under quite different principles, the question of a rapprochement of the systems of law of the individual member states arises not only in connection

---

[52] See the author's article "Základní právní problémy Evropského hospodářského společenství" ("Basic Legal Problems of the European Economic Community"), *Studie z mezinárodního práva (Studies in International Law)*, Vol. 9, pp. 81—123.

with the legal regulation of foreign trade, but also, e.g., in connection with the problem specialization and co-operation in the production sphere,[53] in scientific and technical co-operation, protection of patents, etc. We could, of course, list a number of similar examples from different spheres of the legal regulation of social relations.

We believe that the importance the internationalization of economic and social life in general has for the growth and development of individual legal institutions is not apparent at first sight and tends to be underestimated; here, too, comparative jurisprudence could probably discover a number of most interesting connections and interrelationships. A lawyer raised on his own, municipal law and operating only within its framework is usually not willing to attach any major importance to the process of transformation of systems of law taking place as a result of the internationalization of the whole life of society,[54] which does not apply to Western Europe alone. More is also involved than just the impact of international law and the formulation of the rules of international law, which is increasingly taking place in different spheres not only within the framework of the activities of international organizations of both universal character (the United Nations and its specialized agencies) and special or regional nature (integration groupings, the regional bodies of the United Nations, such economic unions as Benelux in Western Europe, etc.); the vast sphere of contractual arrange-

---

[53] The discussion between lawyers from the socialist countries is still in the beginning on this point. See, e.g., M. M. Boguslavski, *Sovietskoe gosudarstvo i pravo,* 1966, No. 8, J. Růžička in *Časopis pro mezinárodní právo (Czechoslovak Journal of International Law),* 1966, No. 4, p. 322, or P. Kalenský in *Časopis pro mezinárodní právo (Czechoslovak Journal of International Law),* 1967, No. 1, p. 43, P. Kalenský—A. Wagner, "Ke kolizní právní problematice smluv o mezinárodní socialistické výrobní specializaci a kooperaci" (Conflicts of Law in Contracts on Socialist Specialization and Co-operation of Production), *Právník (The Lawyer),* 1971, No. 8, p. 642—654.

[54] See Marc Ancel, "Le rôle de la recherche juridique comparative dans la coopération juridique internationale", *De conflictu legum,* Sijthoff, Leyden, 1962, p. 33.

ments in the field of international law requires that municipal law should be placed in harmony with international law in one way or another. We might quote as a rather recent example the International Covenant on Economic, Social and Cultural Rights or the International Covenant on Civil and Political Rights, both adopted at the Twenty-First Session of the U.N. General Assembly in 1966 (proceeding from the Universal Declaration of Human Rights), which, if ratified, shoud greatly influence the content of municipal laws in spheres which, as spheres reserved for the internal jurisdiction of states, had been, until quite recently, completely or mostly closed to the internationalization trends.

In the present period, when the world has been undergoing a number of radical changes under different influences, in particular the impact of the scientific and technological revolution, comparative jurisprudence, or the use of the comparative method in the individual branches of jurisprudence, has an increasing and a growing scope of activity. In this connection, some ideas have been raised on the role of comparative jurisprudence and the possibility of its social application in the world of today. The realization of the conclusion that the legal world of the last third of the 20th century cannot do with systems of law developed – as regards the principal capitalist states – in the 19th century has often led to a renaissance of the once universalistic and idealistic tendencies. Marc Ancel[55] believes that the situation today parallels to some extent the situation in which the lawyers of the Renaisance and of the late 18th century had found themselves. He notes that the task of the former had been made easier by the role then played by Roman law, which had been considered as the embodiment of rationality and as the common legal method of the world of those days; and at the end of the 18th century the role played by Roman law was replaced by the universalistic concept of natural law. The question then arises, whether this role in the world of today should not be played, *mutatis mutandis*, by comparative jurisprudence which,

---

55 *Ibid.*, p. 33.

of course, cannot fall back on the universalism of Roman law or the rationality of natural law, but whose task it is, allegedly, to rebuild individual municipal laws in order to adjust them to the spirit of international co-operation, called for by the demands of co-existence and international understanding.

André Tunc, another leading French authority on comparative law, discusses the possibilities offered by comparative jurisprudence for the promotion of better international understanding[56] and appreciates the role it could play in its particular sphere for the benefit of both world peace and justice imbued with the spirit of humanism.

Both the aforesaid considerations are, of course, idealistically motivated and inspired; Ancel proceeds from the legal philosophy of François Gény and the distinction this author makes between the concepts of *donné* and *construit*. While the *donné* is concentrated in the systems of law presently in force, it is the role of comparative studies – roughly said – to find the *construit;* this is obviously a certain modification of natural law thinking. André Tunc, in turn, bases his views on the Christian humanism of Teilhard de Chardin.

The universally humanistic approach of the two authors is reflected, for example, in the stress they lay on the "humanistic community of justice", which is to be built also with some help from comparative jurisprudence. This has given rise to a tendency aiming at the mutual adjustment of individual systems of law, which is conceived very broadly and which might be interpreted in its consequences as an endeavour to assert the convergence of the individual systems of law without paying the basic and determining respect to the economic, political, social and cultural conditions and objectives from which these systems proceed. The opinion voiced by a number of authors in the capitalist states also evoked a response from some authors in the

---

[56] A. Tunc, "La contribution possible des études juridiques comparatives à une meilleure compréhension entre nations", *Revue internationale de droit comparé,* 1964, No. 1, pp. ff.; "Le juriste et la noosphère; la fonction possible des études comparatives dans le monde contemporain", *Problèmes contemporains de droit comparé,* Vol. II, Tokyo, 1962, pp. 493 ff.

socialist states, who have raised the question whether there exists comparative jurisprudence "as a science" and whether it is possible to compare on a scientific basis the systems of law in force in the socialist and in the capitalist states, which authors in the latter states have been recently quite often doing.[57]

All these authors at first opposed the view that it was currently possible to prove the existence of comparative legal science as a separate branch of the science of jurisprudence, with its own object of study, whose existence is an essential precondition for the constitution of any independent branch of science. They rather tended towards the opinion – promoted in bourgeois comparative jurisprudence by Gutteridge and his school of thought – that comparative legal science was only a method applicable to all branches of jurisprudence; of course, if this method were to be truly scientific, it had to meet a number of conditions the individual authors listed, naturally laying special stress on the marxist scientific approach towards these comparative studies. We may therefore say that the doubts expressed in the legal science of the capitalist states about the independent existence of comparative jurisprudence also appear in the legal theory of the socialist states.

V. Knapp pointed out as early as in 1963[58] that the question

---

57 In Czechoslovak literature see R. Bystrický, "Za marxistickou srovnávací právovědu" ("For a Marxist Comparative Jurisprudence"), *Právník (The Lawyer),* 1962, pp. 625 ff., and the discussion raised by this article (J. Boguszak, "K otázce tzv. srovnávací právovědy" ("On Comparative Jurisprudence", *Právník (The Lawyer),* 1962, No. 9, pp. 803–806; M. Svoboda, "Ještě k marxistické srovnávací právovědě" ("Once More on a Marxist Comparative Jurisprudence"), *Právník (The Lawyer),* 1963, No. 5, p. 388; V. Knapp, "K otázce socialistické srovnávací právní vědy" ("On a Socialist Comparative Jurisprudence"), *Právník (The Lawyer),* 1963, No. 5, pp. 391–402). Also see V. Knapp, "Verträge im tschechoslowakischen Recht, Ein Beitrag zur Rechtsvergleichung zwischen Ländern mit verschiedener Gesellschaftsordnung", *Rabels Zeitschrift,* 1962, No. 3, pp. 495–518, in which the author reacts to the views expressed by D. Loeber in "Rechtsvergleichung zwischen Ländern mit verchiedener Wirtschaftsordnung", *Rabels Zeitschrift,* 1961, No. 2, pp. 221 ff.

58 "K otázce socialistické srovnávací právní vědy" ("On a Socialist Comparative Jurisprudence"), *Právník (The Lawyer),* 1963, No. 5, p. 391.

of the existence of comparative jurisprudence did not seem to be the principal matter in the whole discussion; the main point continued to be, how socially useful was the comparative study of different systems of law and how and for what purpose such comparison was to be made. His opinion on the existence of what was called general socialist jurisprudence (i.e. one that could produce new, truthful findings also by comparing socialist and capitalist law) was negative, although he did, on the whole, lay great stress on properly executed comparative study, stressing that scientific response to the views (erroneous) on the gradual convergence of the law of the socialist and capitalist states could result in some practically valuable knowledge. The abovementioned discussion indicates that none of the authors who had taken part in it had claimed that it was impossible to make a scientific comparison between the laws of the socialist and the capitalist states because of the differences existing in their political and economic foundations, and that all of them underlined — although using different arguments — the importance of such comparison.

In contrast to this general comparative jurisprudence, Knapp considers as more convincing the existence of socialist comparative jurisprudence limited in its object to the study of the systems of law of the socialist countries, although here, too, he agreed with Boguszak that it did not constitute a special field of legal science.[59] As regards comparison of the systems of law of the socialist countries, all those, who participated in the discussion, pointed to its necessity for bringing these systems closer to each other in different spheres. It was only quite recently that Viktor Knapp began to consider comparative jurisprudence as a special branch of legal science.[60]

We fully agree with Viktor Knapp as regards his original view that the existence of comparative jurisprudence was not the

---

[59] *Ibid.*, p. 400.

[60] See his article "Některé metodologické problémy srovnávací právní vědy" ("Some Methodological Problems of Comparative Jurisprudence"), *Právník (The Lawyer)*, 1968, No. 2, pp. 91 ff.

main topic of the discussion, as well as with the views of all the participants in the aforesaid discussion on the importance of comparative jurisprudence both in relationship to the legal systems of the socialist states and in relationship to the legal systems of the capitalist states.

However, we believe that there are many weaknesses in those assertions, which deny comparative jurisprudence the character of a science and present its problems only as those of a method applicable to individual, specifically defined fields of legal science; this attitude basically proceeds from the categorization of the system of law. Comparative jurisprudence is of primary importance for a scientific study of law not only because it is of great help in solving the problems involved in the individual, traditionally defined spheres of jurisprudence, but also because it facilitates overcoming, by a synthetic approach to the subject-matter, the basically static nature of dividing municipal law into individual fields which, of course, are far from identical in the individual states both in their definition and their content; thus, it provides far greater knowledge of reality than could offer any individual field of municipal law using, perhaps, what is being called the comparative method. At the same time, a thus conceived comparative jurisprudence does not want to be – or can be – a general theory of government and law – something that J. Boguszak seems to "worry" about – although there is no doubt that it is of as major an importance for the general theory, as it is for the other fields of the science concerned with state and law.

We believe that the purpose of all the branches of legal science is basically identical, namely to present a true picture of the complex social phenomenon that law undoubtedly is, and there should be no doubt either about the fact that this picture can be presented not only by the traditional branches of legal science but by legal philosophy, the general theory of state and law, and comparative jurisprudence as well.

What is involved, is not only the fact that the standard branches of legal science, even though they may make use of the comparative method, naturally tend towards concerning themselves only with the subject-matter which is their object in the usual, "municipal" categorization of the systems of law and jurisprudence, and ignore what in other legal systems does not belong to the corresponding branches. As an example, we might confront the Anglo-American and the Continental categorization of law and legal science. What is, however, also involved, is the fact that until quite recently, it was precisely the standard categorization of the system of jurisprudence, which more or less obstructed a comprehensive view of certain development trends manifesting themselves, for example, in the legal systems of the capitalist states in the management of the national economy both on the international and domestic levels (integration, state interference with economic life), which comparative jurisprudence could have detected.

We therefore believe that comparative jurisprudence has a dual character. There is comparative jurisprudence and the comparison of legal institutions viewed as a method, and there is, perhaps, no need to stress that it is not an exclusive method or one which at least tries to claim an appearance of exclusiveness; this method is undoubtedly one of the methods of research and scholarly work, which is applicable in all the branches of legal science, as justly pointed out by Gutteridge. However, in another sense, comparative jurisprudence has also become a social science in the true meaning of the term, which, similarly as the general theory of state and law or legal sociology, is to help us obtain scientifically true knowledge; this should certainly not be an end in itself to the extent where we could speak of "comparative law for the sake of comparative law", but should constitute one, far from insignificant, component of knowledge, which no rigidly defined branch of legal science can offer. This character of comparative jurisprudence, too, serves as an instrument whereby we may overcome legal positivism and an academically rigid approach to the problems under study.

When stressing the gradual formation of comparative jurisprudence as a social science in the true sense of the word (thus far we can probably speak only of science *in statu nascendi*), we do so in the belief that this distinction cannot be claimed by any comparative jurisprudence, but only by a science, which does not use only formally logical abstractions with the objective of obtaining universal concepts, but which views legal form in connection with its socio-economic content. Thus, the same principles apply to such comparative jurisprudence, as regards the method of work, which must be observed in the case of any scientific study in legal science. The criterion of the truthfulness of knowledge must therefore be the combination of legal form and its socio-economic content, which prevents the isolation of the form and the attainment of conclusions which by mere logical abstraction, based on an identity of legal forms, would wrongly identify the socio-economic substance of the law. It is precisely in this field, too, that marxist comparative jurisprudence has great opportunities. In the dispute concerning the nature of comparative jurisprudence as a science or a method, the substance of the matter was sometimes obscured by the fact that while comparison and the comparative method are indeed one of the methods of acquiring knowledge, this in no way signifies that comparative jurisprudence uses the comparative method only; if comparative jurisprudence is to become a true science, it must not limit itself to comparison only, but must also make use of other methods, especially analysis and synthesis, analogy, classification, induction and deduction, and the historical method, while the general basis of knowledge must be the marxist dialectical method. Naturally, the methodological questions of comparative jurisprudence far exceed the scope of the present chapter; let us just note that we view as most unconvincing assertions that comparison is one of the methods of acquiring knowledge, which seemingly precludes the existence of comparative jurisprudence "as a science"; this is as if somebody tried to deny history the character of a science merely because it makes use of the historical method.

Although it is true that it is the essential prerequisite of every science to have its objective and method defined, we must realize that no science is constituted at a single stroke, but that its constitution is a process that takes some time. When we bear in mind the relatively static nature of the categorization of jurisprudence, which basically depends on the categorization or division of the system of law, we may probably assert that we are witnessing the process of the gradual formation of comparative jurisprudence as a new branch of legal science, whose object is not only the knowledge of foreign law but also comparison, which may take place to a different extent and with a different motivation. The social justification and necessity of this branch of legal science is dictated by the internationalization of the life of society, which cannot but also affect the sphere of law and legal science. In the period of peaceful co-existence of states with different socio-economic systems, comparative jurisprudence has become a necessity. The importance of comparative jurisprudence for bringing the legal systems of the states of the socialist community of nations closer together is beyond any doubt.

A thus conceived comparative jurisprudence does not, naturally, strive for an idealistically motivated search of a common law for all mankind or a world law of the 20th century as thought of by Saleilles or Lévy-Ullmann. Comparative jurisprudence (whether viewed as a science or as a method) may be of different importance in different spheres of the life of society, dictated in all cases by the degree of internationalization in the respective sphere. Some branches of law, such as private international law, cannot do without comparative jurisprudence (both as a science and a method); the same is true of the legal regulation of international trade.

## CHAPTER 3
## The Role of Comparative Jurisprudence in Private International Law

We have already mentioned in the introduction to this part of the present work, that the mutual relationship between private international law and comparative jurisprudence was deeply affected by the fact that both private international law and comparative jurisprudence proceeded from the plurality of legal systems, which provided the basis of their existence. This does not mean, of course, that these two fields of study are identical, that one can replace the other, or that the former can suppress the latter and *vice versa.* Since we stated already in the previous chapter our opinion on the character of comparative jurisprudence, the definion of its relations to private international law requires only a brief mention of the object of private international law.

In view of the fact that we discussed the complex of questions relating to the object and nature of private international law in a different place,[1] it will be perhaps sufficient to recall that in our opinion modern private international law should not be understood only as the law of conflict of laws, devised to settle "clinically" conflicts arising between different legal systems, but as that branch of law, which governs civil-law or private-law relations, characterized by the existence of a foreign element, *in toto,* and which therefore also includes rules of substantive and procedural law, that envisage the existence of the foreign element and are designed to govern social relations

---

[1] See Part Four of the present work and the author's article "K předmětu a povaze mezinárodního práva soukromého a k otázce jeho místa v systému práva" ("The Object and Nature of Private International Law and Its Place in the System of Law"), *Časopis pro mezinárodní právo (Czechoslovak Journal of International Law),* 1960 (IV), No. 2, pp. 81–102.

characterized by the presence of the foreign element. Under this concept, private international law thus includes, beside the law of conflict of laws, which constitutes its "classical component", also what is known as direct rules, both of substantive law – either internationally unified or municipal only – and of procedural law, the latter specifically bearing in mind relations with an international element and constituting the international law of civil procedure.[2] This trend is being generally manifested in the modern theory of private international law[3] in contrast to older doctrine, especially German, which viewed private international law and the law of conflict of laws as synonyms. Once we accept this modern concept of private international law, we come to the conclusion that also the law of international trade, which governs the relations between individual subjects, as they arise from international commercial contacts with their foreign trade partners, forms a part of private international law in the aforesaid sense; at the same time, the purpose of the internationally unified law of international trade is not to settle clinically the conflicts that arise between different systems of law, but to prevent their occurrence. We believe, therefore, that this definition of private international law is one of the consequences of the internationalization of the life of society and of the international division of labour, and of the resulting differentiation between relations of a purely municipal character and relations characterized by the existence of a foreign element. In Czechoslovakia this development has quite apparently been expedited by the additional differentiation between relationships under civil law, necessarily brought about – in our opinion – by the enactment of a separate Code of International Trade which in many respects had to include among its

---

[2] See Kalenský, "K obecným otázkám tzv. mezinárodního práva procesního" ("General Problems of the So-called International Law of Civil Procedure"), *Právník (The Lawyer)*, 1957, No. 4, pp. 326–340.

[3] E.g. H. Batiffol, *L'objet général du droit international privé... est l'ensemble des règles applicables aux seules personnes privées dans les relations de la société internationale. (Traité de droit international privé*, 1953, 3.)

provisions civil-law maters that are mostly missing in the new Civil Code.[4]

Private international law and its study are characterized by a number of specific features which ensue from the fact that the object of private international law (irrespective of whether it proceeds from municipal rules or rules of international law) are relations characterized by the existence of an international element; thus, every regulation, if it is to meet its purpose, should also be in keeping with the needs of the international life of society. Although there still "exist as many private international laws as there are states", the science of private international law is maintaining its international character, but, of course, we cannot claim that it is a unified one. Another factor strengthening the international elements in private international law are the links existing between private international law and public international law, which we have already discussed elsewhere in the present work.[5]

Under this situation, the importance of comparative jurisprudence and comparison in general for private international law and for its science appears quite clearly; as we shall further see, we may draw some more detailed distinctions in their concrete functions and the relations between them. A truly scientific application of comparative jurisprudence in private international law is, of course, sometimes hampered by the approach of those authors, who often view the individual problems of private international law in general and of the law of conflict of laws in particular in a static manner, reducing its importance to

---

[4] Although a differentiation was made in the form of separate codes for each sphere of law, this differentiation has not erased the civil-law character of the social relations governed by these codes, and the question remains open, whether it may not have been more expedient not to draw such a drastic line between the individual categories of civil-law relations.

[5] For these links (and differences) see the first, third and fourth parts of the present work and the author's study "K předmětu a povaze mezinárodního práva soukromého a k otázce jeho místa v systému práva" ("The Object and Nature of Private International Law and Its Place in the System of Law"), *Časopis pro mezinárodní právo (Czechoslovak Journal of International Law)*, 1960, No. 2, pp. 81–102.

the status of a mere "technical" aid, a guiding line designed for the court – not the parties – to facilitate the solution of individual problems. Naturally, this concept obscures the substance, development and transformation of private international law and, in particular, the dependence of the individual conflict solutions on the economic system of the society at every stage of its development, which can be rather well detected in this sphere, although it may not always be direct and immediate.[6] In the contemporary theory of private international law, comparative work has become essential, and the comparative method is used by the great majority of all authors; private international law is also frequently taught at universities from the comparative aspect because only comparison can offer a better and more exact understanding of one's own private international law. An example in this respect is provided by the system used by the American author of German origin, Ernst Rabel, whose work on this topic has become a classic.[7] However, as we have already pointed out, comparative study can be successfully used in private international law only if it is not viewed as mechanical comparison but as one of the methods making possible a true understanding of reality in its broader connections.

There exists a fundamental difference between private international law and what is called "comparative law"; while private international law is one of the branches of the valid law of every state, comparative jurisprudence is only one of the branches of legal science or just a method applicable to the individual branches of legal science. If we compare the purpose of private international law and the purpose of comparative law,

---

[6] The outstanding Swiss author M. Gutzwiller expressly underlines in his study "Le développement historique du droit international privé", *Recueil des Cours*, 1929, Vol. IV, p. 376, the assumed independence of private international law of any material conditions, when he says: "*... le droit international privé est absolument étranger à ces considérations matérielles ...* and *... les questions des conflicts des lois civiles renferment un problème purement juridique, voir technique, abandonné dans une mesure bien large aux décisions d'un petit comité d'experts*".

[7] E. Rabel, *Conflict of Laws. A Comparative Study*, 4 vols., University of Michigan Law School, 1945–1958.

we find that the primary importance of the latter rests in the fact that by explaining and assessing the differences existing between individual systems of law, which stand out primarily from the comparative viewpoint, it makes possible both the selective function of the law of conflict of laws, determining which of the laws involved should be applied, and the preventive elimination of conflicts through uniform rules of private international law under the concept explained above. Thus the very existence of private international law and, in particular, of the law of conflict of laws as its component part has rested from the beginning of its existence on the premise of comparison of the provisions of the conflicting systems of law.[8] In this respect, we may once more point to the famous statement made by Master Aldric in the 12th century, that the judge should apply that of the conflicting laws, which he finds more useful and better.[9] We must at the same time see that although comparison is inseparably linked with private international law, the principal function of the law of conflict of laws, namely the choice of the applicable substantive law, is influenced and facilitated by comparison but not replaced or suppressed by it. Similarly, viewed from the other side, private international law cannot suppress or replace the purpose and objective of comparative jurisprudence in the sphere of civil or private law.

Although, quite naturally, the judge who must apply the private international law of his own country and, under its provisions, possibly a foreign law, may not be expected or required to have a special knowledge of comparative jurisprudence, his activity in this sphere calls for comparison. This is envisaged in specially underlined cases also by the valid Czechoslovak law governing private international and procedural law – the Act No. 97/1963 – when it instructs the judge in many places not only to apply the decisive foreign law but also to study, still before applying it, its impact on the possible outcome of the pro-

---

[8] E. Balogh, "Le rôle du droit comparé dans le droit international privé", *Recueil des Cours,* 1936, Vol. 3, p. 578.

[9] See Part Two, Chapter 2, Div. 5, of the present work.

ceedings. In this connection we may point to Section 22 of the aforesaid Act, which provides for the applicable law in matrimonial matters. Under this Section, divorce is governed by the law of the state whose citizens the married couple were at the beginning of the divorce proceedings; however, if a foreign law should be applied, which does not permit divorce or does so under extremely harsh circumstances and the spouses, or at least one of them, have been living in the Czechoslovak Socialist Republic for a longer period of time, Czechoslovak law is to be applied.[10]

However, the connection between comparison of different systems of law and private international law is not manifested only in the cases specifically stressed in the law; we shall try to show further in the present study that it is a connection esential for the purpose of private international law in general, without which private international law could not fulfil its function as a branch of law. In doing so, we shall first discuss the role of comparing different systems of law and of comparative jurisprudence in the law of conflict of laws, and, finally, in the legal regulations governing international commerce.

In private international law more is involved than a mere necessity of knowing and applying foreign law on the basis of the reference contained in the respective conflict rule; in its substance, the application of foreign law is a culmination of the conflict rule, where the homogenous and in a way exclusive sphere of the *lex fori* is invaded by foreign law whose application the legislator must envisage but which, in its own way, disturbs this homogeneity and exclusiveness of the municipal law. A study of the process of application of foreign law in private international law gives rise to a number of theoretical and complex problems; first among these is the assessment of the nature of the foreign law applied from the viewpoint of the legal system of the state whose court is called upon to decide

---

[10] The same principle was applied in the case of Section 20, par. 3, of the Act, concerning the law applicable to adoption, Section 3, par. 2, regarding the legal capacity of aliens, and in other provisions.

the respective case, i.e. the definition of the relations between the applied foreign law and the domestic law – whether the application of the foreign law does not make this law a "fact" which must be pleaded and proven to the deciding court, or whether it remains a law. If the foreign law is not viewed as a "fact", the question arises, whether in the process of its application it does not, perhaps, become a part of the municipal law and is thus "received", "naturalized" or "incorporated" by the law of the forum, or whether its nature remains unaffected by its application and that, to say it briefly, it remains to be foreign law. These are the fundamental, we might say "philosophical", questions involved in the application of foreign law, which we have tried to answer in another place.[11] They are linked with a set of additional problems where the points of friction between the conflicting laws are more specific; some of these we shall point out here.

We may say in general that a judge who is called upon to decide cases involving private international law must compare the conflicting laws both when seeking the decisive substantive law on the basis of the respective conflict rule and when applying foreign law. Such comparison involves in most cases a comparison between the possibly applicable foreign law and the law of the deciding court *(lex fori)*; however, in some cases comparison must be made between two or more foreign laws. We may say that such comparison required by the postulates of conflict-law and justice. Although there are undoubtedly cases where the judge feels that he has fulfilled his task by applying the law to which the respective conflict rule refers him, it should be borne in mind, that private international law calls not only for the determination of the applicable law, but that this determination is inseparably linked with the result of the proceedings as they arise from substantive law. This result must be anti-

---

[11] See Part Six of the present work and the author's study "Podstata a povaha aplikace cizího práva" ("The Substance and Nature of Application of Foreign Law"), *Studie z mezinárodního práva (Studies in International Law)*, Vol. 13, pp. 41 ff.

cipated already when the applicable law is being sought and this, naturally, leads to a comparison of laws, which is essential in the whole sphere of private international law.

Comparison takes place, first of all, in the very sphere of the law of conflict of laws. In many legal systems, as we know, the system of conflict rules is not complete and thus the existing gaps in one's own law of conflict of laws must be bridged. This method of comparing conflict-law solutions is quite common in contemporary private international law; it is quite frequent in England, the United States, France, Belgium, the Netherlands, West Germany, or the Scandinavian countries, usually with the aim of finding in a foreign conflict-law solution of a similar case an inspiration for setling one's own case. Here again, of course, a significant factor is the common, historical background of the private international law of the European continental states on the one hand, and the close relationship existing between the English and the North American law of conflict of laws on the other hand. This method of bridging the gaps existing in one's own law of conflict of laws — thus, for example, the non-existence of written conflict rules in the law of conflict of laws of obligations of a number of states is well known, just as the vagueness of judicial precedents on this point[12] — is promoted by the similarity of the situations to be solved and the endeavour of scholars and practising lawyers alike — which has its historical roots and a rational core — to have conflict problems settled everywhere identically as much as possible, in other words, that the same substantive law should be applied in different coutries on the basis of the same facts of a case.

A special type of comparing conflict rules occurs in the case of *renvoi* and transmission; the question we must ask is whether the reference to foreign law contained in the conflict rule is a reference to foreign substantive law or to a foreign private international law; therefore, any use of *renvoi* calls for the comparison of conflict rules or several systems of law. Naturally, here we cannot deal with special emphasis and at length with

---

[12] P. Kalenský, *Obligační statut (Conflict of Laws).*

the grounds listed in favour of the institution of *renvoi* or against it; let us just point to the fact that this general question of private international law is bitterly disputed in the doctrine of this law. In Czechoslovakia, the legislator expressly permitted the possibility of *renvoi* and transmission,[13] but motivated its applications quite vaguely when he provided that the decisive factor for the admission of *renvoi* was that it should be in keeping with the reasonable and just settlement of the relation involved. *Renvoi* is a classical problem of long standing in the theory of private international law; however, no matter what the opinion concerning it may be, there is no doubt that a comparison of the solutions offered by the law of conflict of laws (and often of substantive law as well) is a prerequisite of any theoretical and practical consideration.

Another general problem arising in private international law is that of the conflict of qualifications, which is again marked by a considerable difference of opinion. It involves basically the solution of the problem of a conflicting placement of certain social relations into legal categories in different systems of law. We know that the placement of these relations under legal provisions differs in different legal systems; consequently, the assessment of this question is of primary importance for the application of the decisive substantive law i.e. also because the law of conflict of laws of every state has only one conflict rule covering whole groups of legal relations which are usually governed in substantive law by a large number of provisions. The answer to the question whether a given case involves movables or immovables, a matrimonial propery settlement or inheritance, a right *in rem* or an obligation, etc., then becomes of primary importance for finding the decisive substantive law. Once again, here we cannot weigh the reasons supporting or opposing the solution of the conflict of qualifications under the *lex fori*, as recommended by Kahn and Bartin, or discuss whether the extremes of such qualification can be corrected by qualification under the *lex causae*, as recommended by Martin

---

[13] See Section 35 of the Act No. 97/1963.

Wolff and many other authors. It is, of course, interesting that Franz Kahn himself, as one of the original promoters of qualification under the *lex fori,* seems to have sensed the untenability of the procedure he recommended, when he pointed out that private international law, which is a part of the municipal law of every state, could be scientifically studied and developed only by the international method; one cannot interpret private international law by considering it only from the viewpoint of one's own municipal law but should constantly compare it with foreign laws and thereby attain the necessary harmony.[14] There is no doubt that the process of qualification and solving conflicts of qualifications rests on the comparative method for which the knowledge of the foreign law is naturally essential. In connection with the solution of conflicts of qualifications, special stress was laid on the use of the comparative method by Rabel and Becket who felt that this method of qualification could eliminate the extreme harshness and injustices resulting from qualification under the *lex fori.*[15] Both these authors essentially believed that certain terms and concepts used in private international law differed (precisely in view of the international element and the international purpose of the respective rules) from the terms used in municipal law; these terms, whose use should be universal in private international law, should be ascertained by study and with the help of the analytical method, which should find general principles with universal applicability to replace terms of a purely municipal scope for the purposes of private international law. Although it may be very controversial to formulate the principles envisaged by Rabel and Becket, the theory promoted by these two authors basically arises from the fact that in solving conflicts of qualifications, one must always proceed from a comparison of the inidividual terms and concepts of the conflicting laws, irrespective of how

---

[14] Kahn, *Abhandlungen,* Vol. I, pp. 311 ff. and 419 ff.

[15] Rabel, "Das Problem der Qualifikation", *Zeitschrift für ausländisches und internationales Privatrecht,* 1931, pp. 24 ff., and "Le problème de la qualification", *Revue de droit international privé,* 1933, No. 1; Becket in the *British Yearbook of International Law,* 1934, pp. 46 ff.

the conflict of qualifications will be settled in the given case. It is also quite certain that the international element and the application of foreign law required in private international law the abandonment of the positivistically exaggerated rigidity in the definition of certain legal categories, which was hardly compatible with the purpose of private international law because it caused unjustifiable harshness.[16]

Another institution of private international law which we encounter in all legal systems, namely the category of public order, which underlines the role played by the fundamental principles of the system of law of the deciding court as the criterion for the possible application of a foreign law, as a certain "safety valve", requires from the judge a knowledge of the foreign law and its comparison with his own law prior to the former's application. But even in this case we should bear in mind that the foreign law as such, *in abstracto,* is not contrary to the public order of the forum, but that the court must always ask whether the public order permits a concrete application of a concrete rule of the foreign substantive law; it is to this substance of the application of public order that the comparison in a concrete case must be subjected. For some experience gained especially with the application of Soviet law in the years preceding the Second World War shows that an abstract comparison of laws and legal systems can result in solutions which purposefully preclude the application of a foreign substantive law even in cases where it is fully warranted.

We have tried to demonstrate on some of the general institutions of the law of conflict of laws how deeply the comparison

---

[16] See, e.g., the reaction to some Czechoslovak cases in Petrů–Steiner, "K problematice pravomoci československých soudců ve věcech péče o nezletilé" ("Jurisdiction of Czechoslovak Courts in Matters concerning Child Care"), *Časopis pro mezinárodní právo (Czechoslovak Journal of International Law),* 1966, No. 1, pp. 41 ff., and Heyer, "K problematice pravomoci a příslušnosti čs. soudů ve vztazích k cizině" ("The Jurisdiction of Czechoslovak Courts in Legal Relation with a Foreign Element"), *Časopis pro mezinárodní právo (Czechoslovak Journal of International Law),* 1966, No. 3, pp. 266 ff.

of legal systems penetrates all of private international law. These examples could, of course, be expanded by other conflict problems of application of substantive law as well as by venturing into the sphere of the international law of civil procedure as regards, for instance, conflicts of judical competence or the recognition and enforcement of foreign judicial decision, or matters of the legal status of aliens, reciprocity, etc.

All these examples show how important it is to know foreign law for solving cases in the sphere of private international law. However, there is more to it than this aspect alone. Comparative jurisprudence has, beside its importance for private international law in solving concrete cases, an additional, far-reaching significance manifested, in particular, in the whole endeavour to develop this branch of law still further by theoretical work as well as by the various efforts at international codification and unification. It is characteristic of the contemporary science of private international law, that it quite frequently uses the comparative method and that the comparison of individual conflict rules and judgements in concrete cases provides it with new material for considering what procedures are most expedient. In this sense we may truly speak of comparative private international law whose existence is essential since it makes it possible to understand the phenomenon of private international law in its whole on the one hand, and, on the other hand, helps to promote the development and drawing together of the individual "municipal" private international laws, which is a difficult and protracted, but essential process. The comparative study of individual municipal laws in the sphere of private international law and the law of international trade shows that in private international law there exists a number of common solutions, and that these solutions provide the starting point for the "rapprochement" of the private international laws of individual states. We could list many examples of such a "rapprochement" and of such solutions. However, since we shall discuss further in our study the questions of the relations between comparative jurisprudence and the legal regulation of international commercial relations, we shall only point to an example from the sphere of the law of conflict of laws of obligations, which is closest to the sphere of international commercial relations and where the comparative approach to the subject-matter made possible a considerable "rapprochement" not only in the solution of such a complex question as the sphere of the influence of the autonomy of will of the contracting parties on the determination of the proper law of contract, but also in finding the method of determining the points of contact in the individual types of synallagmatic contracts which most often occur in foreign trade in cases where the contracting parties failed to choose the applicable law.[17] Other examples are offered when we compare the individual attempts at unification made, for instance, by the Hague Conference on Private International Law and national codifications in different spheres; however, such comparisons are not the topic of the present work and we have therefore merely pointed to them in general.

We may thus say that the science of private international law is gradually acquiring in the present period the character of a comparative science and that precisely this method of work is helping it find a synthesis in the form of general findings and concepts; this approach is dictated by the fact that individual municipal private international laws are to serve in their substance the needs of not only the national but also the international life of society. We believe that the value of comparative jurisprudence for private international law as that branch of law, which is most often involved with foreign systems of law, is quite obvious and that without comparative jurisprudence, private international law could not fulfil its role and purpose.

---

[17] On these questions see the author's monograph *Obligační statut (The Conflict of Laws).*

## CHAPTER 4
## Some Notes on the Law of International Trade

In recent years we have witnessed an unprecedented development of what is being termed – technically somewhat vaguely – as the "law of international trade" or, in some cases, as the "law of world trade". Questions relating to the substance of the law of international trade and its existence were discussed by an important scientific colloquium sponsored by the International Association of Legal Science in London in 1962 also with a view to the question whether this law was developing and, indeed, existing autonomously and, in substance, independently of the legislative activity of individual states.[1] The colloqium rightly pointed out that legal regulations governing questions of international commercial relations showed some obvious similarity in all states,[2] in spite of the fact that the legal systems of these states differ in their basic concepts under the impact of the differences existing in their economic and political structure, their historical development and legal traditions.

Although we have to approach the assertions concerning the origin or existence of a separate and autonomous law of international trade, which is fully or, at least largely, independent of

---

[1] Materials from this meeting are to be found in the publication *The Sources of the Law of International Trade,* edited by C. M. Schmitthoff, London, Stevens, 1964.

[2] See the general report presented at the aforesaid colloqium by C. M. Schmitthoff under the title "The Law of International Trade, its Growth, Formulation and Operation", published in the above publication on pp. 3 ff.; also see the study by the same author, "Das neue Recht des Welthandels", *Rabels Zeitschrift,* 1964/1, pp. 44 ff.

the legislative activity of states[3] with considerable reservations, motivated in particular by the realization that no law, no matter whether at the level of municipal law or international law, can essentially be formed without the legislative activity of individual states,[4] we must at the same time see that individual states devote greater or lesser attention to calls for separate legal rules governing international commercial relations, warranted by the endeavour to achieve legal security and stability of the mutual rights and obligations of the parties in international commercial transactions.

The internationalization of production and exchange of goods, which characterizes the contemporary international economic activity, necessarily has to be reflected also in the legal superstructure not only in public international law, where this influence is quite prominent in many respects, but also in that part of the legal superstructure, which is concerned with the regulation of the mutual rights and obligations of the parties which conclude individual commercial contracts in everyday trade relations.

The principal phenomenon which must be mentioned in this connection are the unification efforts which have been aiming within the framework of different international institutions, both governmental and non-governmental, at unifying solutions of the problems of the law of conflict of laws and of substantive law regarding the international sales contract. It is precisely in this unification effort, that comparative jurisprudence plays an important role. Today we may already take for granted the very limited success of the endeavour to unify conflict rules in the

---

[3] For example, in his above quoted study – pp. 44 ff. – S… concludes that the universal character of the law of int… is increasingly gaining in prominence and warrant… the emergence of a new *lex mercatoria.*

[4] Also Schmitthoff has recently come … clusion that the new *lex mercatori*… *oder indirekte Rechtsschöpfun*… *schweigend ihr Entstehen* … dels", *Rabels Zeitsch*…

sphere of the international law of obligations, which was promoted – after previous failures scored in this field by the International Law Institute at the beginning of the century and by the International Law Association in the period between the two World Wars – by the Hague Conference on Private International Law.[5]

In the sphere of substantive-law regulations governing the international sales contract, the question remains still open as regards the fate of two additional proposals to unify these rules, adopted at the diplomatic conference held in the Hague in 1964, which replaced the older drafts prepared by the Institute for the Unification of Private International Law in Rome.[6] One of

---

[5] After protracted efforts, this institution drew up three proposals for unifying conflict rules regarding the international sales contract; however, the response was meager both as regards the number of states which signed the drafts, and individual ratifications. According to the documents published by the Hague Conference on Private International Law, its *Convention sur la loi applicable aux ventes à caractère international d'objets mobiliers corporels* was signed by ten states and ratified by seven, and, as the only draft, became valid; the *Convention sur la loi applicable au transfert de la propriété en cas de vente à caractère international d'objets mobiliers corporels* was signed by two states and ratified by one, and, finally, the *Convention sur la compétence du forum contractuel en cas de vente à caractère international d'objets mobiliers corporels* was signed by four states but ratified by one.

[6] On these latest proposals see André Tunc, "Les Conventions de la Haye du 1[er] juillet 1964 portant loi uniforme sur la vente international d'objets mobiliers corporels", *Revue international de droit comparé,* 1964, No. 3, pp. 547 ff. In Czechoslovakia, an analysis of the two drafts was made in P. Kalenský, "Poznámky k Haagským návrhům právní úpravy mezinárodní kupní smlouvy" ("Some Remarks on the Hague Uniform Laws on International Sale of Goods"), *Časopis pro mezinárodní právo (Czechoslovak Journal of International Law,* 1965, No. 1. See also O. Riese, "Verlauf der Konferenz und Ergebnisse der materiellen Vereinheitlichung des Kaufrechts", E. V. Caemmerer, "Die Ergebnisse der Konferenz hinsichtlich der Vereinheitlichung des Rechtes des Abschlusses von Kaufverträgen", and Zweigert–Drobnig, "Einheitliches Kaufgesetz und Internationales Privatrecht", all published in *Rabels Zeitschrift,* 1965, No. 1, pp. 1 ff. The same issue contains the text of [illegible] drafts on pp. 166 ff. and 210 ff. For the text of an older draft of [illegible] on the international sales contract, which strongly in-

these is the Uniform Law on the Conclusion of International Sales Contracts, the other the Uniform Law on the Sales Contract.

On the other hand, the General Conditions of Delivery of Goods Between the Foreign Trade Organizations of the Member States of the Council of Mutual Economic Assistance[7] in their new redaction of 1968 constitute the thus far only valid international unification of the law of the international sales contract; of course, they are applicable only to relations between the foreign trade enterprises of the member states and, in contrast to the Hague drafts, do not claim applicability to subjects outside those of the member states, irrespective of their citizenship. These General Conditions govern in a basically obligatory manner (leaving the regulation of some questions to the autonomous will of the parties to individual contracts) the main problems involved in international sales contracts from the viewpoint of substantive law and also contain a conflict rule,[8] which, as regards questions not dealt with, refers to the substantive law of the state of the selling enterprise.[9]

---

fluenced the concept of the Czechoslovak Code of International Trade, see *Projet d'une loi uniforme sur la vente internationale des objets mobiliers corporels,* Imprimerie nationale, The Hague, 1956; an analysis of this text was made by Otto Riese, "Der Entwurf zur internationalen Vereinheitlichung des Kaufrechts", *Rabels Zeitschrif,* 1957, No. 1, pp. 16—116; see also Gunnar Lagergren, "A Uniform Law of International Sales of Goods", *Journal of Business Law,* 1958, p. 131; John Honnold, "A Uniform Law for International Sales", *Pennsylvania Law Review,* 1959, p. 299.

[7] On this point see for general information P. Kalenský, "Ke koncepci právní úpravy zbožních vztahů mezi podniky pro zahraniční obchod členských států RVHP" ("The Concept of Legal Regulation of Commodity Relations Between Foreign Trade Enterprises of the Member States of the Council of Mutual Economic Assistance"), *Studie z mezinárodního práva (Studies in International Law),* 1966, No. 11, pp. 103—135, and the literature quoted therein.

[8] See Section 74 of the General Conditions from 1958 and Section 110 of the amended General Conditions adopted in 1968.

[9] We should also note the fact that in contrast, the Hague Drafts strive as much as possible (perhaps under the impact of the failure of the Ha-

All the materialized or proposed projects of unification of the law of the international sales contract are also — in addition to other factors — the result of the fact that neither the Civil Codes of individual states, nor their Commercial Codes, drawn up, as a rule, still in the last century as a professional law of merchants *(droit professionnel des commerçants, Sonderrecht für Kaufleute)* and marked by the endeavour to regulate social relations then materialized primarily within closed, national economies, meet the legal needs of the highly developed international trade of our era, which expresses the objectively growing trend towards the internationalization of production and exchange of goods.[10] These shortcomings of municipal civil or commercial law are eliminated only in part by the drawing up of standard contracts or delivery terms for individual types of goods, commercial usage and interpretations of the different clauses used in international commerce, all of which may be applied within the scope of the autonomy of will, which is broadly granted in the field of the law of obligations to parties to international commercial contracts by the decisive substantive law.[11] These

---

gue Conference on Private International Law) for the exclusion of questions of the law of conflict of laws; see, e.g., Article I, par. 9, of the Draft Uniform Law on the Conclusion of International Sales Contracts and Article 2 of the Draft Uniform Law on the International Sales Contract; in addition, Article 17 of the same Draft provides that questions not governed by the Draft should be governed by the universal principles on which it is based.

[10] See on this point the opinion voiced by E. von Caemmer, "The Influence of the Law of International Trade on the Development and Character of the Commercial Law in Civil Law Countries", *The Sources of the Law of International Trade,* pp. 88 ff., and John Hannold, "The Influence of the Law of International Trade on the Development and Character of English and American Commercial Law", *Ibid.,* pp. 70 ff.

[11] See, e.g., the Incoterms or the Uniform Rules and Usage for Documentary Letters of Credit drawn up by the International Chamber of Commerce in Paris, or the general terms drawn up by different commercial centres dealing with individual, usually generic types of goods according to such general terms or standard contracts. We should also take note of the general conditions of sale and standard forms of contract drawn up by groups of experts within the framework of the United

general terms and standard forms of contract have been conceived in a manner whereby they could deal with as large as possible a number of questions that may arise. Nevertheless, the idea that they should be viewed as "self-regulatory contracts", i.e. contracts which could exist independently of the law formulated by individual states, has been disproved as unwarranted in view of the fact that they can be applied only on the basis of the autonomy of will granted to the contracting parties by the decisive law.[12] Still, it is a most remarkable phenomenon of a spontaneous unification of the law of international trade, which may, of course, be applied only within the limits set by individual, municipal systems of law.

All this leads us to the conclusion that there is a constant endeavour (even in spite of partial failures, for example in the sphere of the law of conflict of laws) to regulate the legal questions of international commercial relations by rules which would be distinct from the legal rules governing internal trade, provided for under mercantile or civil law. The manifestations of this trend naturally differ in their intensity, technique and form, but there is no doubt that they may be reduced to a "common denominator", which is the generally felt necessity of differentiating between civil or business law regulations of a purely municipal scope on the one hand, and relations characterized by an international mark. All this indicates the growth of the process leading both in the sphere of international unification

---

Nations Economic Commission for Europe for a variety of goods in the endeavour to facilitate the trade between the socialist and non-socialist countries of Europe. On this point see L. Kopelmanas, "La codification des coutumes du commerce international dans le cadre des Nations Unies", *Annuaire français du droit international,* 1955, pp. 370 ff.; P. Benjamin, "The EEC General Conditions of Sale and Standard Forms of Contract", *Journal of Business Law,* 1961, p. 113; A. Tunc, "L'élaboration des conditions générales de vente sous les auspices de la Commission économique pour l'Europe", *Revue internationale de droit comparé,* 1960, p. 108.

[12] See the debate at the London colloquium held by the International Association of Legal Sciences, as published in *The Sources of the Law of International Trade,* in particular on pp. 234 ff.

and in the sphere of municipal legislation to a gradual differentiation between international trade regulations and civil-law rules governing internal trade. However, at the same time we must bear in mind the fact that only legislation by individual states, which has the opportunity of asserting itself in the near future for example through the ratification of both the Hague Conventions introducing the Uniform Law on the Conclusion of International Sales Contracts and the Uniform Law on the Sales Contract, will show whether the states will respect the need to govern these matters, generally felt in professional juristic and commercial circles; nevertheless, we may conclude this discussion by stating that the tendency to provide for special regulations to govern international commercial relations has an objective character and that in spite of certain partial failures, it is asserting itself most vigorously and persistently.

However, in spite of what has been said about the possibilities of unification of the law of international trade on the interstate level, any state which wants to govern the legal questions of international commercial contacts differently from its own civil law where the international element, typical of international trade relations, is absent, may regulate these questions within the framework of its own legislative power; the Czechoslovak Socialist Republic did so in the Act of December 5th, 1963, Concerning Legal Relationships in International Commercial Contacts (the Code of International Trade), No. 101/1963, which has been in force since April 1st, 1964. In contrast to the possibility of international unification (which is undoubtedly questionable as to its early and universal success), the Czechoslovak legislator gave preference to a comprehensive regulation of the legal relationships arising in the conduct of international trade by governing in the Code of International Trade not only the limited set of problems concerning the international sales contract, which is, for example, the object of both Hague Drafts, but also the whole sphere of relationships between non-sovereign subjects arising in connection with international trade.[13]

---

[13] On the Czechoslovak Code of International Trade and its characte-

In this respect, the Czechoslovak codification goes further than the American Uniform Commercial Code, which aims primarily at eliminating confilcts between the laws of the individual States of the Union (and thus does not, in fact, constitute a legal regulation governing international trade in the true sense), or the Yugoslav codification of commercial usages of 1954, which is not a law but a set of rules adopted under a plenary decision of the Yugoslav State Arbitration Agency, necessitated among other factors also by the fact that Yugoslavia has not had a valid codification of civil law since 1945.[14]

---

ristic features see Kalenský, "Die Grundzüge des tschechoslowakischen Gesetzes über den internationalen Handel", *Rabels Zeitschrift*, 1966, No. 3, pp. 296–323; Kalenský–Kopáč, "Quelques considérations sur le nouveau Code tchécoslovaque du commerce international", *Bulletin de droit tchécoslovaque*, 1964, pp. 299 ff.; Kalenský, "Les traits essentiels des nouvelles codifications tchécoslovaques du droit de commerce international et du droit international privé", *Revue internationale de droit comparé*, 1964, No. 3, pp. 565 ff.; Kanda, "Zákon o právních vztazích v mezinárodním obchodním styku (zákoník mezinárodního obchodu) a jeho místo v systému československého socialistického práva" ("The Code of International Trade and Its Place Within the System of Czechoslovak Socialist Law), *Právník (The Lawyer)*, 1966, No. 2, pp. 128 ff. The discussion on where to place this particular law in the system of Czechoslovak law has apparently not yet ended. The author believes that it forms a part of private international law under the concept explained in the present work. Other Czechoslovak authors, like Kanda (in the above-quoted article) or Luby (see *Právny obzor (Legal Review)*, 1970, No. 1) hold a different opinion, asserting that it is a part of civil law.

[14] This usage does not constitute a legal regulation of international trade either, because it applies to all commercial relations, domestic as well as international. Professor Aleksandar Goldštajn points out in his introduction to the German translation of the document, *Allgemeine Usancen für den Warenhandel*, Federal Chamber of Foreign Trade, Belgrade, 1954, p. 8, that the usage itself does not provide the answer whether it also applies to international trade and concludes that it may be applied, if it had been chosen by the contracting parties as the *lex contractus* or if the legal relationships of the parties are to be governed under Yugoslav law. It is interesting that this document, which in its substance is a substitute for a codification of commercial law, also contains some rules of mandatory nature. *Ibid.*, p. 5.

We should, of course, bear in mind that the development and formation of the law of international trade progress at a dynamic pace and that accent is also laid therein on the role played by comparative jurisprudence. In this connection we should point to the fact that the 21st Session of the U.N. General Assembly, held in 1966, adopted a Hungarian-sponsored resolution on the promotion of the law of international trade.[15]

In the preamble of this resolution, the General Assembly underlined the importance of international trade co-operation among states for the growth of friendly relations and for the maintenance of peace and international security, as well as the fact that the differences arising from the laws of different states, governing questions of international trade, constitute a serious obstacle to the continued development of this trade. In view of the fact that in spite of all the efforts in this field, the progress made had not been in keeping with the seriousness and urgency of the problems involved, and feeling that the United Nations should play a more active role in removing the legal barriers obstructing the development of international trade, especially since such activity was in keeping with the purposes of the United Nations, as expressed in Article 1, par. 3, Article 13, and Chapters IX and X of the Charter, the General Assembly decided to establish a United Nations Commission for the Law of International Trade, whose task would be to promote the progressive harmonization and unification of the law of international trade.

The Commission is made up of representatives of twenty-nine states. Its members are elected by the General Assembly for a term of six years; seven of them must be African states, five Asian, four East European, five Latin American, and eight West European and other states. In electing the members, the General Assembly must pay due regard to the requirement of an appro-

---

[15] See Document A/6594; also P. Kalenský, "XXI. Valné shromáždění OSN a rozvoj práva mezinárodního obchodu", ("The Twenty-First General Assembly of the United Nations and the Development of the Law of International Trade"), *Časopis pro mezinárodní právo (Czechoslovak Journal of International Law)*, 1967, No. 2.

priate representation of the principal economic and legal systems in the world, and of the advanced and developing nations.

The first members of the Commission were elected at the 22nd Session of the General Assembly, and the term of office of fourteen of them will expire already after three years. The members of the Commission are to be, as much as possible, individuals who have gained prominence in the field of the law of international trade. The Commission is to hold its sessions once a year alternately at the United Nations headquarters in New York and in Geneva. Its task is to promote a progressive harmonization and unification of the law of international trade by (a) co-ordinating the activities of organizations engaged in this field and promoting their co-operation; (b) promoting greater participation in international conventions already in force, and a broader acceptance of model and uniform laws; (c) preparing the adoption of new international conventions and model and uniform laws, promoting the codification and a broader adoption of international commercial terms, usages and customs, possibly in co-operation with organizations active in this field; (d) promoting the ways and means of a uniform interpretation and application of international conventions and uniform laws in the field of the law of international trade; (e) gathering and disseminating information on national legislations and contemporary legal developments (including case law); (f) establishing and maintaining close co-operation with other United Nations bodies and specialized agencies in the field of international trade; (h) engaging in any other activities it may find useful for fulfilling its tasks.

The Commission is to submit its annual report, including recommendations, to the General Assembly and, at the same time, to the United Nations Trade and Development Conference, which is to forward its opinion and recommendations regarding the materials of the Commission to the General Assembly. The Commission may consult or request the co-operation of any international or national organization, scientific institution or expert, if it finds it expedient for the fulfilment of its tasks. It is also to establish appropriate working contacts with intergovermental and non-govermental international organizations concerned with the harmonization and unification of the law of international trade.

As indicated by the scope of the tasks of the U.N. Commission for the Law of International Trade, we may expect that the Commission will direct its endeavour at the gradual creation of a system of a new legal regulation of international commercial contacts, which, of course, also requires far-reaching legislative activity of states in this field, paralleled undoubtedly by a growing importance of commercial usage (e.g. Incoterms et al.) formulated by non-governmental institutions. For the time being, we cannot envisage, whether the form of model laws or international conventions will prevail in this field, but no matter which of them does, we may assume that there will be an endeavour to regulate gradually all the questions related with international commercial relations, which should also spur the tendency to formulate an international commercial law.

A major question, on which will undoubtedly also depend to some extent at least the success of the endeavour to harmonize and unify the law of international trade, will be the question of the relation between regional and universal unifications[16] and their compatibility or the possibility of their rapprochement. Eörsi rightly points out that it would be wrong to believe that the doctrine of universal unification should and could bring an end to regional unifications, but at the same time shows that both tendencies are compatible. While universal unification of law is unattainable in any other field, as it requires substantial changes in the spheres of the socio-economic structure and ideology, the situation differs in the field of international exchange of goods, where universal unification can be achieved in principle.[17] Such unification is, quite naturally, of tremendous importance for the developing countries as well.

The factors promoting the unification efforts in the field of

---

[16] See Gyula Eörsi, "Regional and Universal Unification of the Law of International Trade", *Journal of Business Law*, 1967, pp. 144 ff.

[17] *Ibid.*, p. 147.

the legal regulation of international commercial relations are quite powerful and include, at the top of the list, the current level of development of the productive forces, which leads to international division of labour and economic integration transcending state bondaries; what is involved, of course, is not the formation of an autonomous international business law which would be created outside or even "above" the legislative activity of individual states, but rather an activity pursued within the scope of the possibilities offered by this legislative work, which is the *conditio sine qua non* of its success. There should be no dispute as to the fact that this activity must proceed from a most thorough and long-range work in the field of comparative jurisprudence.

In this part of the present work we have tried to show the importance of comparative jurisprudence for both the law of conflict of laws and the unification efforts aimed at the prevention of conflicts. It is a common feature of both the fundamental social functions of private international law, i.e. the settlement of existing conflicts and their prevention, that they cannot do without comparative jurisprudence and that in many respects their development depends precisely on scientific studies in the field of comparative jurisprudence.

# PART SIX
# The Substance and Character of Application of Foreign Law

## CHAPTER 1
## Application of Foreign Law as the Consequence and Culmination of the Conflict Rule

In the process of application of foreign law, the overall problem of private international law reaches a special and, one may say, specific culmination. This process brings together a number of problems of a fundamental character, whose importance stands out quite clearly when we realize that it is precisely the application of foreign law, which constitutes, under certain factual and legal premises, the specific feature that has made private international law a *special entity* within the system of law, which in this culmination differs from the other branches.

The application of foreign law as such is not just a more or less perfected operation of legal technique developed over the centuries; as we shall further see, the application of foreign law as such may directly negate or at least greatly influence the purpose followed by the conflict rule which has instructed the judge to apply the foreign law. While the growth of international contacts has evoked in many fields the increased need of applying foreign law, unfortunately, the methods of this application have often remained in many countries at a level which is far removed from the postulates of justice under both conflict and substantive laws. This is precisely why the problem of the application of foreign law closely touches upon the very theoretical foundations of private international law in general and its most substantial part, the law of conflict of laws, in particular.

The process of applying foreign law is the field where conflicts are being settled between the law of the adjudicating court and the foreign law to which the conflict rule refers. It is there that the closed and, we may say, exclusive sphere of the *lex fori* – which constitutes a complete and, from the legislator's and judge's point of view, homogeneous legal entity – is penetrated by foreign law whose application is envisaged by the legislator in the conflict rule but which is, nevertheless, an element that disturbs in its own, specific manner the homogeneity and exclusiveness of the domestic law.

Thus, the fact that under certain circumstances foreign law must be applied, has raised a number of theoretical questions which are, however, of far-reaching practical importance. Private international law is sometimes – at least as regards the law of conflict of laws as its most essential part – interpreted as a set of conflict rules; this viewpoint is one-sided and incomplete if it ignores the final stage to which the conflict rule usually leads, namely the application of foreign law based on its provisions. There exists a number of views on foreign law and its application by domestic courts, which – from the theoretical aspect – are all influenced by the basic tenets of legal philosophy regarding private international law and which may lead in their practical realization, namely in the judicial proceedings where the foreign law is to be applied, to a situation where completely identical conflict rules in the laws of different states, referring to the application of the same foreign law, may result in different decisions. This is, of course, a highly problematic matter from the viewpoint of the scientific study of private international law in spite of the fact that "there are as many private international laws as there are states"; for the science of private international law – precisely because it is concerned with the theoretical explanation and interpretation of the settlement of social relations in the sphere of civil law, containing a foreign or international element – has preserved to a considerable degree its international character, although we do not claim, of course, that it has attained unity.

The look at the process of application of foreign law will make us attempt in this part of the present work to solve the theoretical problem of the character of the foreign law from the viewpoint of the legal system of the state whose court is adjudicating, the central question being whether the foreign law is a fact or a law from the viewpoint of the *lex fori.* If we are to look upon foreign law as a law, we must then define its relation to the domestic law and determine in particular whether its application does not alter its character as a foreign law in the sense that it becomes the domestic law, that it is "naturalized" or "incorporated" into the exclusive body of the *lex fori,* or whether its character as a foreign law remains unaltered by its application and that, in brief, it continues to be foreign law.

Another group of questions that must be answered logically ensues from the study of the substance of the applied foreign law; these are questions of the relation between the adjudicating court or judge and the foreign law as regards the process of its understanding and of proving it. However, the scope of this part of our work does not permit us to deal with these problems in detail and therefore we can only mention them briefly with the understanding that we intend to discuss them separately on the basis of the considerations contained herein as regards the substance of the application of foreign law. What is involved here is to determine the duty of the adjudicating court to learn to know the foreign law not only as regards the extent of this duty acording to different systems of law, but also as regards the grounds given for the existence or non-existence of this duty. At the same time, we shall also have to consider whether the foreign law is to be applied on the motion of the parties which must prove this law to the adjudicating court (the judge himself not being under the obligation to learn to know and apply this law *ex officio*) or whether for some reasons (and which) the judge is to request the aid of the parties in acquainting himself with the foreign law and in proving it, being *ex officio* under the obligation to learn to know and apply it. This group of problems should be followed by a study of the consequences that may occur in cases where for some reason the adjudicating court either does not learn to know the foreign law or the parties fail to prove it.

As we know, these problems also strongly affect the solution of the question whether a wrong application of a foreign law may be reviewed by superior judicial bodies.

There also arise some special questions in connection with the application of foreign law, in particular as regards the competence of the adjudicating court to review the validity of the foreign law which it had learned to know in one way or another and which it is to apply; this review may concern the constitutionality of the foreign law to be applied (i.e. whether its provisions are not contrary to the Constitution of the state which enacted them) as well as some questions of the validity of the foreign law from the viewpoint of foreign intertemporal regulations.

In this part of our work we also intend to touch upon some questions of interpretation of the applicable foreign law; for obvious reasons, the questions of correct interpretation of this law cannot be separated from the problems of application of foreign law.

The fact that under a reference contained in a conflict rule a foreign substantive law is being applied under certain factual circumstances to a greater or lesser degree, determines in a characteristic way – as regards the consequences, not the reasons of this application – the differences between the settlement of relations of a purely municipal nature and the settlement of relations containing a foreign element. Here we shall discuss questions of application of foreign law as the culmination and the consequence of the application of a conflict rule, and, in doing so, we shall also try to define the specific features marking the application of foreign law in contrast to the application of the domestic law.

We feel that there is an inseparable link between the application of foreign law and the substance of private international law. The application of foreign law, which takes place in every state – without the existence of a rule of public international law instructing states to apply foreign law to this or that extent or in a particular manner – manifests the endeavour of individual states and their organs to meet through such application certain needs arising in the life of society, which occur in direct proportion to the frequency of contacts between the subjects of civil-law relations from different states. Since – with the exception of cases of unified law, whose extent is still insignificant compared with the other parts of substantive civil law – it would be illusory to expect in the foreseeable future the formation of a substantive private international law, which would be a comprehensive system applicable to all cases containing a foreign element, there is nothing to be done but to fulfill the demands of justice and logic through a system of conflict rules and the application of foreign law based thereon. Although individual states do not make the requirement of reciprocity in the application of foreign law and the existence or formulation of conflict rules a *conditio sine qua non* for any concrete application and its scope, it ensues from the nature of the matter that they expect a similar endeavour by other states, aimed at settling civil-law relationships with a foreign element through the application of foreign law. We may say that it would be possible to deduce from the principles of public international law, in particular the obligation to respect the principle of equality of states and the obligation of states to contribute to the realization of international co-operation the essential necessity and duty of every state to respect another state as a legislator, which would necessarily lead to the application of foreign law; although there is no state in the world, which would refuse to apply foreign law at all, it nevertheless remains to be answered, whether in such a case such state would not commit a delict under international law. The author tends to support the opinion that such an attitude would represent a breach of the principle of mutual respect by states and, by implication, of mutual respect for each other's system of law, and feels that this principle (i.e. the principle of application of foreign law) forms a part of contemporary international law. At the same time, it is, however typical that the method of applying foreign law is not specified by the rules of public international law and that – with a few exceptions existing in municipal laws – it is not defined in municipal regulations either; these, in their majority, are only limited to questions of determining or proving foreign law, as the case may be. The method of applying foreign law has been developed in judicial decisions, in particular those of the major capitalist states. However, in this field again (as practically everywhere else in private international law), the viewpoints have not been uniform. For a detailed analysis of the methods of applying foreign law shows how frequently and expediently the courts have resorted – mostly on the basis of considerations motivated by a practical approach and preferential treatment of their own law – to analogies comparing or even identifying the foreign law with the factual circumstances of the adjudicated cases, in particular as regards the knowledge and evaluation of the foreign law; a certain corrective factor in this procedure has been the endeavour to influence the anomalies of such one-sided viewpoint by analogy and the application of the domestic law.

Its is precisely the application of foreign law, as a phenomenon occurring under all legal systems, which shows that the legislative activity of a state, proceeding from its sovereignty (even though territorially limited) and thus building its system of law as a united and exclusive entity where foreign legislative jurisdiction has no place, must respect the element of rationality contained in the very idea of law and justice, and give it preference in such an original manner, which disturbs the concept of the unity and exclusiveness of the law of every state, as the application of foreign law. The dilemma of the exclusive character of a system of law, its comprehensiveness and closed nature on the one hand, and on the other hand, of the fact that foreign law must be respected in one way or another, has brought forth legal constructions which are trying to overcome this anomaly. This is true both of the theory claiming that the domestic court does not apply foreign law but merely takes into account subjective rights acquired under a foreign law (the theory of vested rights), and the fiction that foreign law is incorporated into the domestic law and only as such is subsequently applied, or the construction of the judicial formulation of law in concrete cases under consideration by the court according to the "example of foreign law". In our opinion all these theories voluntaristically distort and complicate the reference to a foreign law contained in the respective conflict rule.

We must not exclude from the analysis of the application of foreign law as a phenomenon characteristic of private international law also the question of why foreign law should be applied. There are many answers to this question to be found in the doctrine of private international law, and every one of them proceeds from the theoretical credo of its author. These answers range from views asserting that the source of the application of foreign law must be sought in the *comitas gentium,* which proceed from the extreme concept of the territoriality of law, as promoted by d'Argentré and the proponents of the Dutch statutory theory (not mentioning their English and American disciples), to positivistic views referring to the will of the state as the legislator and to the instruction contained in the conflict rule, and theories asserting that the application of foreign law is the outcome of the supranational character of private international law.[1] In our opinion, however, the ontological explanation of this phenomenon must be sought parallel with the explanation of the existence of law as a social phenomenon with a view to its economic and political dependence, aiming at the creation of a system of social behaviour which would be in keeping with certain — again conditional — criteria of evaluation. In view of the current needs of international life, regulated by law, we may also find in the application of foreign law on the basis of a conflict rule as a rational element, which existed already in the 12th century, when private international law was born,[2] voluntaristic

[1] See the survey of these theories in the third and fourth parts of the present work and in the author's study "K předmětu a povaze mezinárodního práva soukromého a k otázce jeho místa v systému práva", ("The Object and Nature of Private International Law and Its Place in the System of Law"), *Časopis pro mezinárodní právo (Czechoslovak Journal of International Law),* 1960, No. 2, pp. 81—102.

[2] See Lainé, *Introduction,* or Neumeyer, *Entwicklung;* a clear explanation of the principle of rationality in private international law may also be found in Gutzwiller, *Recueil des Cours,* 1929, Vol. IV,

elements which are characteristic of the legislative activity of a state; their mutual dependence and impact are obvious precisely in private international law which disturbs the exclusive nature of the individual systems of law with respect to all other systems of law through the fact of the application of foreign law. At the same time, of course, we can observe the role played by the political and social elements arising from the necessary co-existence and plurality of states and their legal systems, and from the demands of mutual respect and co-operation among them.

The problem of the application of foreign law in the technical sense may be divided into several mutually dependent and consecutive stages. When applying foreign law (if the conflict rule refers to the foreign law as the applicable one), the judge must determine the scope of the reference contained in the conflict rule; in this respect we may speak of a determination of the quantum of the applicable foreign law. From this ensues the next stage, where the judge must evaluate the applicable foreign law, bearing in mind the requirements and the intents of the *lex fori,* on which he must insist (this is where the negative and excluding influence of the reservation of public order may manifest itself). The application of foreign law also calls for the assessment of several questions which might be solved differently according to the *lex fori* or the applicable foreign law; this is true, in particular, of preliminary questions, with a full view of the fact that it is precisely in the case of application of foreign law, that such fundamental and universal institutions of the law of conflict of laws are involved, as *renvoi,* use of the reservation of public order, or the question of qualification and conflict of qualifications.

---

p. 301. Gutzwiller quotes Master Aldric as the author of the opinion that the judge should apply the law which he finds more useful and better *("... quaeritur si homines diversarum provinciarum, quae diversas habent consuetudines, sub uno eodemque iudice litigant, utrum earum iudex qui iudicandum suscepit sequi debeat? respondeo eam quae potior et utilior videtur, debet enim iudicare secundum quod melius ei visum fuerit").* See also Krčmář, *Základy (Bases),* p. 117.

When studying the problems of application of foreign law, we meet in a certain parallel with problems of both substantive and procedural laws. There is no doubt, for example, that the procedural aspect of proving foreign law is deeply influenced by the manner in which foreign law is viewed; very briefly and simply said, whether the adjudicating court views foreign law as a fact or as law. It is these aspects which make some authors include the problems of application of foreign law in those parts of their textbooks or systems of law, devoted to the general institutions of private international law or, in other instances, in chapters dealing with what is known as the international law of civil procedure. In the list of questions with which we must concern ourselves in making a theoretical analysis of the application of foreign law, those of a procedural character or at least with procedural aspects are questions of how a judge acquaints himself with a foreign law and where he obtains information about it, and therefore also the subsidiary question whether the judge may apply a foreign law only if the parties, or at least one of them, pleads the existence of the foreign law and proves it to the court, or whether the judge himself may acquaint himself with the foreign law, or, possibly, whether he may apply the foreign law on the basis of his own, non-procedural, knowledge. Also the question whether it is possible for superior judicial bodies to review erroneous applications of foreign law has procedural aspects. As we shall further show, the procedural aspects of the application of foreign law are inseparably linked with the substantive-law basis of the problem and cannot be forcibly separated from it, if we want to study the application of foreign law as a phenomenon in its entirety. For we must bear in mind that, for example, the very qualification of foreign law as a law or as a fact is, as a rule, dependent on the concept of the theoretical foundations of private international law, which is so prominently reflected in the theoretical explanation of the application of foreign law; the question of proving foreign law in judicial procedure is then only a procedural reflex of this basic problem.

Nussbaum[3] therefore quite justly describes as a sign of absence of a sense for reality in understanding private international law the fact that the question of proof of foreign law is either completely ignored or is left to treatises or discussions in the sphere of procedural law; he himself sees the core of this subject-matter in international and interstate relations.

However, when discussing questions of application of foreign law, we frequently meet with the procedural aspects of the matter (which we have no intention of underestimating in any way), arising from the "practical" and expedient aspect of the fact that we have nothing to do with the application of domestic law – which leads to certain complications – being used as arguments for obscuring the true nature of the application of foreign law, taking place on the basis of a conflict rule. Yet, it is precisely this substance of the application of foreign law, as well as the character of the applied foreign law, viewed in its relation to the domestic law, which are the decisive factors in explaining the whole problem of application of foreign law. It is for this reason that we shall primarily concern ourselves with the substance and character of the applied foreign law, while necessarily touching upon some questions of procedural law; however, in their entirety and from the systematic point of view they would require a separate treatise.

---

[3] *Grundzüge*, p. 32.

# CHAPTER 2
# Application of Foreign Law and Domestic Law

The problem of the substance of the applied foreign law, viewed from the point of view of the law of the adjudicating court and thus defining the relation between the applied foreign law and the domestic law on the basis of the conflict rule of the forum, may be briefly and simply described as antinomy between the thesis that "foreign law is a fact from the viewpoint of the adjudicating court" and the thesis asserting that "foreign law is a law also from the viewpoint of the adjudicating court". As we shall further see, there is a whole range of opinions striving for a compromise between these two extremes.

The thesis about the factual character of the applied foreign law is upheld predominantly in strictly formulated judicature – together with all the consequences ensuing therefrom – especially in countries characterized by an empirical and pragmatic approach to a case, which means primarily in English and American judicature, and, in a somewhat weaker form, in the judicature of some West European countries, in particular France, as well as in earlier Italian judicature. On the other hand, the doctrine often holds an opinion which diametrally differs from the theory of the factual character of the applied foreign law.

## (1) The Anglo-American Doctrine and Practice

Speaking of the common law sphere, Rabel[1] describes the consideration of foreign law as fact as being a dogma proceeding from the assertion that only domestic law is the law of the

---

[1] *Conflict of Laws*, Vol. 4, pp. 473 and 474.

country and therefore foreign law must be proved as a fact.[2] Nussbaum[3] quite fittingly points to the fact that this dogma, which is characteristic of the view held on foreign law under common law, came into existence through the consideration of cases involving not a direct application of a foreign law by the court but rather the influence of foreign law on the facts of the case (e.g. in considering the amount of a foreign interest rate, etc.).

However, in spite of the clear-cut common law concept, there are some highly respected authors who have criticized this concept, pointing to its erroneous aspects. Thus, for example, M. Wolff[4] notes somewhat ironically the nonsensical character of the situation where a court is applying "facts", (i.e. foreign law under the English concept) to facts, and shows that the fact that French law is not the law in force in England does not deprive it of its character of law even in England. Wolff fully supports the conclusion that "the law which is applied is foreign law and remains foreign law".[5]

What is also interesting in the English development is a certain weakening of the thesis that foreign law is a fact, which has manifested itself in English law by the fact that foreign law and proof of its existence as a fact were removed from the competence of the jury and were entrusted to the judge only; this happened under the Supreme Court of Judicature Act of 1925.[6]

---

[2] Also see Dicey's Conflict of Laws, 6th ed., 1949, Rule 194, and the centuries-old English literature quoted, for example by Nussbaum, *Grundzüge,* pp. 236 and 237; in a 1775 decision (in Mostyn v. Fabregas), Lord Mansfield asserted: "The way of knowing foreign laws is by admitting them to be proved as facts". Also see some older decisions quoted in Donner, "Důkaz a použití cizího práva" ("The Proof and Application of Foreign Law"), *Studie z mezinárodního práva (Studies in International Law),* III. pp. 107 ff., in particular p. 124.

[3] *Grundzüge,* pp. 236 and 237.

[4] *Private International Law,* 1st ed., p. 218.

[5] *Ibid.*

[6] The respective provision (Article 102) reads: "Where it is necessary to ascertain the law of any other country which is applicable to the facts of the case, any question as to the effect of the evidence given with

Nevertheless, we may conclude the analysis of the English opinion on foreign law by stating that it is fully subservient to the theory of vested rights, under which the true purpose of private international law is to grant recognition to those rights, which have been acquired under some foreign legal system.[7]

The strict assertion that "only domestic law is law", while foreign law must be proved as any other fact may be viewed as a consequence of the theory of *comitas gentium* as the basis of private international law, which, as we know, proceeds from the dogma of the territorial validity of every law.[8]

The English theory of the character of the applied foreign law also prevailed in American theory; the factual character of foreign law from the viewpoint of the *lex fori* was unquestionable for Joseph Story, the founder of American private international law,[9] and the same opinion is also held by Beale.[10] Nevertheless, the decisions of some American courts reflect certain doubts as to the suitability and expediency of such an *a priori* position.[11]

While the English resistance to and disregard of foreign law goes so far that it also affects Scotch law, for example the indivi-

---

respect to that law shall instead of being submitted to the jury be decided by the judge alone." Quoted from Cheshire, *Private International Law,* Oxford, 1935, p. 69.

[7] *Ibid.,* p. 73.

[8] Nevertheless, we should take note of how the founder of this theory, Ulricus Huber, opposed in his *Praelectiones iuris civilis* — in the chapter *De conflictu legum* — in advance the possible negation of the application of foreign law through an extreme interpretation of the territorial character of laws, when he deduced that there was nothing more harmful to international legal relations, than if what was effective under the law of one place were to be made ineffective elsewhere due to differences in laws. See Yntema, "Die historischen Grundlagen des internationalen Privatrechts", *Festschrift für Ernst Rabel,* p. 524.

[9] Story, *Commentaries,* 8th ed., § 637.

[10] *Conflict of Laws,* 1664, § 621.1.

[11] For example, Rabel quotes the decision of the Supreme Court of New Hampshire, which sums up its doubts as to the true character of foreign law as follows: "...Conceding that foreign law is a matter of fact, yet it also is law in every true sense ... it is a fact as domestic law is." See *Conflict of Laws,* Vol. IV, p. 475.

dual States in the United States were forced by practical needs to modify their laws at least as regards the consideration of the laws of the other States of the Union. Although under the constitutional doctrine prevailing in the United States the law of one State should be considered in the other States as a fact, the rigidity of this doctrine was broken, at least with respect to proving the laws of the other States, by the enactment in 1920 of the Uniform Proof of Statutes Act, which was either fully embraced by or directly influenced the legislation of the overwhelming majority of the States constituting the United States; at the same time, a tendency appeared in some States to take a more benevolent view of submitted evidence of the written law of foreign states,[12] although, as Nussbaum states, little has changed as regards the law of foreign states, wherein, in his opinion, lies the main difference between the understanding of private international and interregional laws in the United States.[13] In this connection, Rabel quotes the opinion of the Commissioners of Uniform State Laws which body, when advocating that the court itself (i.e. without pleas by the parties) should take into account the existence of foreign law (i.e. the law of another State of the Union), wanted to amend two outdated rules of common law, namely the factual character of the law of a sister State, and felt that the decision-making on this question by the jury was the heritage of the insular, English common law, dating back two centuries ago, when all foreign countries spoke different languages and had foreign systems of law.[14]

Thus, as we can see, even in the United States the modern trend to criticize those views which consider foreign law to be

---

[12] For details see Nussbaum, *Grundzüge*, p. 238; the same author discusses this question in great detail – quoting extensively from American judicature – in his study "The Problem of Proving Foreign Law", *Yale Law Journal*, Vol. 50, p. 1018; also see Donner, "Důkaz a použití cizího práva" ("The Proof and Application of Foreign Law"), *Studie z mezinárodního práva (Studies in International Law)*, No. 3, pp. 127 and 128.

[13] *Grundzüge*, p. 239.

[14] *Conflict of Laws*, Vol. IV, p. 476. The Uniform Judicial Notice of Foreign Law Act was passed in 1936; see Nusbaum's above-quoted article.

a fact, seems to be making only little headway; progress in this respect has been made primarily in the sphere of North American inter-local conflicts, and even there the dogma of foreign law being a fact has not actually been abandoned, but merely adjusted so that it does not obstruct the practical need of facilitating the submission of proof of the "foreign" law. On the other hand, as regards truly foreign law, thus far no substantial change has taken place (with a few exceptions quoted in Czechoslovak literature by Donner). Nevertheless, from the practical point of view with respect to the application and proof of foreign law, a considerable step forward was made in Article 344a of the 1943 New York Civil Practice Act, under which the court must take into account a law, statute, proclamation or decree, ordinance or unwritten law, and the common law of a sister State or a foreign country, without the parties pleading it. Nussbaum points out[15] that this change in the law of the State of New York was directly influenced by the criticism expressed in his article.[16] Nevertheless, we must see that in the United States the approach to foreign law still proceeds from the doctrine of comity and vested rights, formulated in American doctrine especially by Beale as the recognition and enforcement of foreign created laws.[17] Beale thus proceeds from the consideration of foreign law as a fact,[18] which leads to the logical conclusion that the court may apply as law only its own law.[19]

---

[15] *Grundzüge*, pp. 240, 235.

[16] "The Problem of Proving Foreign Law" (*Yale Law Review*, 1941, p. 1018).

[17] *Conflict of Laws*, 3, 3, 1968, 1969: "The topic called 'Conflict of Laws' deals with the recognition and enforcement of foreign created laws.. A right having been created by the appropriate law, the recognition of its existence should follow everywhere. Thus an act valid where done cannot be called in question anywhere."

[18] *Ibid.*, Vol. 1, 1916: "The provisions of this (i.e. foreign) law having been proved as a fact, the question is solved by the national law, the foreign factor in the solution – i.e. the foreign contract law – being present as mere fact, one of the facts on which the decision is to be based."

[19] See Beale's preceding idea and the questation in the preceding footnote.

There is no difference between these conclusions and the local law theory of Walter Wheeler Cook, formulated in his studies and the book The Logical and Legal Bases of the Conflict of Laws. This theory, which basically denies the existence of an objective law prior to the consideration of a case by the adjudicating court, also proceeds from the premise that the court never applies foreign law but that the judge who creates the law does so according to the example set by the foreign judge.[20] It is this theory, which is being followed in American judicature, as so clearly expressed in the opinion of Judge Learned Hand in Guiness v. Miller.[21]

Although in many respects there are considerable differences between the theory of vested rights, as formulated by Beale, and Cook's local law theory[22] as regards the approach to the application of foreign law, it is rather irrelevant whether protection is granted to (subjective) rights acquired under a foreign system of law (as asserted by the theory of vested

---

[20] See Cook, *The logical and Legal Bases of the Conflict of Laws*, Cambridge, Mass., 1942, pp. 2021: "The forum, when confronted by a case involving foreign elements, always applies its own law to the case, but in doing so adopts and enforces as its own law a rule or decision identical or at least highly similar though not identical in scope with a rule or decision found in the system of law in force in another state or country with which some or all of the foreign elements are connected... the forum thus enforces not a foreign right but a right created by its own law." (Underlined by the author.)

[21] Quoted from Kegel, "The Crisis of Conflict of Laws", *Recueil des Cours, 1964,* Vol. II, p. 107: "No court can enforce any law but that of its own sovereign, and, when a suitor comes to a jurisdiction foreign to the place of the tort, he can only invoke an obligation recognized by that sovereign. A foreign sovereign under civilized law imposes an obligation of its own as nearly homologous as possible to that arising in the place where tort occurs." Also see Rabel, *Conflict of Laws,* Vol. II, p. 63.

[22] These differences are described by Yntema, "Die historischen Grundlagen des internationalen Privatrechts", *Festschrift für Ernst Rabel,* p. 534. Yntema very strongly opposes Cook's theory and the pragmatism which characterizes it, and accuses the former author of having disrupted the American tradition of private international law established by Joseph Story.

rights) or whether the judge creates his own law in keeping with the example set by the foreign judge.

Among the newer American authors, the application of foreign law is vehemently opposed by Brainard Currie[23] with his typical endeavour to promote the application of the substantive law of the forum; his arguments are based on the assertion that only by applying this law may the judge meet the interests and policy pursued by his own state as the legislator.[24] Under this theory, foreign law may be applied only as an exception if the state of the forum has no interest in the case concerned and provided that the foreign state has such an interest. If neither state has an interest in the case under consideration, the *lex fori* must again be applied according to Currie.

Yet another leading American author, Albert Ehrenzweig,[25] opposes all theories stating that foreign law may be considered as the decisive law, and is against all trends which take the same view of the *lex fori* and the applicable foreign law. In his opinion, a reference to a foreign law should never be understood as reference to such law as a certain body; such foreign law, he claims, is merely incorporated – and that only as an exception – into the substantive law provisions of the *lex fori*. Although Ehrenzweig's system of law of conflict of laws is rather original, the stress he lays on the substantive-law application of the *lex fori* as the fundamental principle of the law of conflict of laws is openly hostile to the endeavour (generally characteristic of the theory of private international law) to achieve on the basis of conflict rules dealing with certain factual configurations with international elements identical adjudications in all countries. This is also why Ehrenzweig's theory met with a most negative reaction on the part of Kegel.[26]

---

[23] Currie, *Selected Essays on the Conflict of Law,* Durham, North Carolina, 1963.

[24] This theory was subjected to sharp criticism in Kegel, *Recueil des Cours,* 1964, Vol. II.

[25] A. A. Ehrenzweig, "The Lex Fori – Basic Rule in the Conflict of Laws", *Michigan Law Review,* Vol. 58, 1960, pp. 637–688; *A Treatise on the Conflict of Laws,* 1962, *Conflicts in a Nutshell,* 1965.

[26] *Recueil des Cours,* 1964, Vol. II, pp. 224 ff.

(2) The Theory and Practice of European States

A negative attitude towards the applicable foreign law "as a law" is taken not only by English and American judicature and most of the doctrine of those two countries. French judicature, too,[27] still proceeds from the old thesis that foreign law must be viewed as a fact, including the consequences arising therefrom as regards the obligation of the judge to know the foreign law and the obligation of the parties to prove this law. A similar position is held in Spanish judicature,[28] although Spanish doctrine upholds a diametrally different view, which – as we shall see later – is also true of the great majority of the French doctrine of private international law. On the other hand, an analysis of the judicature of a number of other states of the European Continent, such as Italy for example (especially as regards more recent decisions), or of older and newer German or Austrian judicature, shows that this judicature – even though it must take into account the specific features arising from the fact that foreign law is being applied – does not deny the applicable foreign law the character of law.[29]

The legal systems of many states – primarily those of the European Continent – provide in the form of valid legal regulations of procedural character quite unequivocally that the foreign law, which is to be applied under a conflict rule, must be

---

[27] See, e.g., Batiffol, *Traité élementaire de droit international privé,* 1949, § 328, § 332; Zajtay, *Contribution à l'étude de la condition de la loi étrangère,* 1958, p. 31, and the judicature quoted therein.

[28] On this judicature and doctrine see Mariano Aquilar Navarro, *Lecciónes de derecho internacional privado,* Madrid, 1964, Vol. 2, p. 214.

[29] See Giuliano, "Le traitement du droit étranger dans le procès civil dans les systèmes juridiques continenteaux", *Revue internationale de droit comparé,* 1962, No. 1; Riezler, *Internationales Prozessrecht,* Berlin–Tübingen, 1949, p. 491; Donner, "Důkaz a použití cizího práva" ("The Proof and Application of Foreign Law"), *Studie z mezinárodního práva (Studies in International Law),* No. 3; Dölle, "De l'application de droit étranger par le juge interne", *Revue critique de droit international privé,* 1955, No. 2; Motulsky, "L'office du juge et la loi étrangère", *Mélanges Maury,* 1960, Vol. I, pp. 337 ff.

viewed as law. These provisions are mostly contained in regulations which instruct the judge how he should or can obtain knowledge of the foreign law he is to apply in the proceedings. A typical example of this group of legal systems is the German Code of Civil Procedure which provides in its Section 293[30] that customary law and law valid in foreign countries need not be proved if it is known to the court, and the court, when determinig its content, is not bound by the evidence submitted by the parties and may also use other sources of information and order any steps whereby it can obtain the knowledge of such law.

The same idea underlies Section 271 of the Austrian Code of Civil Procedure, under which foreign law must be proved only if it is not known to the court; the court may *ex officio* obtain all necessary information in this respect, and, if necessary, also request the co-operation of the Ministry of Justice.

In Hungary, too, Article 200 of the 1952 Code of Judicial Civil Procedure instructs the courts to inform themselves *ex officio* of foreign law which is not known to them, but they also have the option of making use of evidence submitted by the parties.

The same principles served as the background of Section 633 of the old Czechoslovak Code of Civil Procedure of 1950, and Section 53 of the 1963 Act Concerning Private International Law and the Rules of Procedure Relating Thereto instructs the judicial organs to take all necessary measures to ascertain the provisions of a foreign law; if such provisions are not known to them, they may request the information for this purpose from the Ministry of Justice. Identical considerations serve as the basis of Article 1143 of the Polish Code of Civil Procedure, which has been in force since 1965 and which replaced Article 39, par. 1, of the Polish Act Concerning Private International Law of 1926, which also instructed the judge to ascertain the provisions of the applicable foreign law *ex officio* with the co-operation of the parties, if necessary.

Soviet law, too, provides (Article 12, par. 2, of the Founda-

---

[30] This is a provision taken over verbatim from Section 265 of the old German Code of Civil Procedure.

tions of Judicial Civil Procedure of the Union of Soviet Socialist Republics and the Union Republics) that "the court shall use the rules of foreign law in accordance with the present law"; the character of foreign law "as a law" clearly ensues from this provision.

Similar principles also govern Rumanian and Bulgarian law.

In Scandinavia there is a lack of uniformity on this point with Danish cases viewing foreign law as fact rather than law.

Among the continental states of Europe, Greece has thus far been an exception (Article 245, No. 3, of the Greek Code of Civil Procedure);[31] Switzerland switched in 1947 from viewing foreign law as a fact to considering it as law,[32] but according to Niederer the matter has not yet been finally settled.

The idea of applying foreign law *ex officio* as a law is also gradually gaining sway in the legal systems of non-European states, especially those of Latin America,[33] which has also been clearly manifested in the provision of Article 408 of the Código Bustamante, which states that "the judges and courts of every Contracting State shall apply in proceedings *ex officio* the laws of the other Contracting States", but without prejudicing the other means of evidence provided for in the Código Bustamante.

A study of legal provisions concerned with the application of foreign law and thereby also with its substance, some of which we have quoted here, shows the link existing between private international law and what is known as international law of procedure as one of the former's parts. The fact that the legislation of many states deals with such an important question, as

---

[31] For details see Donner, *Studie z mezinárodního práva (Studies in International Law)*, No. 3.

[32] See Niederer, *Einführung in die allgemeinen Lehren des internationalen Privatrechts*, Zürich, 1956, p. 345; Donner, *Studie z mezinárodního práva (Studies in International Law)*, No. 3, p. 119; Gutzwiller, "A propos d'une 'quaestio aurea' en droit international privé suisse, l'application du droit étranger", *De conflictu legum*, Leiden, 1962, (Mélanges R. D. Kollewijn et J. Offerhaus), pp. 181 ff.

[33] See the survey of some legislative provisions contained in M. A. Navarro, *Lecciónes*, p. 208.

the character of applicable foreign law, parallel with the question of the application of such law or the methods of acquiring its knowledge, shows how the realization of the law, and thus also of foreign law, taking place in judicial proceedings, helps to clarify the substance of the law and the relation of the judge thereto also as regards the substance and character of the foreign law. These stand out with special clarity when compared with the substance of the domestic law – applied *ex officio* – and with some additional questions arising from the character of the domestic law.

Thus, if we compare the private international laws of individual states and their relations to the applied foreign law, we discover the existence of basic differences between the Anglo-American practice (and the prevalent part of the Anglo-American doctrine) of private international law and the almost universally accepted viewpoints expressed in the doctrine of the continental states of Europe. Nussbaum[34] shows on the historical development of proving foreign law, that it had been a usual practice also on the Continent of Europe to submit expert opinion and to prove – for example by witnesses – the validity of individual provincial laws which at first were interpreted in the spirit of the *Corpus juris.* The opinion that it was an obligation of the parties to prove foreign law appeared on the Continent earlier than in England, but was denied and never acquired the rigid form as we know it from English law. Since the time when the internationalist theory of private international law began to assert itself in the 19th century, the view also asserted itself, that domestic and foreign laws should be treated equally in judicial procedure. The idea that the court should apply foreign law *ex officio* as a law found especially fertile ground in Germany as early as at the time of von Bar (it was also widely accepted in Holland), and judicature adapted itself to this theory. Nussbaum[35] therefore notes that as regards the approach to the character and ascertainment of foreign law, the private inter-

[34] *Grundzüge*, p. 241.
[35] *Ibid.*, p. 242.

national law of the continental states of Europe stands at a higher level of development than common law. This, of course, applies not only to the consideration of the character and substance of the foreign law to be applied in judicial proceedings, but also to its ascertainment and the methods of obtaining knowledge about it.

Nussbaum's finding does not apply, in principle, to French judicature which is still proceeding from the consideration of foreign law as any other fact that must be pleaded and proved to the adjudicating court.[36] We may say, however, that on the whole, the French doctrine of private international law almost unanimously opposes this approach by French judicature, and its opinion has been persistently promoted in France for a number of years.[37]

Nevertheless, in spite of this general trend in French literature on private international law, such leading French authority as Henri Batiffol, holds an opinion which finds essentially correct French judicial practice under which foreign law is treated as a fact. In his works quoted above, Batiffol proceeds from the premise that foreign law is a heterogeneous element with respect to the *lex fori* and that the judge applies it as he would, for example, the statutes of a business corporation. Although the foreign law arises from the will of a legislator who exercises his jurisdiction which is similar to the jurisdiction of the domestic legislator, but this jurisdiction cannot be exercised on territory which is under the jurisdiction of the domestic legislator. Batiffol quite obviously proceeds from indisputable facts, but the results he reaches may be defined as meaning that foreign law

---

[36] On this point see, e.g., the judicature quoted by Zajtay, *Contribution*, or by Motulsky, *Mélanges Maury*, Vol. I, pp. 337 ff; also see Batiffol, *Traité de droit international privé*, § 328 ff.

[37] See the works quoted above and Maury, *Recueil des Cours*, 1936, III, pp. 376 ff., "La condition de la loi étrangère en droit français", *Travaux du Comité français de droit international privé*, 1948–1952, pp. 97 ff., and "Observations sur les 'Aspects philosophiques du droit international privé'", *Revue critique de droit international privé*, 1957, pp. 238–246.

is to be applied as any other factual circumstance.[38] This view is also supported by the argument that the applicable foreign law is of an incidental character compared with French law, and this in two respects.[39] First, the foreign law is officially unknown to the French court since it was neither promulgated nor published in France and, secondly, the foreign law proceeds from the jurisdiction of a foreign legislator, which does not exist in France. On the other hand, the domestic law, i.e. the *lex fori,* is of a quite different character, namely one of necessity *(raison de nécessité);* it is what it should be and not what is found that it is.[40]

Although law is a social phenomenon (which is true both of domestic law and foreign law), its character as such in the broad sense does not mean that a comparison between the *lex fori* and the applicable foreign law could and should lead to a conclusion which denies the foreign law the character of law and identifies it – as regards its application in proceedings before a domestic court – with all other factual circumstances which are decisive for the adjudication of the case,[41] which means that only domestic law can have the character of law.

In our opinion, Batiffol's arguments – if we subject them to a critical legal and logical analysis – do not support this conclusion. In spite of the fact that foreign law is indeed the result of the will of the foreign legislator, Batiffol has failed to identify

---

[38] See Batiffol, *Aspects philosophiques,* p. 111: "*Quand on dit par conséquent que la loi étrangère apparaît comme un élement de fait, on veut dire, qu'elle se présente au juge saisi, d'une part comme extérieure aux ordres du législateur au nom duquel il rend la justice, d'autre part comme faisant abstraction de l'élément impératif qu'elle comporte à l'étranger. On ne nie pas sa nature de proposition générale applicable à des cas particuliers, on ne nie pas sa nature impérative à l'étranger, mais on constate qu'il manque dans le pays considéré un élément de la notion de droit, celui de constituer l'ordre du pouvoir.*"

[39] Batiffol, *Traité,* p. 383.

[40] *Ibid.*

[41] Martin Wolff, *Private International Law,* 1st ed., had this sarcastic comment to make on this point: "It is meaningless to say that a judge applies a 'fact' to fact... The law which is applied is foreign law and remains foreign law."

it with the factual circumstances of a case; his arguments merely prove the fact that foreign law is not domestic law and that it is – and also remains to be for purposes of its application by a domestic court – foreign. On the one hand Batiffol stresses the element of the will of the domestic legislator (*a contrario* to the imperative of the foreign legislator), but on the other hand he at the same time overlooks the fact the conflict rule of the *lex fori*, under which the foreign substantive law is being applied, is also a part of the imperative of the domestic legislator. The purpose of such conflict rule is in this sense to replace the will of the foreign legislator, aiming at the application of the foreign law, by the will of the domestic legislator to apply foreign law to certain factual configurations. At the same time, the conflict rule undoubtedly contains beside the element of will also an element of rationality, influenced by the postulates and ideas of justice under the law of conflict of laws as well as under substantive law.

The arguments used to support the conclusion that from the viewpoint of the adjudicating court foreign law is but a factual circumstance (which must as such be pleaded and proved by the parties) frequently mix up the explanation of the substance of foreign law – which in our opinion is and remains also from the viewpoint of the adjudicating court a law, even though a foreign one – and some specific features of procedural nature with which we meet in the legal systems of some states and which arise from the fact that foreign law applied in judicial proceedings on the basis of a conflict rule of the *lex fori* is not the domestic law.

Foreign law is usually identified with factual circumstances because the judge is not obliged to know foreign law (in contrast to domestic law); such law must be referred to either by both parties or at least by the party which bases its claim thereon, they must prove it (just as any other factual circumstance), and the judge is not obliged to apply this law (again in contrast to domestic law) *ex officio*. However, are these features which are inherent to foreign law in view of its substance and character, or are they merely procedural specialties?

A survey of mostly procedural rules of a number of states, concerning the status of applicable foreign law, has shown that also from the procedural viewpoint the judge may be instructed to apply foreign law *ex officio* and that he himself, or with the co-operation of the parties to the proceedings, should obtain its knowledge (e.g. by inquiring at the Ministry of Justice, etc.).[42] We may deduce therefrom that the special treatment of foreign law in the process of its application ensues from the fact that foreign rather than domestic law is involved, which does not mean, of course, that these special features of procedural character could erase the substance of foreign law.

### (3) A Critical Assessment of the Opinion that Foreign Law Is a Fact

We shall now try — naturally to the extent permitted by the scope of this part of the present work — to explain some of the special features with which we meet in the application of foreign law in judicial proceedings with regard to arguments asserting that from the viewpoint of the *lex fori* foreign law is not law but a fact.

The basic argument raised by the advocates of these theories is frequently the assertion that the principle *iura novit curia* concerns only the domestic law, which the judge must apply *ex officio*, while foreign law must be pleaded and proved to the court as a fact in accordance with the principles *da mihi factum, dabo tibi ius* or *secundum allegata et probata iudex iudicare debet.*

We believe that arguments asserting that the judge is not obliged to apply foreign law *ex officio* avoid the very essence and focal point of the application of foreign law, which is the conflict rule.[43] It is precisely in relations with a foreign

---

[42] See the brief survey of some existing rules made above.

[43] See Mustafa Kemal Yasseen, "Problèmes relatifs à l'application du droit étranger", *Recueil des Cours*, 1962, II, p. 514.

element, that conflict rules constitute the basis on which foreign law is being applied, and the attitude of the judge towards the decisive foreign law must therefore depend on the structure and character of the respective conflict rule. Thus, if the judge must *ex officio* apply a conflict rule of his own legal system, he must also heed its instruction to apply foreign law. This argument should not be weakened by the fact that not all conflict rules have the same character and that there exist conflict rules which, for example, offer the parties the possibility to choose themselves the applicable law. But even if we carried to the extreme the argument that conflict rules – or at least some of them – do not have the character of mandatory rules but of optional rules, this character of theirs would in no way warrant the conclusion that they lost the character of legal rules and that they became a fact for adjudicating court.

The argument asserting that the judge is not obliged to apply foreign law *ex officio* has given rise to another argument, claiming that the judge is not obliged to know foreign law but that the parties must plead and prove the validity of the foreign law involved. However, does this involve a change of the substance and character of the applicable foreign law, which would make such law a fact? We believe that this is not so. In our opinion, this aspect of the matter ensues from the needs of judicial procedure in states where the principial guiding line of civil procedure it its dispositional character under which the parties to the proceedings are *domini litis*. Under such procedure there occurs a necessary distribution of roles between the parties, which supply the judge with fact, and the judge who issues the legal finding in accordance with the principle *da mihi factum, dabo tibi ius*. The parties therefore have the right to plead and prove a complex of factual circumstances on which they base their claims or defence, while the judge has the obligation to assess the factual state of the case in accordance with the objective law which is to be applied to the assessment of this factual state of affairs. We believe that a proper assessment of the importance of conflict rules shows beyond any doubt that even under the dispositional principle of judicial procedure, the applicable foreign law falls within the category of legal rules to be applied to the given case. The conflict rule, in particular a multilateral conflict rule specifying *in abstracto* what substantive law is to be applied to the respective case, views domestic law and foreign law as fully equal, and in no way indicates that foreign law should be considered merely as just a fact. The foreign law which is to be applied on the basis of the conflict rule is not binding upon the judge under any instructions of the foreign legislator, which are territorially limited, but on the instructions of his own, domestic legislator, which are contained precisely in the conflict rule. Therein lies the actual purpose of the conflict rule, which on the basis of instructions of the domestic legislator introduces into the body of domestic law a foreign law which could not be otherwise applied.

It is certainly remarkable that Batiffol, whose views on the application of foreign law we have already outlined in brief, bases his theory on an alleged absence of the imperative element in the foreign law,[44] which makes him compare the application of foreign law by a domestic court to the application of the statutes of a business corporation, which, he argues, do not include the imperative element either. At the same time, of course, Batiffol completely ignores the fact that the imperative of the conflict rule subjects the given legal relations to the foreign law which – viewed from this aspect – cannot be identified with the factual circumstances of the case under consideration, but preserves its character of a rule of law applicable to the case. Thus the parallel comparing the applicable foreign law with the statutes of a business corporation, which Batiffol obviously based on the provisions of Article 1134 of the French Civil Code,[45] is quite inappropriate.

Thus, if the judge is to apply foreign law, his role cannot be limited to a mere ascertainment of the existence of such law,

---

[44] See the quotation from his *Aspects philosophiques*, p. 111, given above.

[45] Article 1134 of the *Code civil* reads: "*Les conventions légalement formées tiennent lieu de loi à ceux qui les on faites.*" On the above arguments also see M o t u l s k y, *Mélanges Maury,* Vol. I, 1960, p. 361.

but he is obliged to apply the foreign law and adjudicate the case in accordance with its provisions. The concrete solution of the case must be based on a written foreign law, or on a foreign precedent, and the law must be applied in the same manner as if it were applied by a judge in the state whose law is involved. Under the conflict rule of the *lex fori* the role of the judge in applying foreign law is therefore the same as in the case of application of the domestic law. This means that the judge must apply the foreign law on the basis of the conflict rule also in proceedings of a dispositional character as well as in cases where the parties do not plead the applicability and validity of the foreign law; in our opinion, this conclusion ensues from the fact that the decisive foreign law which is applicable under the conflict rule of the *lex fori* is the law in accordance with which the case is to be decided.

We must, of course, bear in mind the fact that the applicable foreign law is applied on the basis of the imperative contained in the conflict rule of the *lex fori.* This fact, in our opinion, is decisive for defining the relationship between the domestic and foreign laws in the sense that the domestic law is superior to the foreign law in that the latter is not applied originally but derivatively. This means that under certain conditions foreign law may be excluded from application, this again on the basis of special provisions of the *lex fori* concerning the non-applicability of foreign law which would disturb public order of the forum. The foreign law therefore stands lower than the domestic law in the hierarchy of the two laws, but this fact again does not change the former's substance as a law. We should at the same time take notice of the fact that foreign law is something different from a dispositional agreement between the parties, to which it is compared by Batiffol when he makes a parallel between foreign law and the statutes of a business corporation. If Batiffols's parallel were to hold water, it would not be necessary to resort to such an exceptional institution as *ordre public* for excluding the application of foreign law, and foreign law, as a basically dispositional category, would have to be excluded from application whenever it would run-counter to the mandatory provisions of the *lex fori.*[46] When, of course, there are no reasons for rejecting the application of foreign law on the grounds of violation of public order, foreign law enjoys full equality with domestic law as the basis for settling the given case. One consequence of this relationship between domestic and foreign law is that in certain cases the judge must act in the same manner as the foreign judge would, for example, in filling the gaps that may exist in legal provisions, in interpreting the foreign law and foreign legal institutions, or even in the judicial creation of law. Here his role with respect to the foreign law may go quite far; it is defined by his obligation to act in the same manner as would in the given case – within the scope of the applicable foreign system of law – the foreign judge. This role, which seems to us to be of extreme importance for the proper application of foreign law, at the same time negates Batiffol's thesis that in applying foreign law (i.e. a fact under his concept) the judge is obliged to seek only "what there is", while his role in applying domestic law (i.e. law as such) consists of seeking what there should be.[47]

Rabel, too, stresses[48] that when applying foreign law, the judge cannot do without the typical judicial operations which differ from his consideration of the factual circumstances of the case.

Batiffol's theoretical deductions on the substance of foreign law and its relation to domestic law have many weak points and cannot be interpreted otherwise than as an attempt to justify the practice of the French Cour de cassation, which does not consider as a ground for quashing a decision of a lower court the fact that the latter court did not apply a foreign law whose applicability the parties had failed to plead.[49] It should be remembered that this judicature has been strongly critized in France, beginning with Maury, and that the great majority of contemporary French authors oppose it.

---

[46] See Motulsky, *Mélanges Maury,* 1960, Vol. 1.

[47] Batiffol, *Aspects philosophiques,* p. 109.

[48] *Conflict of Laws,* Vol. 4, p. 477.

[49] See Maury, *Recueil des Cours,* 1936, III, p. 403.

Batiffol's arguments concerning the character of foreign law are based on a wrong definition of the relation between the applicable foreign law and domestic law, which has led to the conclusion that foreign law is a fact and therefore does not have the character of a law. On the other hand, even if the character of foreign law as a law is not denied, the question may arise – and, as we shall further see, has indeed arisen – whether the foreign law which is being applied in judicial proceedings remains to be f o r e i g n law and whether its application does not turn it into domestic law.

## (4) "Reception" of Foreign Law by Domestic Law

The authors who proceeded in their arguments from the dogma of the exclusiveness of domestic law deemed it incompatible with this exclusiveness to have foreign law "penetrate" domestic law and therefore felt it necessary to resort to a construction under which the foreign law becomes through its application a part of the domestic law and is "received" by it. This is why this theory has become known as the reception theory. It is typical of the Italian doctrine of private international law[50] and is therefore frequently referred to as the Italian reception theory; however, more recent Italian literature is opposed to it.[51] Ago feels that foreign law is incorporated into the domestic law and argues that the foreign law should be in keeping with the postulates required of a rule of law, a legal provision, which can be achieved only if it is incorporated into the domestic systems of law.[52]

Although it may not seem so at first look, this theory has in

---

[50] See, e.g., A g o, "Les règles générales des conflits des lois", *Recueil des Cours,* 1935, IV, pp. 302 ff.

[51] See C a p p e l l e t t i, "Il trattamento del diritto straniero nel processo civile italiano", *Rivista di diritto internazionale,* 1966, Nos. 3–4, pp. 299 ff.

[52] *Recueil des Cours,* 1935, IV.

fact much in common with Cook's and Lorenzen's American local law theory, which is based on the premise that the judge never applies foreign law but always domestic law created according to the example of the foreign judge. Rabel points – in our opinion quite justly – to the unnecessary artificial intricacy of the Italian reception theory.[53]

Although the reception theory does not view foreign law as a fact which must be proved by the parties, its weak point lies in the fact that foreign law, which (seemingly) loses its foreign character and becomes a part of domestic law, must be applied and interpreted as domestic law, i.e. out of the context of the whole systems of law, inorganically and restrictedly, which greatly reduces the fundamental purpose of its application. Maury quite rightly criticizes a number of Italian authors for incorrectness, lack of logic and the absurd consequences of the procedure they advocate.[54] For the question of interpretation of the applicable foreign law is exceptionally important when we realize that two fully identical regulations may be interpreted quite differently under the legal systems of two states; therefore, a foreign legal provision should always be interpreted in accordance with the foreign rather than the domestic law, but this is not at all possible under the Italian reception theory. We must, of course, bear in mind the fact that some advocates of the reception theory have abandoned the impossible consequences of their initial construction and, as Maury points out,[55] began to assert that foreign legal institutions should be incorporated within the domestic law as they are understood under the foreign law; here we might speak of a weakened reception theory. The question which arises in connection with this form of the reception theory may be formulated so as to ask whether this construction of incorporating foreign institutions within the domestic law in the meaning they have under the foreign law under which they were creat-

---

[53] *Conflict of Laws,* Vol. I, p. 62.

[54] *Recueil des Cours,* 1936, III, p. 385.

[55] *Ibid.*

ed is necessary and expedient. It seems that such weakened construction makes it posible to apply and interpret foreign law as it was created. At the same time we must ask what has been left of the original purpose of the reception of foreign law by the domestic law and whether it would not be simpler to say that — as it corresponds to the substance of the whole phenomenon — the court applies foreign law. When we realize that the reception theory had been formulated in its original form in order to turn foreign law into domestic law, it is difficult to imagine that the domestic law could acquire such a diversified content and form as ensue — under the interpretation of the weakened reception theory — from the fact that it might incorporate legal provisions of all states. We believe that the content of foreign laws and their interpretation depend on the jurisdiction of the foreign legislators and the foreign courts, and that it is practically impossible to incorporate this jurisdiction within the scope of the jurisdiction of one's own state organs. The reception theory can in no way explain the contradiction which is inherent to its weakened form, namely that the foreign law incorporated in the domestic law should be applied and interpreted differently from the provisions of the *lex fori.*

We believe that the initial thesis of the exclusiveness of one's own law against foreign law is wrong in so far as it overlooks the function of the conflict rule which, in particular as a multiple conflict rule, itself envisages the application of foreign law and thereby undermines the assumed exclusiveness of the domestic system of law. This position is also borne in mind by Rabel, who stresses the utter uselessness of the foreign law reaching the court on crutches (i. e. with the help of the reception theory) when it is quite sufficient that the conflict rule of the *lex fori* orders its application.[56] The theory of incorporation of foreign law in the domestic legal system, which proceeds from the thesis of the exclusiveness of domestic law, is in our opinion unnecessary when we realize that the sovereignty

---

[56] Rabel, *Conflict of Laws,* Vol. I, p. 63; also see Dölle in *Revue critique de droit international privé,* 1955, No. 2, p. 235.

of the domestic legislator and the exclusiveness of his law are not violated by his own order as to when, to what extent and under what conditions the foreign law is to be applied.[57]

(5) Conclusions

An analysis of the views regarding the substance of the application of foreign law and the relations between the applicable foreign law and domestic law underlines the role played in such application by the conflict rule. If we leave aside considerations of why foreign law is applied, which might be called something of a "philosophy" of private international law, we find that the role of the conflict rule – as far as the application of foreign law is concerned – is to introduce into the body of domestic law, ensuing from the jurisdiction of the domestic legislator, under certain conditions and within a certain scope the rules of a foreign law. Since the validity of every legal system is territorially limited by the boundaries of state sovereignty, the conflict rule of the forum, as the source of the application of foreign law, becomes the instrument whereby the legislator gives validity to foreign law within the framework of his own body of law. The foreign law which is applied on the basis of the conflict rule does not change its character by such application; it does not become either a factual circumstance of the given case or a part of domestic law. The applied foreign law is and remains foreign law. This is reflected in the principle that the judge has the obligation to apply the decisive foreign law in the same manner in which it would be applied by the foreign judge, which is true, of course, not only of the application of the foreign law but of its interpretation as well. This is a principle expressed some time ago also by the Permanent Court of International Justice in the Hague.[58] Only

---

[57] See M. K. Yasseen, *Recueil des Cours,* 1962, II, p. 525.

[58] See *Journal du droit international,* 1929, p. 1027: *"La Cour étant arrivée, qui'l y a lieu d'appliquer le droit interne d'un pays déterminé, il ne*

thus it is possible to meet the will of the domestic legislator that certain legal relationships should be governed by foreign law.

This principle naturally gives rise to some additional problems, in particular the problem of *renvoi* and trasmission whose core involves the solution of the question whether the legislator's reference to a foreign law should be understood only as a reference to foreign substantive law or, also, to a foreign law of conflict of laws which may, of course, take a quite different view of the question of the applicable law than the conflict rule of the *lex fori.* However, these questions and their special character go far beyond the scope of the present work.

Nevertheless, it would be wrong to believe that no further problems arise from the substance and character of the applicable foreign law. On the contrary. It happens frequently – as we have already shown – that precisely these problems obscure the true substance of the application of foreign law and its character. All these problems arise in connection with the specific character of the foreign law which, as such, is usually unknown to the adjudicating court, and the methods whereby the judge acquires such knowledge and which, in our opinion, depend on the principles governing the procedural law of the respective country, differ; however, they may lead to a situation where foreign law is wrongly identified with the factual circumstances of the case, which may have some serious, practical consequences not only as regards the questions of ascertaining the foreign law and proving it in the judical proceedings, but also with respect to the possibility of reviewing a decision where a foreign law was wrongly applied.

However, even when solving these questions, we must not forget that the application of foreign law is not an end in itself but that the actual purpose of this application is the endeavour to settle certain social relations (containing a foreign element)

---

*semble guère douteux qu'elle doit s'efforcer de l'appliquer comme on l'appliquerait dans ledit pays. Ce ne serait pas appliquer un droit interne que de l'appliquer d'une manière différente de celle dont il serait appliqué dans le pays où il est en vigueur."*

justly from the viewpoint of both conflict and substantive laws.

The question of the proper elucidation of the character of foreign law applied in judicial proceedings is therefore of primary importance for the whole body of private international law. It is a question whose practical consequences may manifest themselves in any case where foreign law is to be applied. Since today we lay such stress on the security of legal relations in international relations, in particular international trade, it is obvious that the explanation of the substance of foreign law and its application is important not only for the judicial realization of a right in relations with a foreign element, but also for the parties to a variety of civil-law relations with a foreign element, on whose moves in the proceedings it will often depend whether they succeed in pleading the validity of a foreign law, which is in a number of countries the main principle of the application of foreign law, whether they succeed in duly proving it, and whether the decision in which the foreign law may have been wrongly applied may be reviewed on this ground by a superior court.

The questions related with the character and substance of the application of foreign law also clear up the key problems of private international law, primarily the role of the conflict rule in the case of conflict of the laws of several sovereign states, whose validity is territorially limited. A proper elucidation of this role, which we have tried to offer, should clear up the theoretical confusion which is still considerable and which does not spur a proper understanding of the role played by foreign law in private international law. The extreme views which are put forward in many respects in this field, irrespective of whether they are the older and more recent Anglo-American theories, the Italian reception theory, or Batiffol's apology of the decisions of the French Cour de cassation, undoubtedly call for a scientific reaction which would try to determine in broader relations, and not merely with respect to the practical questions of proving foreign law in judicial proceedings, the substance of the application of foreign law, which represents the culmination of the conflict rule and its purpose.

If the conflict rule is an instrument for transplanting into the territorially limited body of domestic law (which is otherwise assumed to be exclusive) the law of a foreign state, which has some special aspects as regards the relation between the two laws, the question arises at the same time of the scope of replacing the domestic law by the foreign one. What is involved here is not only the safety valve of the reservation of public order, but also the assertion of the principle of applicability of foreign law in its integrity and entirety as regards the interpretation of the foreign law and filling any gaps that may exist therein.

A proper application of foreign law in civil-law relations with a foreign element is of far-reaching importance in daily life for solving social situations of an international character and thus also for the mutual respect of different state entities and their systems of law.

# BIBLIOGRAPHY


A g o, R., *Lezioni di diritto internazionale privato, Parte generale,* Milano, 1955.

A n c e l, M., "La tendance universaliste dans la doctrine comparative française au début du XXème siècle", *Festschrift f. E. Rabel,* 1953, pp. 7 ff.

– "Le rôle de la recherche comparative dans la coopération juridique internationale", *De conflictu legum,* Leiden, 1962, pp. 31 ff.

– "Valeur actuelle des études de droit comparé", *XXth Century Comparative and Conflict Laws,* Leiden, 1961, pp. 15 ff.

A q u i l a r N a v a r r o, M., *Lecciónes de derecho internacional privado,* Vol. 1, Madrid, 1963, Vol. 2, Madrid, 1964.

A r m i n j o n, P., "L'objet et la méthode du droit international privé", *Recueil des Cours,* 1933, Vol. 44, pp. 5 ff.

– *Précis de droit international privé,* 3rd ed., Paris, 1956.

B a b i ń s k i, L., *Zagadnienia współczesnego polskiego prawa międzynarodowego prywatnego,* Warszawa, 1958.

B a l o g h, E., "Le rôle du droit comparé dans le droit international privé", *Recueil des Cours,* 1936, Vol. 57, pp. 577 ff.

B a r, L. v o n, *Theorie und Praxis des internationalen Privatrechts,* 2 vols., Hannover, 1889.

B a r i l e, "La fonction historique du droit international privé", *Recueil des Cours,* 1965, Vol. 116, pp. 305 ff.

B a r t i n, E., *Principes du droit international privé selon la loi et la jurisprudence française,* 3 Vol., Paris, 1930–1935.

B a t t i f o l, H., *Aspects philosophiques du droit international privé,* Paris, 1956.

– *Les conflicts de lois en matière de contrats,* Paris, 1938.

– "Les tendances doctrinales actuelles en droit international privé", *Recueil des Cours,* 1948, Vol. 72, pp. 5 ff.

– "Principes de droit international privé", *Recueil des Cours,* 1959, Vol. 97, pp. 431 ff.

– *Traité élémentaire de droit international privé,* 3rd ed., Paris, 1959,

Beale, J. H., *A Treatise on the Conflict of Laws*, 3 vols., New York, 1935.

Becket, A., "What Is Private International Law", *British Yearbook of International Law*, 1926, pp. 73 ff.

Blagojević, B., *Medjunaradno privatno pravo*, Beograd, 1950.

Bobrov, R. L., "Povaha základních principů mezinárodního práva" ("Nature of the Basic Principles of International Law"), *Časopis pro mezinárodní právo (Czechoslovak Journal of International Law)*, 1961, No. 1, pp. 52 ff.

Boguszak, J., "K otázce tzv. srovnávací pravovědy" ("On Comparative Jurisprudence"), *Právník (The Lawyer)*, 1962, No. 9, pp. 803 ff.

Bühler, O., "Der völkerrechtliche Gehalt des internationalen Privatrechts", *Festschrift Wolff*, 1952, pp. 177 ff.

Bystrický, R., "O vztahu mezinárodního práva veřejného a soukromého a o předmětu mezinárodního práva soukromého" ("The Relationship between Public and Private International Law and the Object of Private International Law"), *Časopis pro mezinárodní právo (Czechoslovak Journal of International Law)*, 1962, No. 2, pp. 134 ff.

— *Právo mezinárodního obchodu (The Law of International Trade)*, Prague, 1967.

— *Základy mezinárodního práva soukromého (Principles of Private International Law)*, Prague, 1958.

— "Zákoník mezinárodního obchodu (ZMO) v systému československého práva" ("The Code of International Trade in the System of Czechoslovak Law"), *Právník (The Lawyer)*, 1966, No. 3, pp. 251 ff.

— "Za marxistickou srovnávací pravovědu" ("For a Marxist Comparative Jurisprudence"), *Právník (The Lawyer)*, 1962, No. 8, pp. 625 ff.

Bystrický, R. — Kalenský, P., "K některým otázkám navrhované osnovy zákona o mezinárodním právu soukromém" ("Some Aspects of the Bill on Private International Law"), *Časopis pro mezinárodní právo (Czechoslovak Journal of International Law)*, No. 3, pp. 214 ff.

Cappelletti, M., "Il trattamento del diritto straniero nel processo civile italiano", *Rivista di diritto internazionale*, 1966, Nos. 3—4, pp. 299—341.

Cheshire, G. C., *Private International Law*, 6th ed., Oxford, 1961.

Cook, W. W., *The Logical and Legal Bases of the Conflict of Laws*, Cambridge, Mass., 1942.

Cúth, J., "K problematike práva medzinárodného obchodu", ("Problems of the Law of International Trade"), *Časopis pro mezinárodní právo (Czechoslovak Journal of International Law)*, No. 1, pp. 3 ff.

David, R., *Les grands systèmes de droit contemporains*, Paris, 1964.

— *Traité élémentaire de droit civil comparé*, Paris, 1950.

De Nova, R., "Current Developments of Private International Law", *American Journal of Comparative Law,* 1965, No. 4, pp. 542 ff.

– "Historical Comparative Introduction to Conflict of Laws", *Recueil des Cours,* 1966, Vol. 118, pp. 313 ff.

*Dicey's Conflict of Laws,* 6th ed., edited by J. H. Morris. London, 1949.

Diena, G., "La conception de droit international privé d'après la doctrine et la pratique en Italie", *Recueil des Cours,* 1927, Vol. 17, pp. 343–447.

Donner, B., "Důkaz a paužití cizího práva" ("The Proof and Application of Foreign Law"), *Studie z mezinárodního práva (Studies in International Law),* 957, No. 3, pp. 107 ff.

Droz, G. A. L., "La conférence de la Haye de droit international privé et les méthodes d'unification du droit; Traités internationaux ou lois modèles", *Revue internationale de droit comparé,* 1961, No. 3, pp. 507 ff.

Ehrenzweig, A., *A Treatise on the Conflict of Laws.* St. Paul, Minn., 1962.

– *Conflict of Laws. Part One. Jurisdiction and Judgements.* St. Paul, Minn., 1959.

– "The Lex Fori – basic rule in the conflict of laws", *Michigan Law Review,* Vol. 58, 1960, pp. 637–688.

Esser, J., *Grundsatz und Norm in der richterlichen Fortbildung des Privatrechts,* 2nd ed., Tübingen, 1964.

Etter, K. M., *Vom Einfluss des Souverenitätsgedankens auf das internationale Privatrecht,* Zurich, 1959.

Evrigenis, D., *L'applicatioi du droit étranger,* Salonika, 1956.

Falconbridge, J. D., *Essays on the Conflict of Laws,* 2nd ed., Toronto, 1954.

Franceskakis, Ph., "Droit naturel et Droit international privé", *Mélanges offerts à Jacques Maury,* 1960, Vol. 1, pp. 113 ff.

– "Droit naturel et Droit international privé", *Revue critique, 1961,* No. 3.

– *La théorie du renvoi en droit international privé,* Paris, 1958.

Frankenstein, E., *Internationales Privatrecht (Grenzrecht),* 4 vols., Berlin, 1926–1936.

– *Projet d'un code européen de droit international privé,* Biblioteca Visseriana, Vol. XVI, Leiden, 1950.

– "Tendances nouvelles du droit international privé", *Recueil des Cours,* 1930, Vol. 33, pp. 245 ff.

Giuliano, M., "Le traitment du droit étranger dans le procès civil dans les systèmes juridiques continenteaux", *Revue internationale de droit comparé,* 1962, No. 1.

Goldschmidt, W., "Jacques Maury et les aspects philosophiques du droit international privé", *Mélanges Maury,* 1960, Vol. 1, pp. 153 ff.

— *Sistema y filosofia del derecho internacional privado,* 2 vols., 1st ed., Barcelona, 1945—1949; 3 vols., 2nd ed., Buenos Aires, 1952—1954.

Graveson, R. H., "Aspects philosophiques du droit international privé anglais", *Revue critique,* 1962, No. 3, pp. 397 ff.

— "Comparative Aspects of the General Principles of Private International Law", *Recueil des Cours,* 1963, Vol. 109, pp. 7 ff.

— *The Conflict of Laws,* London, 1960.

Gutteridge, H. C., *Comparative Law (An Introduction to the Comparative Method of Legal Study and Research),* Cambridge, 1946.

Gutzwiller, M., "A propos d'un 'quaestio aurea' en droit international privé suisse: l'application du droit étranger", *De conflictu legum,* Leiden, 1961, pp. 181 ff.

— *Der Einfluss Savignys auf die Entwicklung des Internationalprivatrechts,* Freiburg, 1923.

— "Fünfzig Jahre Internationalprivatrechts", *Rabels Zeitschrift,* 1958, No. 3—4.

— "Le développement historique du droit international privé", *Recueil des Cours,* 1929, Vol. 29, pp. 291 ff.

Hall, J., *Comparative Law and Social Theory,* Louisiana State University Press, 1963.

Jagmetti, M., *Die Anwendung fremden Kollisionrechtes durch den inländischen Richter,* Zurich, 1961.

Jitta, J., *La méthode du droit international privé,* The Hague, 1890.

Kahn, F., "Über Inhalt, Natur und Methode des internationalen Privatrechts", *Abhandlungen zum internationalen Privatrecht,* 2 vols., Munich—Leipzig, 1928.

Kahn, F.—Freund, O., *The Growth of Internationalism in English Private International Law,* London—Jerusalem, 1960.

Kalenský P., "Ke kolizní problematice vzniku obligačních smluv" ("Some Problems of the Conflict of Laws Concerning the Formation of Contracts"), *Studie z mezinárodního práva (Studies in International Law),* 1961, pp. 191 ff.

— "Ke koncepci právní úpravy zbožních vztahů mezi podniky pro zahraniční obchod členských států RVHP" ("The Concept of the Legal Regulation of Commodity Relations between Foreign Trade Enterprises of the Member States of the Council of Mutual Economic Assistance"), *Studie z mezinárodního práva (Studies in International Law),* 1966, Vol. 11, pp. 103 ff.

— "K některým soudobým aspektům mezinárodního práva soukromého jako společenského jevu" ("Some Contemporary Aspects of Private International Law as a Social Phenomenon"), *Časopis pro mezinárodní právo (Czechoslovak Journal of International Law),* 1968, No. 2, pp. 119 ff.

– "K obecným otázkám tzv. mezinárodního práva procesního", ("General Problems of the So-called International Law of Civil Procedure"), *Právník (The Lawyer)*, 1957, No. 4, pp. 326 ff.

– "K předmětu a povaze mezinárodního práva soukromého a k otázce jeho místa v systému práva", ("The Object and Nature of Private International Law and Its Place in the System of Law"), *Časopis pro mezinárodní právo (Czechoslovak Journal of International Law)*, 1960, No. 2, pp. 81 ff.

– "K soudobým teoretickým problémům srovnávací pravovědy" ("Contemporary Theoretical Problems of Comparative Jurisprudence", *Právník (The Lawyer)*, 1968, No. 4, pp. 289 ff.

– "Základní právní problémy Evropského hospodářského společenství" ("Basic Legal Problems of the European Economic Community"), *Studie z mezinárodního práva (Studies in International Law)*, 1964, Vol. 9, pp. 81 ff.

– *Obligační statut kupní smlouvy v mezinárodním obchodním styku (Conflict of Laws in International Sale)*, Prague, 1960.

– "Některé současné tendence v oblasti právní úpravy zahraničního obchodu" ("Some Current Trends in the Sphere of Legal Regulation of Foreign Trade"), *Časopis pro mezinárodní právo (Czechoslovak Journal of International Law)*, 1963, No. 1, pp. 52 ff.

– "Podstata a povaha aplikace cizího práva" ("The Substance and Nature of the Application of Foreign Law", *Studie z mezinárodního práva (Studies in International Law)*, 1968, Vol. 13, pp. 41 ff.

– *Právní otázky řízeni vzájemného zahraničního obchodu členských států RVHP (Legal Aspects of the Management of Foreign Trade between the Member States of the Council of Mutual Economic Assistance)*, Prague, 1966.

– "Současná činnost Haagské konference mezinárodního práva soukromého a její další program" ("The Current Activity of the Hague Conference on Private International Law and Its Future Agenda"), *Časopis pro mezinárodní právo (Czechoslovak Journal of International Law)*, 1962, No. 1, pp. 20 ff.

– "Univerzalismus a nacionalismus v doktríně o mezinárodním právu soukromém" ("Universalism and Nationalism in the Doctrine of Private International Law"), *Časopis pro mezinárodní právo (Czechoslovak Journal of International Law)*, 1968, No. 4; 1969, No. 1.

Kalenský, P. – Steiner, V., "K návrhům nových úprav československého práva soukromého" ("Comments on the New Provisions Governing Czechoslovak Private International Law), *Právník (The Lawyer)*, 1963, No. 6, pp. 480 ff.

Kanda, A., "Zákon o právních vztazích v mezinárodním obchodním styku (zákoník mezinárodního obchodu) a jeho místo v systému československého socialistického práva" ("The Code of International Trade and Its Place Within the System of Czechoslovak Socialist Law"), *Právník (The Lawyer)*, 1966, No. 2, pp. 128 ff.

Kegel, G., "Der Gegenstand des internationalen Privatrechts", *Festschrift für L. Raape*, Hamburg, 1948.

– *Internationales Privatrecht*, Munich–Berlin, 1960.

– "The Crisis of Conflicts of Laws", *Recueil des Cours*, 1964, Vol. 112, pp. 275 ff.

Knapp, V., *Filosofické problémy socialistického práva (Philosophical Problems of Socialist Law)*, Prague, 1968.

– "K otázce socialistické srovnávací právní vědy" ("On Socialist Comparative Jurisprudence"), *Právník (The Lawyer)*, 1963, No. 5, pp. 391 ff.

– "Některé metodologické problémy srovnávací právní vědy" ("Some Methodological Problems of Comparative Jurisprudence"), *Právník (The Lawyer)*, 1968, No. 2, pp. 91 ff.

– *Předmět a systém československého socialistického práva občanského (The Object and System of Czechoslovak Socialist Civil Law)*, Prague, 1959.

– "Verträge im tschechoslowakischen Recht. Ein Beitrag zur Rechtsvergleichung zwischen Ländern mit verschiedener Wirtschaftsordnung", *Rabels Zeitschrift*, 1961, No. 2, pp. 221 ff.

Kopelmanas, L., "La théorie du dédoublement fonctionnel et son utilisation pour la solution des problèmes des conflits des lois", *Hommage prof. G. Scelle*, Paris, Vol. 2, pp. 753.

Krčmář, J., "Beiträge zur Geschichte des internationalen Privatrechts", *Festschrift zur Jahrhundertfeier des österreichischen ABGB, 1911*, Vol. 2, pp. 133 ff.

Kubeš, V., *Právní filosofie XX. století (Legal Philosophy of the 20th Century)*, Brno, 1947.

Kutikov, V., *Mezhdunarodno chastno pravo na Narodna Republika Balgariya*, Sofia, 1958.

Lainé, A., *Introduction au droit international privé contenant une étude historique et critique de la théorie des statuts et des rapports de cette théorie avec le Code civil*, Paris, Vol. I, 1886, Vol. II, 1892.

Lerebours-Pigeonnière, P., *Précis de droit international privé*, Paris, 1962.

Lewald, H., *Das deutsche internationale Privatrecht auf Grundlage der Rechtsprechung*, Leipzig, 1931.

– "Règles générales des conflicts des lois", *Recueil des Cours*, 1939, Vol. 69, pp. 5 ff.

Louis-Lucas, P., "Conflits des méthodes en matière des conflits des lois", *Clunet*, 1956, No. 4, pp. 774 ff.

Luby, Š., "Pohľad na buržoáznu porovnávaciu právnu vedu" ("A View of Burgeois Comparative Jurisprudence"), *Právny obzor (Legal Review)*, 1966, No. 5, pp. 413–429.

L u n t s, L. A., *Mezhdunarodnoe chastnoe pravo, Obshchaya chast*, Moscow, 1959, 2nd ed. 1971.

*Mezinárodní právo soukromé, (Czech Translation from the Russian), (Private International Law)*, Prague, 1952.

"O predmete mezhdunarodnogo chastnogo prava v otnosheniyach mezhdu stranami socialisma", *Voprossy mezhdunarodnogo chastnogo prava*, Moscow, 1956, pp. 5 ff.

L u n t s, L. A., "Otázky mezinárodního práva soukromého v základech občanského zákonodárství a základech občanského soudního řízení svazu SSR a svazových republik" ("Questions of Private International Law in the Fundamental Principles of Civil Law and Procedure of the U.S.S.R. and the Union Republics"), *Časopis pro mezinárodní právo (Czechoslovak Journal of International Law)*, 1963, No. 2, pp. 111ff.

M a n c i n i, P. S., "De l'utilité de rendre obligatoires les règles générales du droit international privé", *Clunet*, 1874, 1, pp. 221 ff., 285 ff.

M a u r y, J., "Observations sur les 'Aspects filosophiques de droit international privé' ", *Revue critique*, 1957, No. 2, pp. 229 ff.

– "Règles générales des conflicts des lois", *Recueil des Cours*, 1936, Vol. 57, pp. 329–569.

M e i j e r s, E. M., "L'histoire des principes fondamentaux du droit international privé à partir du Moyen-Age", *Recueil des Cours*, 1934, Vol. 49, pp. 547 ff.

M e l c h i o r, G., *Die Grundlagen des deutschen internationalen Privatrechts*, Berlin, 1932.

M o t u l s k y, H., "L'office de juge et la loi étrangère", *Mélanges Maury*, 1960, Vol. 1, pp. 337 ff.

N e u h a u s, P. H., *Die Grundbegriffe des internationalen Privatrechts*. Berlin–Tübingen, 1962.

N e u m e y e r, E., *Die gemeinrechtliche Entwicklung des internationalen Privat- und Strafrechts bis Bartolus*, Munich, Vol. 1, 1901, Vol. 2, 1916.

N e u m e y e r, K. H., "Fremdes Recht und Normenkontrolle", *Festgabe für A. N. Makarov, Rabels Zeitschrift*, 1958, Nos. 3–4, pp. 573 ff.

N e u n e r, R., *Der Sinn der internationalprivatlichen Norm*, Brno, 1932.

N i b o y e t, J. P., *Cours de droit international privé*, Paris, 1947.

N i e d e r e r, W., *Einführung in die allgemeinen Lehren des internationalen Privatrechts*, Zurich, 1954.

– "Internationales Privat- und Völkerrecht", *Schweizerisches Jahrbuch für internationales Recht*, 1948, pp. 63 ff.

N u s s b a u m, A., *Deutsches internationales Privatrecht*, Tübingen, 1932.

– *Grundzüge des internationalen Privatrechts*, Munich–Berlin, 1952.

O u t r a t a, V., "K pojmu obecných a základních zásad mezinárodního práva" ("The Concept of General and Basic Principles of International

Law"), *Časopis pro mezinárodní právo (Czechoslovak Journal of International Law)*, 1961, No. 3, pp. 177 ff.
– *Mezinárodní právo veřejné (Public International Law)*, Prague, 1960.
– "Předmět mezinárodního práva" ("The Object of International Law"), *Časopis pro mezinárodní právo (Czechoslovak Journal of International Law)*, 1961, No. 1, pp. 1 ff.

Peretерski, I. S., "Sistema mezhdunarodnogo chastnogo prava", *Sovietskoye gosudarstvo i pravo*, 1946, Nos. 8–9, pp. 17 ff.

Pereterski, I. S. – Krylov, S. B., *Mezhdunarodnoe chastnoe pravo*, 2nd ed., Moscow, 1959.

Pillet, A., *Traité pratique de droit international privé*, 2 vols., Paris, 1923, 1924.

Pillet, A. – Niboyet, J. P., *Manuel de droit international privé*, Paris, 1934.

Pound, R., "Some Thoughts About Comparative Law", *Festschrift für E. Rabel*, 1953, pp. 7 ff.

Quadri, R., *Lezioni di Diritto Internazionale Privato*, Naples, 1961.

Raape, L., *Internationales Privatrechts*, 4th ed., Berlin–Frankfurt, 1955.

Rabel, E., *The Conflict of Laws – A Comparative Study*, Vols. 1–4, Chicago, 1945–1958.

Réczei, L., *Internationales Privatrecht*, Budapest, 1960.
– "Zur Frage des Gegenstandes des internationalen Privatrechts", *Staat und Recht*, 1955, pp. 488 ff.

Rheinstein, M., "Ernst Rabels vergleichende Studie des internationalen Privatrechts", *Rabels Zeitschrift*, 1955, No. 3, pp. 457 ff.

Savatier, P., *Cours de droit international privé*, Paris, 1963.

Savigny, F. C. von, *System des heutigen römischen Rechts*, 8 vols., Berlin, 1849.

Scelle, G., *Manuel élémentaire du droit international public*, 3rd ed., Paris, 1948.

Schmitthoff, C. M., "International Trade Law and Private International Law", *Festschrift Dölle*, pp. 257 ff.
– *The Sources of the Law of International Trade*, London, 1964.

Schnitzer, A. F., *De la diversité et de l'unification du droit*, Basel, 1946.
– *Handbuch des internationalen Privatrechts*, Basel, Vol. 1, 1957, Vol. 2, 1958.
– *Vergleichende Rechtslehre*, 2 vols., 2nd ed., Basel, 1961.

Schwind, F., "Von der Zersplitterung des Privatrechts durch das internationale Privatrecht und ihrer Bekämpfung", *Rabels Zeischrift*, 1958, Nos. 3–4, pp. 449 ff.

Steiner, V., "Cizí právo v občanském soudním řízení" ("Foreign Law in Civil Procedure"), *Časopis pro mezinárodní právo (Czechoslovak Journal of International Law)*, 1968, No. 1, pp. 91 ff.

Szászy, I., "L'évolution des principes généraux du droit international privé dans les pays de démocratie populaire", *Revue critique de droit international privé*, 1963, No. 1, pp. 1 ff., No. 2, pp. 233 ff.

– *Private International Law in the European People's Democracies*, Budapest, 1964.

Triepel, H., "Les rapports entre le droit interne et le droit international", *Recueil des Cours*, 1923, No. 1, pp. 77 ff.

Tunc, A., "La contribution possible des études juridiques comparatives à une meilleurs compréhension entre nations", *Revue internationale de droit comparé*, 1964, No. 1, pp. 47 ff.

Tunkin, G. I., *Ideologicheskaya borba i mezhdunarodnoe pravo*, Moscow, 1967.

Valladaõ, H., "Private International Law, Uniform Law and Comparative Law", *XXth Century Comparative and Conflict Laws*, Leiden, 1961, pp. 98 ff.

Vallindas, P., "Droit international privé 'lato sensu' ou 'scricto sensu' ", *Revue critique de droit international privé*, 1961, No. 3.

Walker, D., *Internationales Privatrecht*, 4th ed., Vienna, 1926.

Weiss, A., *Traité théoretique et pratique de droit international privé*, 6 vols., Paris, 1908–1913.

Werner, M., *Der Begriff des wohlerworbenen Rechts im internationalen Privatrecht*, Zurich, 1955.

Wiebringhaus, H., *Das Gesetz der funktionellen Verdopellung*, 2nd ed., Saarbrücken, 1955.

Wiemann, H., "Die Bedeutung des internationalen Privatrechts in der DDR", *Staat und Recht*, Berlin, 1954, pp. 743 ff.

– "Zur Frage des Gegenstandes des internationalen Privatrechts", *Staat und Recht*, Berlin, 1955 pp. 988.

Wolff, M., *Das internationale Privatrecht Deutschlands*, 3rd ed., Berlin–Göttingen–Heidelberg, 1954.

– *Private International Law*, 2nd ed., Oxford, 1955.

Wortley, B. A., "The General Principles of Private International Law from the English Standpoint", *Recueil des Cours*, 1947, Vol. 71, pp. 1–109.

– "The Interaction of Public and Private International Law Today", *Recueil des Cours*, 1954, Vol. 85, pp. 239–342.

Yasseen, M. K., "Problèmes généraux du droit international privé", *Recueil des Cours*, 1965, Vol. 116, pp. 387 ff.

– "Problèmes relatifs à l'application du droit étranger", *Recueil des Cours*, 1962, Vol. 106, pp. 499–595.

Yntema, H., "Die historischen Grundlagen des internationalen Privatrechts", *Festschrift für E. Rabel*, 1953, pp. 513 ff.

– "Les objectifs du droit international privé", *Revue critique de droit international privé*, 1959, No. 1, pp. 1 ff.

Zajtay, I., *Zur Stellung des ausländischen Rechts im französischen internationalen Privatrecht*, Berlin–Tübingen, 1963.

Zitelmann, E., *Internationales Privatrecht*, 2 vols., Munich–Leipzig, 1897, 1912.

Zweigert, K., "Die dritte Schule im internationalen Privatrecht", *Festschrift für Leo Raape zu seinem 70. Geburtstag*, Hamburg, 1948.

– "Méthodologie du droit comparé", *Mélanges Maury*, 1960, Vol. 1, pp. 579.

Žourek, J., "Kritika učení o tzv. primátu mezinárodního práva" ("Critique of the Doctrine of Primacy of International Law"), *Studie z mezinárodního práva (Studies in International Law)*, No. 1, pp. 68 ff.

# INDEX